The modern banking system manufactures money out of nothing... if you want to continue to be the slaves of bankers and pay the cost of your own slavery, then let bankers continue to create money and control credit.

— Sir Josiah Stamp, President of the Bank of England and the second richest man in Britain in the 1920's, speaking at the University of Texas.

THE KINGS HAVE WON

THE BATTLE FOR THE WEALTH OF OUR NATION

A NOVEL BY

ADRIEN GOLD

This book is dedicated to Jackie, for her eternal optimism and joyful heart, Lila and Miles for their kindness, wondrous spirits and immense talent, Ruth for her brilliance and artistic mind, and to my angels Simone and Desmond for reminding me that life is a wonderful mystery.

TABLE OF CONTENTS

PROLOGUE

While time and the winds of destiny drew near,
The warnings I bestowed upon them,
The Kings ignored.

But as seasons passed, the worst I feared.
So, I dared repeat my plea,
"Beware, my Kings, for you are the prey!"

Troubled by such audacity, their scornful eyes met mine.
"Dear Sir, it is gold, not counsel, we seek from our bankers."

Soon, the fires of fury raged on.
Spears lowered. Blood drawn.
In time, the Kings of old no longer ruled Nations.

But far from the limelight these Kings so cherished.
Unnamed, unseen, and unspoken for.
I,
The miserable creditor they abhorred.
I,
The wretched old banker they dismissed.
I
Became the King.

CHAPTER 1

THE PAUPER MADE KING

Give all the power to the many, they will oppress the few.
Give all the power to the few, they will oppress the many.
— Alexander Hamilton

We've become, now, an oligarchy instead of a democracy. I think that's
been the worst damage to the basic moral and ethical standards to the
American political system that I've ever seen in my life.
— Jimmy Carter

NEW YORK, 1804

"This is a mortal wound, Doctor," I say to the frantic old man. His hands move from my wrist to my neck, desperately searching for a pulse. Footsteps surround me, heavy, rushed. They slowly fade. Dr. Hosack calls for help. More footsteps soon break the silence. Men arrive.

"Hamilton has been shot," the Doctor shouts. "Hurry up."

They lift me off the ground. We move through the tall grass and down the path. The gentle rush of the river stirs the waiting boat in which I am carefully laid. I sense the body I do not feel and fall out of consciousness.

The light drowsiness which had first appeared, I ignored, the logical response of an invincible thirteen-year-old boy. But the dull condition worsened. A high fever, intense diarrhea, and wrenching vomiting now inflict me. Weakened, I can no longer rise from the bed I share with my sick Mother. Our mortal bodies motionless, statues inadvertently discarded on a soaked and rancid mattress.

From my feverish dream, I wake to see my mother's face. Her bright blue and immensely peaceful eyes stare tenderly back at me. It warms my

3

heart. Within seconds I succumb to sleep once more, her gentle stare forever frozen upon my soul.

The sunlight casts familiar patterns on the wall. It is morning. Half awake, my head throbbing, voices echo all around me. "Alex, the disease has taken your mother."

I straighten, panicked, as the unbearable truth hits me. What little strength I had regained deserts me. My head falls back onto the pillow. The strong woman who incessantly fought for our survival, the Mother I so loved, was forever gone.

Within a day, our house is taken away to repay our mother's massive debt. Inconvenient witnesses to a life lost and the subjects to its immediate devastation, my brother James and I stand outside our home in disbelief.

Slaves with muscular bodies, their faces covered with rags to protect themselves from the disease that killed my mother, carry our furniture into the yard. When a carriage appears, the inventory from our mother's small store is hauled away. Another carriage arrives, followed by another, and soon nothing of our life in this house remains—nothing but memories. The front door is slammed shut by an irritated landlord who scowls at us in disdain.

Helpless, I sit on the ground and lean back against the lone tree in our yard. Exhausted from my illness, I fall into a slumber, and the odor of medicine is replaced by the unbearable stench filling our house a day earlier. The pain in my throat, temples, and legs return as a deep sorrow fall upon me. Ours was a dark house full of sadness, lies, and despair. My Mother's beautiful eyes stare into mine once more.

"Mother! Oh, dear mother."

A loud burst snaps me out of this dream. I smell the gunpowder floating in the air. I now remember—Burr, Weehawken, and the duel. I look up at the branch I just shot. But instead of a clearing in the woods, I find myself in the middle of a rowdy tavern.

Rows of tables surround me. Shaken by the palpable reality of the dream I just had; I wonder what brought these memories back from such a distant past.

Out of the cacophony of voices filling the boisterous room, silence seems to surround a single man. Alone, in a dark corner of the room, the man holds a pint of beer before him.

My father. I wonder.

I recognize the features of the man who deserted us. But I am unsure. So much time has passed since I last saw him. I decide to go greet him.

As I sheepishly move forward, a hand grabs my right shoulder and holds it firmly. I turn.

"This way, our table is right here, Sir," a man says.

Still in a daze, I comply, though quite unsure who my companion is. Perhaps he is a businessman whose appointment I have forgotten or a potential client needing legal counsel. I follow him.

The man is tall, with broad shoulders, long, black, wavy hair, a goatee, and dark, peaceful eyes. He wears a wide-brimmed hat, and his clothes are made of quality fabric.

"He was a crooked son of a bitch," announces a postulant man at a table nearby. A repulsive skin condition ravages his face, his nose swollen from an excess of enormous pimples.

A damned soul lost in hell. I judge him to be.

Slamming his fist on the table, the man continues. "Lies upon lies, upon lies. A pauper made king by the wealthy bankers who controlled him."

Across from this obnoxious man sits his identical, though healthy twin. Well-dressed and clean-shaven, he bears none of his companion's repulsive attributes. I watch as he reaches out and lays his gloved hand on his companion's forearm. "Dear brother, it is the path of the vicious to judge, the ignorant to lecture, and the damned to accuse. Who are we to trust? Certainly not our reason, when false is the mind that leads it. And who are we to decide the rights and wrongs of others when we are ceaselessly at odds with truth, honor, and love? Alexander Hamilton, the man you so despise, was no different from you or I, for he embraced the gifts and opportunities God placed before him."

But his brother, furious, can no longer listen. "Brother, your kind words warm my heart, but you are the ignorant who lectures me. Alexander Hamilton was a snake, the son of a whore."

"How dare he speak of my mother in such a despicable manner?" I say to my companion, who stares back at me blankly. When I turn to confront the insolent, of the two men, only one remains. Half of the man's face is ravaged, the other half healthy. He is now both the clean and the dirty, the vile and the proper, the sane and the insane.

My companion reaches out. "Sir, may I suggest we depart from this dreadful place?"

I nod.

Suddenly, the voices around the room seem to grow louder, every conversation thundering in my head.

To the left, the distinct sound of a high-pitched and familiar voice startles me. Three rows away stands an Irish soldier I had befriended long ago and whose voice I recognize. The voice had strangely never matched the sturdy physique of the handsome and educated man I had gotten to know.

"How stupid could Hamilton be to share the lurid details of his affairs with that Reynolds woman? Hamilton wrote in his Reynolds Pamphlet; *'...my real crime is an amorous connection with his wife...'* the soldier says mockingly, quoting me. "What an idiot. Hamilton should have embraced a braver posture. It could have gone like this: I was approached by the most ravishing of women. She arrived at my house one evening. Unknown and uninvited, she begged for financial help. What is a good man to do, I ask? I offered the poor beauty the help she desired. She thanked me in the most appreciative of manner. The woman was, after all, irresistible. I assume you see nothing wrong with my behavior, Gentlemen, do you?" Laughter grows louder around the table.

"Instead, Hamilton offers this *'...confession is not made without a blush. I cannot be the apologist of any vice because the ardour of passion may have made it mine."* the soldier continues. "Hamilton was a horny bastard. No need to blush. Every man understands. But in the end, he was an easy prey for the shameless Mrs. Reynolds, who partook in this unscrupulous and sinful transaction to blackmail the poor idiot." The man concludes.

At the table, the men are now hysterical.

My confession had been made with the belief it would remain private. But a victim, I am not, and a guilty man must bear the label with which he is marked. True, I had fallen madly for the penniless Maria Reynolds, the woman who had mysteriously appeared at my door one evening to solicit pecuniary help. Her purse was empty, but her bosom was full, delicate, and inviting. So, with overflowing lust, I embraced this ill-fated affair.

I stand in the middle of the tavern, unresponsive as the memories come flooding back: Maria Reynolds' porcelain skin, firm breasts, full lips, and gentleness in the heat of passion. I now long for her tender touch, for her body, for her kisses. I long to be with her once more.

A voice snaps me out of my reverie. I look to see an aristocrat sitting a few rows away. Proudly he interjects. "My dear fellow, allow me to impose upon you the words of John Adams, who faithfully described our famed Secretary of the Treasury; words I so dearly enjoyed at the time. John Adams said, *'That bastard brat of a Scottish peddler! His ambition, his restlessness, and all his grandiose schemes come, I'm convinced, from a superabundance of secretions, which he couldn't find enough whores to absorb!'*"

The group roars once more.

Adams, what a vile creature, I tell myself. Should I slap the aristocrat?

But the soldier's high-pitched voice is heard anew. "The husband was a crook who perverted his wife to collect the rewards of a nefarious plan."

As the man speaks, I feel anger growing within me. But the voice, which was so clear a second ago, blends with the many and disappears, lost in a sea of sound.

"He was a thug working on behalf of the English bankers," someone says behind me.

"You idiot! I made a fortune speculating on the Bank Scrip. Hamilton is my hero," another man exclaims excitedly.

Though comforted by the kind words, I feel dizzy. The room comes in and out of focus. I reach for the back of a chair and hold on.

"Hamilton was a monarchist," another man says. "Jefferson was right when he said, *'Hamilton was not only a monarchist, but for a monarchy bottomed on corruption."*

"I am not a monarchist," I scream across the room.

But no one reacts, no one blinks, no one stops. Instead, the tavern grows louder.

One of the men counters with, "Hamilton believed the ruling class an essential part of the economy and thought to reward them; corrupt actors who benefited from the imperious Secretary of the Treasury. He was a traitor."

Overwhelmed, I turn to my companion, whose hand gently reaches over, tugging at me. "This way, Sir."

I am disoriented and feeling faint. A slight pain has appeared above my right hip, and great sadness overwhelms me.

But as my companion turns left, I find myself staring at a man I knew—a man I believed I would never, ever meet again.

Surrounded by wealthy merchants, he sits among honored guests, and away from the commoners. I recognize the fine, black, leather gloves he wears. The red and gold threads cross each other the whole length of the fingers and merge to create a design of five gold arrows.

"Dear Alexander," the man said to me years ago. "These gloves were made by Silverio De Cartahina, the Spanish King's glover, who secretly manufactured these for our dear patron."

I also recognize the three small letters sewn on the cuffs, C.I.I; Concordia Integretas, Industria; Latin for harmony, integrity, and industry, the Rothschilds' family motto, and the five arrows symbolizing the unity of the five brothers.

But the ring, worn above the glove, confirms the identity of the man before me. "A gift from Crown Prince Regent Frederick the VI of Denmark," the man had revealed.

The ring is stunning, and even in the darkness of the tavern, it could not be confused with another. A large square blue sapphire is framed by a line of slightly yellow diamonds. On each side, the line of diamonds was interrupted by a single ruby, cut in a square and mounted delicately into the thick, gold hoop. The wide rim of his black hat hides the man's eyes, but I have little doubt of his identity. He remains quiet, immobile, head slightly tilted down.

How strange that he had promised we would never see each other again. But there he is, sitting quietly across from me, unperturbed. The gloved hand reaches for the pint, which he proudly raises. He looks in my direction, but I realize he does not see me.

"My Lords, I hope you will forgive me," the man says, the exceptional ring catching the light. "But I have ignored the formalities I was to confer upon you. The report on our stakes in the First Bank of the United States, I have not presented. But let me not bore you and just declare our bank has become the most powerful ever to exist, more powerful than the Medici, who only controlled Europe. The profits in America, through the implementation of our central bank, have been enormous. The powers we have acquired are immense."

Disheartened, I reach for a chair close by and sit. My thoughts drift back to my dear Mother, then to Eliza, the gentle wife I had so often betrayed, then to the Department of the Treasury, which I had built out of pure will. But all are eclipsed when the tender moments I shared with Maria Reynolds resurface but slowly disappear.

I now see the faces of my mother's many lovers, and soon I am overcome by the memory of Thomas Stevens, the man who, upon my mother's death, welcomed me into his home while my brother was left to fend for himself—the man who some believed was my birth father. For years, the question had emerged because his son, Edward, and I looked so much alike. Upon meeting Edward, many believed he was my brother. It was an unspoken but obvious truth. Thomas Stevens, I now believe, was probably my father.

In a flash, I remember my wish for a war, and the poem I wrote, for it attracted so much attention. I remember the donation which led me to America. I remember James Hamilton, the father who left us, and George Washington, the father figure I grew to dislike, and each step replays in my mind. I wonder, "Have I surrounded all to exalt my station? Married

9

into the Schuyler family for status? Embraced the shadows to elevate my stature?"

But I did not. Or so I tell myself.

Suddenly, I see Burr and our duel. I see guns firing, the snap of the branch I hit, and the blurry scene before me as I fall to the ground. It all replays in my mind.

Burr shot me. "This is a mortal wound, Doctor."

My body is limp at the bottom of the small boat traveling back to New York City. I listen to the four men rowing frantically, their breathing heavy. I feel the hand of Dr. Hosack pushing firmly on my wound as the sky floats above me in a slow westward motion.

"Concordia, Integretas, Industria," exclaim the men in the tavern.

It startles me.

The gloved hand rises. The extraordinary ring sparkles once more. "Gentlemen, may I offer a toast?" The man says.

The wealthy merchants around him turn to face him.

"Of the Founding Fathers, no dream was too grand to dismiss, and I salute them. However, I wish to dedicate all the honors to the builder of Nation, to the man who transformed ideas into realities, to the corruptible genius, to the man so blinded by honor it led him to his death, to the pauper made King; Alexander Hamilton, who helped us, in the words of Thomas Jefferson; *"...form the most corrupt government on earth."*

The men cheer, raising their cups.

I listen in disbelief, at once dejected and resentful. Suddenly weakened by the pain above my hip, I become dizzy.

My companion pulls me to my feet. As we exit the tavern, I pass by a few coastguards. The youngest of the three is emaciated; a thin scar covers the length of his left cheek, and part of his ear is missing. But his stare is powerful, profound; and strangely, I hear his voice within me. It says, "I am neither here, nor there, neither you nor I. I am neither the water nor the air, the fire, or the earth. I am all and I am none."

"Sir," my companion says sternly.

But I am unresponsive.

He pulls me away and outside of the tavern.

I sit on the ground, trembling. My head bowed, I fall into darkness, the pain throbbing.

"Eliza, my Dear, in my final act, I have, once more, failed you. I hope you will find the strength to forgive me, my Love."

I can hear the oars battling the water in a constant and furious motion. The sound of bells in the distance rings softly.

I am a dead man. I tell myself.

"This way, Sir."

I stand. The fresh air helps, and I regain strength. I realize we are on Whitehall Street in Manhattan.

We turn right onto Broadway. A crowd has gathered to witness a funeral procession. The mood is somber. The sorrowful crowd pushes me forward in the direction of Trinity Church.

In the middle of the street, eight dignified pallbearers march. On their shoulders rests the mahogany casket they transport wearily. Placed atop the casket, I recognize my hat and sword.

The scene strikes through my heart like an arrow. This time, I reach out for my companion's arm. I squeeze it tightly, holding on to a reality that isn't.

My horse follows. The boots and the spurs I had worn days ago reversed in the stirrups. At this sight, a hush falls over the crowd.

My three sons follow. James, John, and William solemnly lead a group of individuals I do not care to look at.

Where is Eliza? I wonder.

"We must go now, Sir."

I spent my entire life in a constant battle for survival; my youth, the war, Washington, and the country I fought so hard to build. But I am exhausted from it all and no longer able to fight. I turn around and walk away from all I know, from all I love.

The cobblestones of Manhattan slowly turn into dirt. Silence has returned, a silence free of the sounds of men, free of the spirit of men. It is an unfamiliar stillness. The small road we travel on winds between two towering walls. At each step, I feel an unbearable weightlifting gently.

In the distance, a sliver of light pierces through the opened panels of a large door. The light is beautiful, and warm, penetrating my soul. We march on.

The door we have now reached is wide open.

My companion steps inside.

I follow.

We enter a long and wide colonnade. The walls, Corinthian columns, and ceiling are built of white marble. A line of the darkest black marble frames the floor, and within it is the most beautiful and asymmetrical design. The most delicate green, red, and white marble fills diamonds, rosettes, and circle shapes. Gold lines intertwine with each other.

Thirty feet away, an old man is hunched over a table covered with manuscripts. His long, white hair is pulled over his shoulders and down his back. I notice his wrinkled hands resting on a manuscript before him. The fingers are gnarled like dried roots. At once, his index finger moves down the page and onto the next in an agile motion, scanning each word deliberately and steadily.

As he carries on, page after page, I think of the letter I wrote Eliza a week ago. I see my hand scrolling down the page, asking for forgiveness from the wife I repeatedly betrayed. The words I then wrote come back to me: *The will of a merciful God must be good.*

The quiet individual leading me moves forward and toward the desk. He passes it and turns, now facing me.

The old man stops reading and straightens back into his chair. To my surprise, his face is handsome, stern but amiable, rugged but sophisticated, and his eyes are void of condemnation.

"Alexander Hamilton, please do tell me, who am I to judge? The destitute or the lord, the husband or lover, and which of your machinations am I to overlook?"

"I am a sinner, My Lord. I beg for His mercy," I say.

The man smiles. "A man who has not sinned is a God, Sir. My duties limit me to the concerns of men and, therefore, sinners." The man pauses as his finger scrolls down another page. "The list of your deeds is so long. I am unsure where to start."

"My Lord, if you would allow me," my companion begins. "Alexander Hamilton was the son of Rachel Faucette Lavien, a woman of French Huguenot origins, who sadly possessed very questionable ways."

The old man waves his hand and says to me, "You desired a war, Sir. Why?"

"I wished for a better life and a reason to escape the miserable conditions I suffered. In the end, the war I longed for defined the honorable steps I pursued. The war led me to the impotent Washington, to write fifty-one of the eighty-five Federalist papers, to create the Treasury Department, the Revenue Cutter Service, to compose a Report on Credit and a Report on Manufacturing which led to the creation of an entirely new American industry. Without a war, I may have become a scholar. Instead, I became a builder of Nation."

The old man stares into my eyes, a blank stare, his wrinkled face at peace within and without.

I say, "But the carnal and promiscuous appetite I carried, the deceits, falsehoods, and corrupt schemes were all the fruits of my rotten youth—a childhood filled with greed born from the poverty and injustices I suffered. The misery, the violence, the sexual looseness, and the pernicious influence of my loving Mother, who, sadly, was indeed a woman of questionable morals, but a woman I loved dearly."

The man says, "A builder of Nation. How so?"

"America was like a complex child who knew not what it desired. The country was void of any of the functional systems it required. It lacked a real financial system, an army, or a modern industry. America was a house built on ideals by a pious and proud populace with little understanding of finance on the scale our country demanded. John Adams acknowledged this simple fact when he stated: *"All the perplexities, confusion and distress arise not from the defects of the Constitution, not from want of honor and virtue so much as from downright ignorance of the nature of coin, credit and circulation."*

"Tell me about the Bank of New York," the man says. "Where did the money come from?"

"The Bank of New York was an attempt at creating a central bank located in Manhattan. Though the Bank of North America in Philadelphia had been created to serve as America's central bank, it lacked the management and financial support allowing it to flourish. However, New York was the center of all commerce but lacked a strong bank. I fought with and lost to New York Governor George Clinton, who seemed more inclined to seek my failure than to act for the benefit of all. So, instead of a central bank, we settled for a common bank."

My answer appears incomplete, for only silence follows, so I continue.

"At first, the bank failed to raise the initial capital we had hoped for. I owned one-and- half shares. Burr had three shares. Approximately 200 people owned shares in the bank; they were mainly wealthy individuals and foreign interests. Of course, British investors partook in this endeavor, and it certainly included the largest banks in London."

The man stares at me and says, "You were repeatedly accused of having given too much to the elite, the financiers, the English Bankers. Were you corrupt, Alexander Hamilton?"

"I surely favored a certain class—one who deserved to gain from their financial investments. It is understandable some called the benefits of these transactions corrupt and undeserved. Though never did the ones who accused me of creating a corrupt system offer any solutions to the financial woes plaguing our young country. To me, these wealthy creditors, bankers, and businessmen were the engine that fed our economy. Their greed was of little concern to me because I believed a government couldn't function without wealthy creditors. I was accused of corruption. But corruption was never found, and no discrepancies were ever discovered. I wondered if one could despise the British for trying to submit our country to its imperious orders yet admire their financial system. But I soon realized this view was not acceptable."

The old man couldn't care less. His eyes fixed on mine, still and relaxed. "Duer?" he says firmly.

"Duer," I repeat. "I was a fool and now recognize the error of judgment it was to nominate William Duer to be the Assistant Secretary of the Treasury. He was a conniving profiteer who used secret information to speculate..."

The man cuts me off, "Sadly, the issue was not particular to Duer. Your father-in-law, Philip John Schuyler, benefited from private details known only to you."

I do not respond. The relationship between the government and the wealthy creditors was an intricate tool from which both sides benefitted. Our country relied on creditors to function. They, in return, desired nothing less than maximum return and cared little whether their profit was rendered in currency or access to power, for either satisfied their greed. Ultimately, I could not satiate their monstrous thirst. Had I given them too much? Probably.

I look at the wrinkled face before me and into the peaceful blue eyes. They stare back into mine. Behind him, my companion stands erect, silent, and patient. The sumptuous colonnade extends past him to infinity it seems.

"Dear Alexander Hamilton, you were indeed the builder of a nation," the old man says. "Brave during the Revolution, you penned most of the Federalist Papers. The United States Treasury and the First Bank of the United States were the results of your immense efforts. The Report on Credit, followed by the one on Manufacturing, spelled out the intricacies you desired to expose in magnificent ways. Your work gave birth to an entirely new American industry, which created the city of Paterson in New Jersey, where thousands were soon employed. When an issue arose from the smuggling and pirating off the American coast, you developed the Revenue Cutter Service. Your actions led to a period of economic prosperity. Upon returning to private life, you became one of the finest lawyers in your country, often taking righteous cases with little pecuniary benefit."

The old man turns a page. "The eminent Charles Maurice de Talleyrand considered Napoleon, Charles James Fox, and you, Sir, as the greatest men of this period. But had he been obliged to select *'between the three, I would give without hesitation the first place to Hamilton'*, De Talleyrand said. Oliver Wolcott, Jr, your successor at the Treasury, said, *'Thus has perished one of the greatest men of this or any age.'* It is clear the gift you were given did not go to waste."

As if time had momentarily stopped, the old man pauses, motionless, his eyes locked on mine. The silence feels like the eternity I am about to face.

The old man continues, "And yet, here you are, Sir. Clouds of doubt remain over your intentions, over your association with the British Bankers, and over your honor. Your endless machinations, and your pettiness, especially toward Jefferson, justify every one of the criticisms you ever received. You once stated, *'All communities divide themselves into the few and the many. The first are the rich and the well-born, the others, the mass of the people... The people are turbulent and changing; they seldom judge and determine right. Give therefore to the first class a distinct, permanent share of government.'* The old man leans back into his chair and asks.

"Sir, over and over, you favored the wealthy at the detriment of the people you were to serve. The few chosen ones received inside information to further their speculations, while the rest lost their meager wages on your deceitful schemes. Soon the balance of power vanished from the government itself and into the hands of the few who pillaged all."

The spoken truth pains me. My body stiffens.

"You were vain and opinionated, an elitist whose self-importance led you to accept corruption as a necessity, not a burden on the weak," the old man says.

My legs tremble, my heart races, and tears run down my cheeks. The scathing words, the truth exposed in such plain details. I fall to my knees.

The man readjusts his stare. Void of any expression or judgment, he continues: "you said; *Has it not . . . invariably been found that momentary passions, and immediate interests, have a more active and imperious control over human conduct than general or remote considerations of policy, utility, and justice?* Quite eloquent, Sir. You may have been one of the greatest men of your time but do tell me. If 'momentary passions' had such 'imperious control over human conduct,' why is it your wife is, at present, left to pay your debts?"

Tears fall uncontrollably. The burden I have caused Eliza to suffer is unforgivable. I lower my face into my hands. I try to console myself, to justify the misery I left behind. But I remember the man with the gloved hand, the unfulfilled promises, and the deceits I was subjected to; the 15,000 words I wrote on behalf of the hidden rulers to persuade Washington to approve America's first central bank. Because of me, the Bank of North America became the Nation's Central Bank, but I gained nothing.

I see the ring flash into the darkness of the tavern and realize what a failure I had been. A pawn in a game I was not meant to play. I recall the many clandestine communications with the British agent, Major George Beckwith.

The old man knew my betrayals had been too numerous to count.

I try to speak but cannot. My eyes flood with tears of shame, tears of guilt.

There are no excuses or justifications for my many failures. While lust controlled my senses, self-importance misguided me into complacency, and honor blinded my vision. I ignored those close to me to serve the people I knew not. I deserted my duties.

My companion leaves his post to fetch me. He pulls me to my feet.

The old man has returned to the parchments on his desk. Ignoring my presence, he writes. We walk further into the colonnade.

The landscape now appears clearer between the columns. To my left is a green pasture filled with joyous individuals frolicking among the colorful bushes of delicate flowers. To my right is a muddy land where scattered fires burn randomly. Men are shoved into mud pits. Others are pushed onto the fires they were forced to build while huge and hairless rats run free.

When the sound of bells appears, I straighten. Horns follow. An odd stringed instrument soon joins, playing an unending low note. It vibrates within me. Voices of angels singing in a mysterious language emerge as the instruments fade away. There must be a thousand angels singing in unison. The melody is simple, yet glorious; primal. My fears vanish, replaced by inner peace. Soon their melodic words become clearer.

In their strange dialect, they say my name, "Alexander Hamilton." I freeze. The stringed instrument, a cello perhaps, has returned. Alone, it plays an endless and hypnotic note. The voices continue.

"Alexander Hamilton, you have been found guilty of giving birth to an American Oligarchy. This oligarchy will spread its tentacles over your cherished country for centuries to come, and while your intention may have been honorable, this crime will perpetuate the enslavement of the nation you helped build. For this crime…

CHAPTER 2

WASHINGTON IS BURNING

Our whole banking system I ever abhorred,
I continue to Abhor, and I shall die abhorring...
— John Adams, 1811

WASHINGTON, D.C., 2018

"Context and Justification..." Jameson Hunt Thouroux kept repeating quietly to himself. "Context and Justification..."

In an abundance of care, the young librarian maneuvered his way to the lab slowly and deliberately. Before him, on the grayish plastic tray, he held firmly, was a two-hundred-year-old letter.

Earlier in the morning, the research director had confirmed the authenticity of the letter Jameson transported. A request for a rushed, high-resolution digital copy had been ordered. He arrived on the sub-basement floor of the Library of Congress, where the archival lab was located, and spoke to Chris, the youngest of the technicians, whom he had briefly met during his orientation day.

Chris freed him of the valuable document.

Jameson returned to his desk where, upon receiving the scan, he would attempt to decipher the letter's content.

"Remember, to truly understand such a document, one must first discover its context, and from there, deduce its justification," Mr. Trumbull had proudly stated. "You need not learn every event that occurred when Madison wrote this letter; only the important ones, for they will provide you with context, and from there, young man, you will discover its *Raison D'être*, if I may."

Trumbull was the head Archivist at the Library of Congress, where

Jameson had been employed for less than a month. The young librarian cared little for his pedantic superior. He disliked Trumbull's tawdry appearance, the rancid smell of alcohol on his breath, and his desperate attempt to impress all.

Two weeks ago, Miss Louise Helen Curtis donated an assumed precious document to the Library. The story was that Ms. Curtis was a descendant of Lieutenant Maxfield H. Thorp, who, between 1811 and 1816, served as President James Madison's Secretary and, when in battle, his *aide- de-camp*. President Madison had supposedly written the letter. Were it proven to be authentic, she desired to donate it to the Library of Congress. The letter proved to be from James Madison and would now be cataloged and legally registered in the Library's collection.

The high-resolution scan would help Jameson decode each word, each sentence. It would certainly speed up translating the letter into a more modern version of the English language.

A formal presentation would soon take place to honor the donation; a celebration, during which the Secretary of the Library of Congress would present the letter and deliver remarks. The Secretary's discourse would be based on the report Jameson Hunt Thouroux had been assigned to create. Though translating the letter appeared to be a simple assignment, the young man felt it was an important one.

On his way back to his office, Jameson took a quick detour to the cafeteria to purchase a small latte. In truth, it was an excuse to see Lucie, the new cashier, whom he had timidly invited to go to "Jazz in the Garden" at the Smithsonian's National Gallery of Art Sculpture Garden. She had welcomed the invitation, and tonight was the night. While taking his order, Lucie kindly commented on his slightly growing beard. The shy and somewhat overweight Jameson blushed but smiled as she confirmed they were still on. He left the cafeteria a little happier. While he waited for the scan to arrive, Jameson searched Google for what historical events took place around August 25, 1814, when the letter had been written. At three in the afternoon, the young librarian had completed enough research to start writing a rough outline. Jameson took one last sip of his now cold latte and wrote:

On the morning of August 24, 1814, while emissaries of the President of the United States of America, James Madison, were negotiating a peace treaty to end the war of 1812, violent battles still raged on in the United States.

British Major General Robert Ross led his troops into the Battle of Bladensburg. President Madison, defiant, rode north from Washington to defeat him but was unsuccessful. Defeated, Madison and his troops found refuge in Brookeville, Maryland, approximately 60 miles northwest of Washington.

Meanwhile, Major General Ross, empowered by his success, led a British force into Washington. Under his leadership, the British troops burned many important buildings, including the Presidential Mansion, known today as The White House. The English continued and set fire to the Capitol, the United States Department of War, and the United States Treasury. It was a violent, calculated, but unjustified act.

The Superintendent of the Public Buildings for the City of Washington, Thomas Munroe, concluded the loss amounted to $787,162, an enormous sum at the time.

Enraged by their inability to find the loot they sought, the British troops turned to the Washington Navy Yard. However, their furor grew when they saw that the Americans had torched many of the navy ships rather than leaving the British a chance to acquire undeserved bounties. The Americans had destroyed two prized vessels: the 44-gun Frigate USS Columbia and the 22-gun USS Argus, both near completion.

In a dramatic and foreboding sign, a massive storm, possibly a hurricane, fell furiously upon Washington. Though the torrential rain put the fires out, it also weakened unfinished buildings and flooded entire neighborhoods. The burning of Washington and its occupancy by the British force lasted only twenty-six hours.

Dejected so little loot had been found, Major General Ross decided to continue toward Baltimore, which he correctly believed would be a much more rewarding target. On September 12, 1814, however, Ross was shot by two American snipers. They were believed to have been the two best shooters available to Madison, who personally assigned them to the mission. Major General Ross died en route to receive medical assistance.

While historians have offered various explanations as to why President James Madison signed a declaration of war against Great Britain in 1812, most agreed with historian Henry Adams, who described the war of 1812 as *"an aimless exercise in blunder, arrogance, and human folly."*

Upon hearing the news of the British departure from Washington, President Madison and his troop journeyed back to the city. Four miles from the Capitol and the White House, the President ordered his company to stop on the grounds of what would one day become the United States Naval Observatory.

Distraught by the sight of the smoldering city in the distance, he ordered everyone to leave him and continue toward the city. Within minutes, the troop had gone. Alone, President Madison remained with a small group of eight experienced soldiers led by Lieutenant Maxfield H. Thorp, his secretary. Madison requested the Lieutenant guard him at a short distance. The rest of the soldiers stood guard further out, on the access road.

Jameson heard a sound coming from his computer. An email had just come in with the high-resolution image of Madison's letter. To his surprise, along with the scan came a PDF of the text. He read it. The letter had been translated into modern English. The translation, he later learned, had been created by a custom application that detected each letter and, through a custom algorithm, translated them into coherent words and sentences. Jameson was grateful to have an exact translation of the text; it would spare him hours trying to decode the handwritten document.

About to read a letter of historical importance written two hundred years ago, Jameson felt suddenly excited.

The young librarian closed his eyes and pictured President Madison, all alone, sitting on a broken tree trunk, perhaps. The sight before him was tragic, and desperation must have overwhelmed him. The location, Jameson deduced from an internet search, offered a broad view of the city.

Madison, who had requested pen and ink from Thorp, soon scribbled this letter. A few minutes later, upon its completion, the President stood, crumpled the letter, and threw it to the ground. We possess it today, thanks to Lieutenant Thorp, who had collected it surreptitiously. The following is the note Madison wrote:

August 26, 1814

How can I continue to be the impotent witness to such senseless crimes, unable to punish the savages who committed such absurd acts without honor and void of reason? I know these evil men acted on behalf of the shadows, the dark powers controlling the puppet government across the sea.

"Teach these impudent Americans a lesson. Bring them back to colonial status," Rothschild is assumed to have ordered. Were these acts committed on his behalf? Would they care for nothing to pilfer our country?

The British troupes marched on. Unopposed, they burned Washington, tearing at the frail symbols of our democracy. Their red coats unsoiled, these vile mercenaries, strictly intent on

23

destruction, left Washington unpunished, their miserable souls tarnished forever.

The smoke billowing over the city breaks my heart in an infinite constellation of tears I dare not share. Washington is burning. I was unable to defend the city I presided over.

How can one justify these actions? In Ghent, my emissaries are negotiating a fair and amicable peace treaty in good faith. It is a sad illustration of how evil these criminals are.

Should I apologize for the many errors I committed? Yes, I did proudly announce the war in 1812. But in my defense, I possessed little doubt we would fail to defeat these foreigners. I soon realized my delusion and the time has come for the battle to be judged, its futility accepted as our future appears dreadful.

Our economy is in shambles. Gallatin, the genius whose financial plan ignored to calculate so many basic and logical costs the war would bring on, has led us to ruins. Soon, millions upon millions of dollars were needed to operate the government. Trusting Gallatin was undoubtedly my mistake, for, on this very morning, it appears he has led us to the brink of bankruptcy. In two years, our national debt has doubled to just over $124 million. Our union is fragile.

I should never have trusted the wealthy bankers from the Northeast as they secretly smuggled their precious gold and silver to Canada for safety. I know they support the shadow powers, for they also desire a damned Central Bank. "We want stability," they humbly declare. But in darkness, they plow the seeds of discord to destabilize our union.

We now suffer a shortage of precious metals. Their evil goal may soon be reached, for our economy could fall into disarray. The creditors now refuse to finance our war. "Re-charter our bank now, or else," they warned. Desirous to re-charter their Central Bank, they were willing to exploit every avenue. Even willing to bring our country to its ruin. Fortunes are to be made, and the beggar desires no less than a legal permit to their unbridled pillage.

William Pinkney, our ambassador to the United Kingdom, was told by Nathan Rothschild, *"Either the application for the renewal of the charter is granted, or the United States will find itself involved in a most disastrous war."*

But how can I embrace the institutions I fought so hard to defeat? This war is led by the shadows, the bankers, and the creditors eager to enslave us to debt.

Will I follow in the footsteps of the man I so despised, that illegitimate son, Alexander Hamilton? Will I charter a new central bank? The freedom we dearly claim is but a dream, and far away, in a foreign country, the masters rejoice.

Our prospects diminish as our crippling debt grows. Tonight, I tremble at the steps before me, for never did I foresee the darkness befalling onto our country, our union.

James Madison

Jameson breathed in. The context in which Madison's letter had been written was clear. Behind the pretense of a disagreement over commerce, the War of 1812 had grown from one event: America's refusal to renew the First Bank of the United States' charter. He started to type a draft for his report.

Madison had been one of the Bank's most forceful opponents. He had ignored repeated calls to renew its charter. Upon its expiration, the First Bank of the United States, one of Hamilton's greatest achievements, was no longer America's Central Bank. The British bankers, who owned as much as 70% of its stock, saw its value quickly depreciate. Within months, the War of 1812 was declared.

Across the sea and led by John Quincy Adams, Madison's emissaries negotiated, agreed, and signed the Treaty of Ghent on December 24, 1814, four months after the burning of Washington. The peace treaty restored the borders between the United States and Canada as they were prior to the war.

"Is it possible that Gallatin, the former Secretary of the Treasury and one of Madison's emissaries in Ghent, secretly reached an agreement with the Rothschilds?" Jameson wondered. They were, at the time, the most powerful bankers in the world, and for them, nothing was impossible.

The scheme to create the Second Bank of the United States was hatched. The British creditors rejoiced, for soon, they would have their central bank in the United States. America would have peace. A week later, the Prince Regent signed the Peace Treaty into law.

Madison was unable to solve America's rising debt. Left with no other option but to follow in the footsteps of Alexander Hamilton, the man he so detested, President Madison signed an act establishing the Second Bank of the United States, a private central bank.

Modeled after the Bank of England and its predecessor, the Second Bank of the United States was a private corporation with public duties. The bank handled all fiscal transactions for the United States Government and would be somewhat accountable to Congress and the U.S. Treasury. The federal government owned 20% of its capital. Four thousand private investors, including one thousand Europeans, held 80% of the bank's capital. A few hundred wealthy Americans controlled the bulk of the stocks, often on behalf of their English masters.

On August 24, 1814, witnessing Washington burning in the

distance, President James Madison may have been overtaken by a mood of deep sorrow. The letter supports the idea, but one wonders if Madison had begun to sense the inevitable and unstoppable force compelling him to charter a new central bank.

Jameson lifted his fingers off the keyboard. He heard a knock on the door as he leaned forward to review part of his notes. He quickly glanced at his screen. It was 5:15 p.m. "Lucie."

He jumped to his feet and rushed to the door.

There she was, Lucie, the adorable young woman he was falling for, a big smile on her face. Petite, her pale face was framed by shoulder-length green hair. She had hazel eyes, a straight nose, and full lips covered with a dark mauve lipstick. Without a word, she approached him and kissed him.

Though delighted, he was a little nervous and the kiss was awkward.

"I have been meaning to do this all afternoon," she said as she stepped back.

"I have been waiting for this to happen from the moment I met you," Jameson responded as he moved closer to Lucie and hugged her tenderly.

They left his dark office at the Library of Congress holding hands. Jameson was excited and very talkative. "Most of my life," he confessed, "has been spent writing about my life. In my diaries, I recounted every moment, every event in my life for no one but myself. The losses, the happiness, the love, the sadness. Each event was dissected under a microscope and turned into long paragraphs. A simple exercise in writing and self-analysis."

Lucie was attentive.

"Over the last couple of years," he said, "I realized writing had been a defense mechanism for my insecurities. A shield branded as a self-exploration into the foundation of my being. But it was also a rabbit hole in which I hid my fears."

The night was cool. He reached out for her hand.

"Six months ago, I stopped writing altogether," Jameson continued. "Though I loved the process of writing, I sensed the need to withdraw from being the subject of my literary investigations. I needed to live without the constant analysis. Today, I stumbled upon the subject of my first book."

Lucie turned to look at him. Her eyes demanded more information.

Jameson Hunt Thouroux, the timid young librarian, stopped, faced Lucie, and kissed her tenderly.

"I was waiting for someone. I was waiting for you, I guess." They held each other on the Capitol grounds.

Lucie also felt the longing for someone to love her.

Jameson interrupted this tender moment and proudly announced he would name his book: *1812; A War for the Wealth of a Nation.*

Looking perplexed, Lucie asked, "What is so fascinating about the War of 1812? I barely remember hearing about it in school."

He was about to answer when they arrived at the National Gallery of Art Sculpture Garden. The music was loud, and the garden was busy. They agreed to continue and purchase a sandwich at one of the food trucks populating the mall.

Lucie pulled his arm around her shoulder.

Jameson talked about the letter from Madison. The War of 1812 was a war neither the British nor the United States desired. Upon its completion in 1816 and the signing of the peace Treaty of Ghent, no winner or loser had been proclaimed.

"So why such a long and costly war?" Jameson asked for emphasis. "In truth, I believe European creditors had become enraged at the failure of the Congress to renew the charter of the First Bank of the United States. Lucie, the Bank was a private entity but acted as the Central Bank of the United States. It controlled the critical functions of our young government."

The Rothschilds, who supposedly owned many shares in the First Bank of the United States, were enraged when the Bank's charter was not renewed, Jameson explained. They had lost control of America's Central Bank and, therefore, America.

Nathan Rothschild threatened America with "*a most disastrous war.*"

"I believe they forced the British government into complying with their order because a year later, war was declared," he said.

Jameson explained his book would feature General Major Ross as the protagonist and describe his arrival in the United States, the rogue troop he led in the burning of Washington, and the rage he felt when the promised loot was never found; his decision to move toward Baltimore to acquire undeserved treasure, his untimely death at the hand of two American snipers, and the charter of the Second Bank of the United States."

Jameson, who continued excitedly, described Madison's letter and shared its content and the lament Madison had probably experienced.

"The War of 1812 was disguised as an instrument to regulate fair trade, but its only purpose was to choke America's young government into submission by weighing it down with enormous debt while stopping the flow of money from its creditors. America was forced to fight a war it could not afford financially or otherwise."

"In a final burst of fury, an overt attempt to change President Madison's mind, General Major Ross was probably sent to destroy Washington. The city was burned to the ground."

Lucie pulled him toward a bright yellow food truck. According to its large sign, the truck served the best vegetarian burgers. Jameson smiled at her. She was so pretty, so sweet.

After a few minutes, their orders were ready. They walked to a bench on the National Mall. The night was warm, and the area was filled with people from all over the world enjoying a beautiful evening in this magical city.

"You mean to tell me all of this was destroyed by a troupe of English Red Coats," Lucie said, waving a French Fry toward the Capitol.

"Well, Washington was quite different then, but yes."

"Still, a war for a Bank?"

"Lucie, we often associate war as a necessity to fight some unconscionable act, some evil miscreants deserving to die. But sadly, the truth is quite different, and often armies go to war to protect the interests of a few."

Lucie leaned forward and kissed him on the cheek. She waved her arm from left to right, saying she never actually thought of the British soldiers possibly camping right where they were seated. "I am sure Ross and his Red Coats camped here for a while," she concluded. She took a bite of her burger and paused. Finally, she asked Jameson what he meant by "...armies go to war to protect the interest of the few."

"There is currently a territorial dispute in the South China Sea. You may have heard of it. In truth, the specific location is believed to contain 11 billion barrels of oil and 190 trillion cubic feet of natural gas. Throughout history, the ruling class has repeatedly forced our puppet governments to go to war in order to pillage some random country. Most often, it's about commodities: oil, gemstones, or some other rare and precious material. Sadly, our government has always complied.

"The American people always carry on the enormous cost of the war. The Iraq war brought enormous wealth to Halliburton and inconceivable debt to the United States of America. Africa, with its incredible natural resources, should be the wealthiest continent on earth. But sadly, it has been pillaged by every private colonialist enterprise imaginable, and as a result, its population is one of the poorest. Why has the war in Afghanistan lasted so long? Natural resources. Afghanistan possesses large quantities of lithium, iron, copper, cobalt, niobium, and gold deposits. It is assumed to have chromium, silver, mica, marble, ruby, emerald, and lapis lazuli. War for profit."

Lucie listened patiently.

An interesting date, she thought.

Jameson was unlike most guys she had dated; certainly not as handsome, but much brighter and kinder.

"The War of 1812," she said, turning to kiss him. "A war for a bank?" Lucie leaned her head on his shoulder. Before them, the Capitol looked glorious.

"We should go listen to the concert," Jameson said, detecting a touch of wonder in her eyes. Lucie stood and held her hand out. He took it, and they walked toward the National Gallery of Art Sculpture Garden. Jameson could have discussed Madison and the War of 1812 for hours. In his pocket was a note he had scribbled earlier. On the note were two quotes by Thomas Jefferson. The first one, *"...I sincerely believe that banking institutions are more dangerous to our liberties than standing armies..."* certainly reflected Madison's concerns.

But considering America's $20 trillion debt, Jefferson's other quote seemed more prophetic, *"If the American people ever allow private banks to control the issue of their currency, first by inflation, then by deflation, the banks...will deprive the people of all property until their children wake up homeless on the continent their fathers conquered.... The issuing power should be taken from the banks and restored to the people, to whom it properly belongs."*

Jameson ignored the note, looked at Lucie, smiled, and walked hand in hand with the woman he hoped he would one day marry.

CHAPTER 3

MESSENGERS

Knowledge becomes evil if the aim be not virtuous.
— Plato

Knowledge itself is power.
— Francis Bacon - Meditationes Sacrae (1597)

UNITED KINGDOM OF THE NETHERLANDS, JUNE 1815

Caillou was a one-eyed beast of sorts—a disfigured being ravaged by fear and the violence of men. Part cyclops, part gargoyle, and part man, A soldier amongst the thousands about to die on this dreary battlefield, he sat, sheltered from the torrential rain; silent, immobile, and apprehensive, waiting for the giant before him to move.

A dark night had fallen upon these errant soldiers. Lost in a cruel world, they shivered from fear, cold, and despair. Like ghosts reaching for a world long gone, they stared into the darkness and through the rain— innocent souls blindly waiting to die in the battle at Waterloo, all hope and resolve washed away by the rain. They now trembled, cold and afraid, wishing for better times, wishing for yesterday and their homes far away, wishing that the night may never end.

On the late afternoon of June 17th, 1815, the world offered a welcome respite from the battlefield's stench, oppressive heat, and deprivation. These soldiers had traveled hundreds of miles on foot and suffered through the relentless heat and dust for weeks. They had dug trenches and freed animals stuck in the mud.

As the sun slowly melted over the horizon, the gentle drops of rain sparkled of gold. As it began to drizzle, the soldiers welcomed the rain.

Most men suffered from various stomach bugs. All had become unaware of their own stench. Raising their faces to the sky in unison, thousands of men slowly took off their shirts to let the rain wash away the dirt. Sadly, the drizzle they had at first embraced soon turned into a steady rain. What followed was a torrential downpour that went on for hours. It washed away all in its path. Mud ran along the battlefield in brown rivers of sludge. With nowhere to take cover from the downpour, the lightning, or the wind, they shivered in the mud, knowing these could be their last hours on earth, for the dark cloak of death had descended upon the battlefield.

Of the roughly 60,000 men in the Coalition armies, a few lucky ones found refuge from the rain. The others quickly gave up. Caillou, the one-eyed French cook, had let the rain roll down his scarred and grisly face. But as the rain came down in torrents, he retreated for cover beneath a supply wagon. The kind and once tender young man was a monster with a disfigured face that, on such a dreadful night, would frighten even the most fearless of men.

A poor Frenchman with little education, Caillou had found his way into the Seventh Coalition Army as a cook. Despite his deformity, he was well-liked around the camp. Truth be told, most men pitied the poor soul. Some nights, around the campfires, soldiers shared his story. He had recounted it so many times he now preferred to let others relate the events that shattered his world. His English was poor, at best, and it was easier. Soon the rowdy soldiers who had mocked him incessantly reached out to lay their hands on his shoulder; a silent touch of compassion for the poor soul they nicknamed "Caillou."

Julien Dessanges was his birth name; a name he had long forgotten. Caillou was the French word for the rock that mutilated his face and took his left eye. Julien was the name Marie de Latour had softly murmured in his ear, the name he carried when accused of raping Marie, the local Viscount's daughter. The evil Lord, who considered himself religious, decided to have the young man stoned for his atrocious crime. Violence and horror were common parts of life. He was captured and locked into a basement room for two days.

On a beautiful Sunday morning, men dragged Julien Dessanges to the town center. Accused of a crime he had not committed and claiming his love for the victim, their mutual love, he screamed desperately, confused, as no one had told the young man of his fate. They pushed him in front of the castle wall, where he stood desperately wondering what would happen. A cretin from a nearby village threw the first stone. It broke his nose. What followed was a scene of horror. Minutes felt like hours, days, a lifetime. He fell to his knees, bleeding from deep cuts all over his face when one last unmerciful soul threw a rock so hard, he fell backward in silence, his left eye forever lost. The young girl, the supposed victim, shrieked in horror while her handsome lover cried tears of blood.

It took Julien's mother weeks to get him back on his feet and months before she could leave his side. Monsieur De Villier, the local doctor, took pity on the poor Julien. He stopped by every day, gently mending the wounds. Until Julien fully recovered, the doctor looked over the infected eye, the scars, and the bruises.

Daily, the doctor wiped the blood slowly dripping from the eyelids where the boy's left eye had once been.

Within a year, Julien recovered and attempted to live a normal life. But no longer would his life ever be normal. He had lost his left eye, and while the doctor's generosity was boundless, his skills were limited, and the scars were hideous. His long nose, once attractive, was now deformed with many cuts. The left eye socket was empty and flattened. The right eye socket had so much scar tissue it was twice its prior size. As a result of many cuts to the lips, which had been poorly repaired, his misshapen mouth forever drooped, showing the many spaces where teeth had once been.

The local children, when not terrorized, made fun of him. The rest of the populace thought of him as a rapist, regretting that it was only his face that had been taken away. "It should have been his life," they murmured behind his back.

One morning Julien disappeared, leaving no notes, a broken mother, and the only world he had known.

Caillou, the disfigured and tormented soul, cherished his time alone with his mother as she tended to his wounds.

His father, a stone artisan, traveled to repair damaged structures for months.

The young Julien learned to cook with his mother during his long recovery. He had not seen her in fifteen years and most likely would never lay his one eye on her ever again. He often prayed for his mother, who was probably as lonely as he was. Julien was nothing but a memory.

Planted on a wooden box under the storage wagon, Caillou sat motionless, his mind racing. The subject of his fascination was a mountain of a man—a giant, standing just a few feet away. Questions came faster in his mind than he was able to answer them.

The man before him firmly held a binocular. As if frozen in time, the giant had barely moved an inch in over an hour.

Caillou was fascinated. He had heard of him and the two other men he'd arrived with, but they were the kind of men you stayed away from.

As the sun rose, the giant slowly moved the aim of his binoculars to his right and then carefully to his left, where he froze. Behind him, a man pulled apart the flap of the tent. The man's eyes of steel locked in on Caillou. Sensing the terror this man could afflict, he looked away—away from the fear, away from the ominous possibilities he knew too well. Caillou crawled out from under the wagon and left his shelter for his work. He turned to look at the two strangers one last time when a hand grabbed him by the collar, lifting him off the ground.

"Calm down," ordered a firm, but calming voice. The hand of steel around his neck relaxed a bit, so he did as well.

Though his entire body still trembled, he stopped flailing. Caillou raised his eye to see who had grabbed him so violently. He instantly recognized the other man who had arrived with the giant and his frightening companion. The man's handsome appearance was memorable—long, dark, and curly hair framed his high cheekbones. He had a perfectly trimmed Royale Beard, dark blue eyes, and fair skin. The man noticed Caillou's stare and offered a kind and warm smile but carelessly released him from his grip.

Caillou landed at the feet of the giant, who, surprisingly, did not move an inch. Before he could straighten, he was again pulled off the ground by the handsome man, who plopped him down on a wooden box.

"Why were you watching us all night? Are you a spy?" A raspy voice asked. Caillou turned toward the voice in disbelief. Before him, inches from his face, was the man who had, a minute before, sent fear through his entire being. Caillou did not respond. Instead, he turned his stare toward the handsome man.

Is he for real? A spy? Me? Caillou thought but remained silent.

"My name is Germain de Montieux. This is Rothworth. The tall one is Gustafson."

But Caillou already knew—Rothworth, the evil-looking brute, Gustafson the giant, and De Montieux. He remained quiet.

A series of questions followed, some in French, others in English. De Montieux quickly realized the poor French cook may not be spying on them after all. The rain had forced him to seek refuge under the supply wagon. Caillou could converse in either language, so he settled on English.

"Me cook. No spy. Me no spy." Caillou kept repeating, shaking his head for emphasis. After a few minutes, Rothworth laid a hand on the terrified creature and said, "We are hungry and would love a warm cup of tea. Could you help us, Caillou?"

Caillou nodded his head timidly. He left for the kitchen. De Montieux joined him, and the two conversed in low voices.

Strangely, Caillou felt comfortable with De Montieux, who did not stare at him as the freak that he was, nor speak to him as he if were an imbecile. It had been an eternity since someone had treated him like a human being. They discussed France. De Montieux came from Beynac in the Perigord Region, where he had served the local nobility. It was an area Caillou had traveled through on his way to England. He could still remember the formidable castle built on top of a hill. It was a fantastic sight.

The two returned twenty minutes later with a kettle full of hot tea, a couple of loaves of bread, some ham, a piece of cheese, and some jelly.

"Sit with us," said Rothworth.

Caillou complied.

The three men conversed about the battle to come. The giant pointed in the direction of the battlefield and described the movement of the French troops.

It was around four o'clock in the morning. The camp was still quiet. Most soldiers were asleep.

"This isn't our battle to win or lose, gentlemen. But the battle is near, and death closer. Let's be vigilant," Rothworth said, his voice trailing off into the wind.

For these men, the journey had begun in London, ten days earlier and was now near its end.

Caillou could feel their sense of excitement.

The battle was near.

The giant decided to rest a bit, a well-deserved break from his night watch.

Rothworth grumbled something, stood, and left, and De Montieux refilled his cup with warm tea. He broke off a few pieces of bread and handed one to Caillou. In French, he talked about their mission and journey through England.

"Do you know the Red Shield?" De Montieux asked Caillou, who responded negatively. "We work for them. Everyone knows the Red Shield," he insisted. "In German, Rot for red, and Schild for Shield. The Rothschild?"

"No, I do not know them."

"Do you know why this battle is about to take place?"

"No."

"Well, it's about gold, my friend. Gold and power. French gold, Prussian Gold and English Gold. The Red Shield controls all of it. They may be the richest family in the world. Anyway, we are almost done here. Once Rothworth acquires the information the Red Shield desires, we will leave for London swiftly. It is the most important part of our mission, and we planned for it. We have horses waiting in Rainham, ten leagues from London, and in Stanford le Hope, where Captain Howsmith will anchor once we cross the channel. The captain and his crew of two are waiting for us in Ostend, pretending to be making the light repairs the boat needs."

"There is a boat waiting for you?" Asked Caillou.

"Yes, Caillou. They will be paid handsomely for very little work. The sailors believe Rothworth was a man of importance, maybe a spy for the King; certainly, a person they had no desire to cross. Only one order had been shared with the sailors; upon our return, the sail back to England would be immediate, regardless of the time of day or the weather."

"Captain Howsmith is waiting for you in Ostend. What kind of boat does he sail?" Wondered Caillou. He pictured a schooner, perhaps a boat with a small crew; a small, two-masted schooner, maybe.

De Montieux interrupted his daydream; "His ship is an English Smack. It has a dark blue hull and auburn sails. Easy to navigate with just a few men."

Caillou could imagine the boat and the journey. He would have loved to have been a soldier, to be one of them.

De Montieux continued to describe their trip. It had been an uncommonly warm spring. June felt like August as they drudged through northern Europe. The damp nights and hot days made their travel grueling. But they were men of war, and no complaints were ever uttered. As they were closer to their destination, the group crossed paths with many civilian caravans traveling away from the battlefield. Most were farmers, mothers, and children departing for safer territories.

"On the morning of June 12th, 1815, the signs of the battlefield appeared on the horizon. Gustafson and I changed into the uniforms of the 1st King's Dragon Guards. A document had been handed to a guard upon their arrival. It had been immediately delivered to the Duke of Wellington. Upon reading the note, the Duke asked the three of us to be brought to him at once."

"You met Wellington?" Caillou interrupted in disbelief.

"Yes," he replied. "But after a few minutes, the Duke requested that Rothworth ask his 1st King's Dragon Guards to give them a few minutes in privacy. Gustafson and I walked out of the tent and stood by its entrance. Our service had now begun. Though our uniforms and demeanor would keep most away, war was all around, and any moment could be our last."

Wellington came out of his tent and spoke to his aide de camp. "This is

Rothworth." No first, last, or middle name. No title, rank, or uniform. "Provide these guests with whatever they need. If Rothworth needs to see me, bring him to me at once."

Rothworth returned and sat next to Caillou, who felt he was in a dream by then. He looked at the man who had so frightened him. *Darkness filled his entire being. There is no joy within this man.* Caillou thought, and suddenly the irony struck him, for he was the one pitying the beast by his side.

Caillou reached out for the tea kettle they had placed over the fire. He poured a cup and offered it to Rothworth. The gruff man looked at him from the corner of his eye and nodded, a silent appreciative nod.

At around five on the morning of June 18th, 1815, the activities around the Duke of Wellington's tent intensified. His aide de camp came running to fetch Rothworth. Within a few minutes, he stood outside the Duke's tent.

There were no formalities between the two men. Wellington knew Rothworth acted on behalf of someone else, someone important, someone he also worked for, in a way.

"Sir, I would advise you to leave the camp as soon as possible. A victor will be crowned today. If the French win the battle, I fear they might not show mercy," said the Duke.

Rothworth straightened a bit. "On behalf of my employer, I want to thank you for your hospitality. I will inform him of your courage and brilliance in battle. Your actions, sir, are the reflection of a great warrior. If I could stay a little bit longer and leave when I felt necessary my Lord, I would greatly appreciate it," Rothworth said.

"Of course. But from now on, you are on your own. Godspeed, Rothworth." The Duke of Wellington turned around and walked over to his lieutenants.

Rothworth scrutinized the Duke as he prepared for the battle to come. *Was there fear in the Commander of the Seventh Coalition army?* He wondered. It did not appear to be so.

"Gentlemen. Our stay is coming to an end," Rothworth said when he rejoined his companions. "The battle will be decided today. Prepare to leave upon my order for the Auberge Ein Frien in Halle. I will meet you there as soon as I am able, and as planned, we will depart immediately for Ostend."

Gustafson made a half step forward and said, "Sir, Caillou informed us of a location with a high point from where to survey the battlefield somewhat safely. It is a mile to the east and offers an excellent vantage point. With your permission, I would like to look at this place. We will take you there if it feels like a suitable location."

"Thank you," said Rothworth. "Gustafson, stay with me and prepare for our departure. De Montieux, take a couple of horses and check out the place with Caillou. Make it as quick as possible."

Slowly turning his head toward the battlefield, he spoke. "Over the next hours, the battle's outcome will be decided. I would greatly appreciate it if you could share your expertise in the art of war. Please, inform me of any signs of victory you may notice, whether French or by the Coalition. It will serve me as I make my final judgment. Thank you."

The group separated.

Thirty minutes later, De Montieux was back and described the location. They agreed it would be a perfect place to settle. The three left the battlefield and led Rothworth on the road north and east toward Waterloo. They soon reached a small, run-down church hidden behind a group of trees. They tied the horses and climbed inside the steeple. Up above, within the roof, was a landing where the roof tiles had been removed, leaving the beams exposed. It provided a 180-degree view of the battlefield.

"Well done, Gentlemen," Rothworth said.

"Thanks to Caillou, sir. This is an amazing location." De Montieux pointed his index finger to the sky.

His companions looked up.

Perched on the highest beam sat Caillou, who, upon hearing his name, looked down and waved.

Rothworth and his men took their positions on the landing.

Gustafson knocked off more roof tiles and widened their view.

The massive movements of troops fascinated Caillou, but the heavy silence and inactivity inside the steeple weighed on him. His thoughts drifted to the two French cooks he had worked with for the last month.

They would indeed wonder of his whereabouts. He felt guilty for not being with them and serving the troops.

For the roughly 130,000 men on the battlefield of Waterloo, the heat was unbearable, the air humid, and death waiting. The terrible rainstorm of the night before had left men drenched and muddied. Most knew in the battle to come, thousands would perish. Death was near. They trembled from fear, despair, and the misery that comes when all appears to be lost.

For the Duke of Wellington, the battle had begun many hours ago. At around two in the morning of June 18th, 1815, he awoke and sent his aide de camp to fetch him a warm cup of tea. Wellington wrote a note to his mistress, Harriet Arbuthnot, in Brussels. It was couriered promptly. Over the following hours, he wrote many letters and messages to his commanders.

Field Marshal Von Blücher, who led the Prussian army, had communicated his positions. Messages were transmitted all night between Von Blücher and Wellington. Messengers raced back and forth between them. For Napoleon and his troops to be defeated, Von Blücher would need to play a significant role. Their communications would be crucial.

The Duke, a tall man with a long, angular nose, was admired by his troops. His eyes were clear and bright blue. As the morning progressed around the command post of the Seventh Coalition Army, activities intensified. Messengers were still departing at full gallop and in all directions. Others arrived on the backs of exhausted horses.

Many of the Seventh Coalition troops were inexperienced, young, and afraid. They often spoke different languages and had little in common with each other. The Duke wondered whether his troops would follow orders and keep to their positions in the heat of battle. Holding a formation while knights on huge horses flew toward them was easy in practice, but in war, a forceful and overwhelming fear emerged. Wellington prayed the soldiers would remain steadfast and follow his orders.

Napoleon knew the Coalition's weakness. He knew he could break the Coalition's lines. The French Army was far superior, with 14,000 cavalrymen against the 11,000 of the Seventh Coalition. He possessed almost 100 more cannons than Wellington. Napoleon had the imperial guards, experienced soldiers, and a better strategy.

At around ten in the morning, the French General launched a furious attack at Hougoumont, a farm on the left of Wellington's army. But the farm hosted some of the more experienced Coalition soldiers. They had prepared for many days and were ready for the attack.

The battle was fierce. On the ridge overlooking the battlefield, the Duke rode Copenhagen, his war horse, from east to west to ensure clear communications of his orders. He and his lieutenants sent commands at a furious pace and in all directions.

Two days earlier, Napoleon Bonaparte had won the phenomenal Battle of Ligny against the Prussians led by Field Marshal Von Blücher. Fear had settled for the French troops appeared invincible. As the morning rose, the men knew a decisive moment was upon them. They quietly prayed.

In their perch, Rothworth studied the battlefield. He had barely moved except to ask pointed questions to clarify his interpretation of the battle. The Battle of Waterloo had raged on for hours now. As the hours passed, his inquiries grew steady, and the three men spoke continuously.

The action now enthralled Caillou.

The battle for Hougoumont started and the French gave it their all, but to no avail. The Coalition forces repelled them and held the farm at Hougoumont. Rothworth and his companions agreed it was a strategic area. The French followed with an infantry attack. Eighty guns drew up in the center of the battlefield and started to fire.

Cannons could be heard for miles. The earth shook from their power. It was close to noon. The Prussian Army appeared far to the east of Napoleon's forces at around 1 p.m. Rothworth thought Wellington would be delighted to see the Prussians.

At four, the English cavalry, in a wild attack, charged at lightning speed, blew the French lines away, and quickly pulled back.

The Duke of Wellington ordered a realignment of his forces. Some soldiers were to move back as others shifted to the side.

To the French commanders observing the activities from the opposite side of the ridge, it appeared the English were retreating. Acting upon this belief, the French cavalry, led by Maréchal Ney, was directed to charge across the battlefield.

In response, the Duke of Wellington ordered squares to be formed by the Coalition soldiers. These formations were massive, impenetrable shapes in which five hundred or more soldiers would group. Men fired rifles at the rushing cavalry. Others firmly held their bayonets hidden behind heavy shields. The horses refused to charge directly into these human porcupine formations and roared in fear, often throwing their riders off in terror. Wellington knew that as long as his soldiers held their position, the attack would fail. He was right. Soon, Maréchal Ney and his troops were forced to retreat.

On and on, the Coalition forces were able to defend against the furious French attacks. La Haye Sainte, on the center-right of Wellington's line, was finally taken over by the French when the German troops ran out of ammunition and gave up. To the east, at Plancenoit, the Prussian IV corps arrived, and another furious battle ensued.

Rothworth and his two soldiers frantically exchanged opinions. Their binoculars had become part of their bodies. The continuous motion of the troops, the roar of the cavalry, the cannonballs hurled through the air—the battle was difficult to read. It was six in the evening, and thousands lay dead on the battlefield. The trio had scanned the battlefield for hours. The outcome was upon them, Rothworth believed.

As Napoleon's Imperial guards attacked, he stiffened. "Prepare to leave," Rothworth said.

Neither moved.

"Do you believe they will get through the English lines?" Gustafson asked.

"The imperial guards have never lost." De Montieux said.

Their eyes were fixed on the battlefield.

"They know not of the coalition artillery hiding in the tall grass," Rothworth said. "Leave now."

Gustafson and De Montieux climbed down the makeshift ladder and exited the church.

Caillou descended from his perch. He had no intention of staying there alone with Rothworth.

As he was about to return to the camp, the soldiers waved him over.

"Be safe, my friend," said De Montieux. "I know Rothworth would want you to have this." The handsome French man pulled a couple of gold coins from his pocket.

"However, this is from me to you, Caillou," he said as he pulled a striking folding knife. Caillou extended his hand to receive the gift. The knife was beautiful and heavy. Its handle was made of black ebony. Silver had been used to create an intricate design within its handle.

Caillou raised his one eye from the knife and thanked De Montieux.

The giant, with whom he had barely conversed, kneeled before him, and said, "Fear only engenders fear, Caillou. Be courageous and ignore this enemy. Godspeed, sir." Gustafson stood, and the two left for the auberge in Halle.

Rothworth heard the immense sound of the Coalition's artillery as the Imperial guards charged. Now all alone, he scanned the battlefield.

The Duke had defended and pushed back every French attack admirably.

Napoleon had pushed and pushed, but the Coalition Armies defended themselves honorably and survived.

The Imperial Guards could be the French last chance. They had to break through, but they were taking significant casualties.

Suddenly, the Prussian forces led by Marshal Von Blücher emerged from the east. They roared behind Napoleon's lines. The Prussians were strong and well-trained, and the fighting grew furious.

Rothworth took one last look at the battlefield, slowly scanning it from east to west. He wanted to be as sure as humanly possible of the battle's outcome. He stared at the movement of troops once more—the Imperial Guards, the Prussians, and the Iron Duke raising his sword.

Rothworth left the protection of the steeple and jumped on his horse, riding toward Ostend and London.

At the Auberge, Gustafson and De Montieux ate dinner quietly while the horses were being prepared. On the road, they had changed out of the uniforms of the 1st King's Dragon Guards. Neither drank a sip of alcohol nor made acquaintances with strangers. The two soldiers were ready for their journey back to London.

Rothworth soon arrived and joined the men in the darkest corner of the dining room. He ordered a warm meal as the others prepared the horses for their journey.

The night was a blur. They slowed a few times to avoid attracting attention. North of Ostend was Fort Napoleon and its many French troops, and while Rothworth held documents protecting them from either of the fighting armies, the three just hoped to avoid delays.

Mist rose from the earth. A gray morning, quiet, protective. The smell of the sea became palpable.

The three knew the harbor would soon appear on their left. The horses, at a working trot, their natural pace, were led to the grassy edges of the road to keep the sounds of their hoofs muffled. The sawmill they were looking for finally appeared, and they slowed the horses to a walk. They were just outside of town and within minutes of the harbor.

De Montieux, intending to take heed of their surroundings, raised his right hand. They stopped. Still early in the day, the town was quiet.

The noises of riggings clapping against the ships' masts in the distance were all that could be heard.

They dismounted. It would not be long before they would reach Captain Howsmith. The horses were tied, saddles and bridles removed. With the saddlebags over their shoulders, they walked to the docks.

A tattered flag flew steadily atop the small boathouse—the lucky sign of a steady wind, deduced the wishful Rothworth. Captain Howsmith would be anchored to the left.

Upon seeing them, the ship's first mate, Young John, jumped into action. He scrambled to his feet, set two planks on the gunwale, and rushed to the round cowl vent. His low voice informed the others of Rothworth's arrival. Young John quickly returned to help them aboard and grabbed the gear.

Captain Howsmith appeared, followed by his other crew member, who, without a word, undocked in a series of rehearsed, decisive motions.

Rothworth and his two guards headed for the stern where blankets waited. After a sleepless night of riding, they needed to rest. Warm cups of bitter coffee arrived a few minutes later and were most welcome. As the ship quietly proceeded to leave the harbor, eggs, bacon, and warm bread were served. It may have been the best food they had ever tasted.

It is upon the gods to dictate the wind's strength and direction. It is upon the gods to hold off the rain while the travelers complete their journey. It is upon the gods to watch over their safety or the dangers they may face.

The gods were good to Rothworth, for the wind blew steadily while the sea remained calm. A belated reward for some unknown kind act he may have committed once upon a time, perhaps. He couldn't care less; the gods were good to him.

Miles away and to the south, the tumult of the battle could still be felt. Smoke billowed across the horizon. Horses neighed furiously. Shots rang endlessly. The howls of dying men filled the darkness of the twilight. Curious, the fearful Caillou embraced the courage he had forever ignored and left the safety of the trees along the road for the open field. Caillou wanted to witness the outcome of the battle of Waterloo.

He stopped at the ridge of a small mound and surveyed the landscape before him. Thousands of bloodied, dismembered, and mangled bodies were strewn across the land. The surreal cruelty of the battle overwhelmed his senses.

Hell on Earth, he thought, as a tear rolled down his cheek. "This war is about gold, my friend," De Montieux's voice reverberated in Caillou's mind. "Gold and power. French gold, Prussian Gold, and English Gold. The Red Shield desires it all."

"Gold," he murmured.

Lost in a nightmarish state, he never heard the roaring stallion charging straight at him. The enormous beast never slowed. The stallion's forelimbs pushed Caillou to the ground. The hind legs crushed his chest—the last violent act Caillou would endure.

Hours later, local scavengers armed with pliers, small hammers, and chisels arrived on the battlefield to extract the front teeth of the dead, a treasured commodity at the time.

A tall, scrawny man found Caillou's body; his one eye fixed to the sky. It laid there with open arms. His left hand held the two coins, his right, the folding knife from De Montieux. The scavenger took them. Satisfied with his reward, he ignored Caillou's single front tooth.

CHAPTER 4

THEATER

Give a man a gun and he can rob a bank;
give a man a bank and he can rob the world.
— Mr. Robot, USA. Networks

LONDON, JUNE 1815

At precisely five o'clock, Nathan Mayer Rothschild retired to the grand living room of the impressive New Court on St Swithin's Lane; a most deserved moment of peace. A few days earlier, the rain had begun to fall over London, and while it varied in intensity, it had never ceased.

As a timid ray of sunshine attempted to break through the thick fog, an intricate light pattern momentarily grew sharper on the crimson red oriental rug. Rothschild, eyes fixed on the shapeless burst of light, wished it to be a good omen.

Nathan Mayer Rothschild cherished the feeling of tranquility that these moments alone provided him. His long days at the London Stock Exchange were demanding. The constant buzz of questions and decisions to be made were exhausting.

Hannah, his wife, could be heard in the room above, asking Charlotte about her homework. The other children were probably playing. He was content and took a sip of the liquor.

Nathan Mayer Rothschild was a calculating man who possessed a rare and brilliant analytical mind. So refined was his talent, he could interpret any event, define its circumstances, discover its various remedies, and correctly deduce the most beneficial solution. The true miracle was in the incredible speed at which he accomplished such prowess. But this skillful mind required rest. Of late, Nathan Rothschild had embraced a new routine and for the last few months, from five to six in the afternoon, he would retreat to the grand living room, where he would rest quietly. But today, his mind would not be quiet. What troubled him was a conversation he had had earlier with Sir Dingham.

"Napoleon will win this damned war, I tell you. Oh yes, you wait and see, my Dear Nathan. Just remember, when the news arrives, I told you so." The comments had been unsolicited and now rumbled uncontrollably in his mind. Though Rothschild could tolerate Sir Dingham's rants, he could hardly look at the man. The poor man suffered from an extreme case of rosacea, and red pimples of varying sizes and colors disfigured his face. Furthermore, Sir Dingham's shockingly large nose was the primary victim of his terrible affliction. A most disagreeable and pustulant sight.

Damned war, Sir Dingham, you foolish, ugly man, thought Nathan Mayer Rothschild, as his eyes moved toward the window. He wondered whether it was the conversation or the nose that bothered him the most. He breathed in deeply to clear his mind. Of course, there had been rumors around London that Wellington had fallen to the French General. Unsubstantiated speculations, he believed. The only official word from the battlefield was delayed news of various skirmishes.

To Nathan Mayer Rothschild, the whole enterprise was ironic. His bank, the N.M. Rothschild & Sons Bank, officially supplied the British army with gold. While secretly, his brother Jakob, through Rothschild et Fréres in Paris, conferred the same to Napoleon's troops. One family and its two banks funded opposing sides of the war.

"We are not in the business of deciding whether a war is good or bad," the brothers had agreed. "All wars are bad. But their financial benefit was quite rewarding. We earn a lot of interest on these loans—lots of interest," Jakob had proclaimed. Loaning to governments granted the Rothschilds unimaginable wealth. The government guaranteed these loans, and in war, the victor would honor the debts of the vanquished. To the Rothschilds, it did not matter which country won or lost this cruel and unnecessary war, for no matter the victor; their loans would be repaid with interest.

Rothschild grabbed the glass and took another sip. Over the past few years, he and his four brothers had developed a network of agents, shippers, and couriers to transport gold and information throughout Europe. Information was power. They believed it was to be their key to unimaginable wealth.

The sunlight that had briefly returned quickly disappeared, and the patterns of light on the carpet vanished. A few more moments of peace before someone from a distant location came seeking advice, money, or insurance.

Nathan Rothschild took a deep breath and returned to his office, a floor below.

At eleven in the evening, Nathan Rothschild closed the book on his desk and said good night to the last visitor. Though tired, the conversation about Napoleon possibly winning the Waterloo battle still troubled him. He fell into a daydream and was soon fast asleep. Within minutes a recurring dream faded into his mind. He could hear the sea rolling gently onto the shore, stirring around the small beach stones. But darkness prevailed. A desolate landscape surrounded him. A man's voice, now familiar, started to recite the haunting poem:

While time and the winds of destiny drew near,
The warnings I bestowed upon them,
The Kings ignored,

Another wave rolled, and a gentle breeze lifted as the voice echoed.
"I...Became the King."

Nathan Rothschild was interrupted from his slumber by the slamming of a door and stomping of footsteps. Briefly panicked, he woke up to see Goodwyn's flushed face charging toward him.

"He has arrived, Sir," Goodwyn said.

"Yes, Goodwyn. Thank you." Rothschild paused briefly to look at the large man. Goodwyn was his right-hand man, or maybe his right arm; the man who pushed people away when they came too close or stood when they raised their voices. Rothschild had grown fond of Goodwyn, the kind and gentle brute. Coming to his senses, Rothschild finally said, "Now,

Goodwyn, take a deep breath and tell me, who has arrived at this time of the night?"

"Rothworth is here," the gentle brute answered. Rothschild almost fell off his chair when he heard the name.

The poor Goodwyn looked like a proud dog, panting with excitement.

"Well, go get him, you silly man, and bring him to the grand living room at once. What are you waiting for? Go, now."

Without a word, Goodwyn turned around and flew down the stairs.

Rothworth was exhausted and stunk, a mix of sweat and mud, war and death. He felt like a pauper in a palace about to break a crystal glass and knew not where to stand or sit. His mind raced. Traveling day and night without rest had been a challenge, but here he was, in London. He had left Gustafson and De Montieux at the Moore Gate. The three would meet at the stables later.

"You must avoid attracting attention," Rothworth had said upon leaving them.

De Montieux, the most presentable of the three and had been sent to the London Gate. He presented their documents to the guards. Slightly anxious, they entered London and wondered if they were the first to bring the news. Would their fate be rewarded with the promised gold?

While mainly silent throughout their frenzied journey, the three had, at times, discussed the last stages of the battle. Rothworth shared what he had witnessed. The French charge. The imperial guards. Von Blücher's troop.

At first, De Montieux's instincts had brought doubts. He disagreed with his companions' deductions of the battle's outcome. By the time they entered London, however, the three agreed. They knew who came out victorious.

"Follow me, my Lord," said Goodwyn.

"Please tell the Master I have been traveling for days now and coming from a battlefield. May I suggest we meet in the guard's hall by the stables?" Rothworth suggested.

Goodwyn made a full circle back to Rothworth, scratched the top of his head, and said, "So you want to meet Sir Rothschild in the guard's hall?

Because you stink." Goodwyn confirmed. After a brief pause, he flew up the stairs.

Still groggy and troubled by his recurring dream, Rothschild waited patiently when his clumsy right-hand man returned. Goodwyn quickly explained the situation.

"I see," said Rothschild. "Collect some clothes, have the maid prepare a bucket of warm water, and give Rothworth a room where he can wash and change into clean clothes. Then order food and tea to be brought here. I'll wait for him."

A young woman, the night maid, appeared in the foyer. She led Rothworth to the second floor, where he was shown to a room lit by a few candles. The maid had set a bucket of warm water, soap, and perfume. She pointed at the clean clothes on the bed and said, "The Master is waiting for you in the grand living room. Please meet me outside when you are ready. I'll take you there." She smiled and left.

Rothworth would have to be brief. He hated for anyone to wait for him. Especially the man who had financed his journey. Soon ready, he exited the room.

The maid stood, turned away from him, and marched toward the end of the corridor.

Rothworth followed her and soon entered the grand living room.

Nathan Rothschild could not contain himself. "Come in, Rothworth. Sit. Right here. Perfect."

Goodwyn stood outside the door where he would wait for their meeting to end.

A minute later, all was quiet. Rothschild wanted to know everything. He demanded every detail be shared slowly, chronologically, and with as many trivialities as possible. Rothworth shared his tale; his two guards, travel, planning, the ship, and the battlefield.

It was past midnight on Tuesday, June 20th, 1815.

Rothworth continued. The battle of Waterloo had been fierce The French troops were far superior. Only a well-led coalition could defeat them. To be victorious, the Duke of Wellington's army could not back down. One mistake, and the French would claim victory. Wellington had been steady and strong, but the French were powerful. Had there been mistakes?

Yes, the first and possibly fatal mistake had been on June 16th. With a formidable force of 20,000 men under his command, Marechal Ney arrived at "Quatre Bras." In the battle to come, the location would be critical. Had Ney, upon his arrival on the battlefield, engaged the coalition forces, who were only 8,000 strong, then he would have quickly taken over the position. However, Marechal Ney, uncharacteristically, decided to rest for the night. He believed a morning battle would ensue. Unfortunately, by then, Ney was outnumbered, coalition troops having arrived continuously throughout the night. "Quatre Bras," a critical position, would not be under French control.

On the East side, Marechal Grouchy, for Napoleon, was fighting Prussian Marshal Von Blücher, whose horse was shot from under him. Von Blücher remained pinned under the beast.

With their commander possibly lost, Von Blücher's generals decided to retreat from the ferocious French attack. The Prussian troops escaped from the field in good order. Von Blücher was rescued and rejoined his troops. Though it looked bleak for the Prussians, they had avoided a decisive French victory, which would have obliterated the coalition's ranks.

As they retreated, Marshal Von Blücher ordered his troops to march west with the French in pursuit. Incredibly, the French lost track of the Prussians—a colossal error, and one the French would dearly regret the next day.

Rothschild was fascinated, transported into a world he had never known, war with its tragic outcome, all its horrors, and the future of nations on the line. The build-up was masterful.

Slowly, Rothworth recounted every minute of his last day on the battlefield. The coalition forces, while fighting bravely, seemed to be chasing their tails; fighting for their survival, he believed.

The two men stopped and refilled their glasses. A small bite of the bread with cheese was a welcome treat. It was two o'clock in the morning.

Rothworth shared his last conversation with Wellington.

"Did he seem worried?" Rothschild inquired, trying to assess the Duke's behavior.

They heard Goodwyn's loud snoring outside the door and laughed. Rothworth continued. He shared the various movement of troops—the many powerful attacks by the French forces. June 18th, 1815 was when the battle of Waterloo would ultimately be lost or won.

Lord Uxbridge's cavalry charged from the center of the coalition's line. But the charge had been too forceful. It led them into the heart of the French troops, where some of the men were lost.

Rothworth shared his companions' concerns and insights. They talked through the night. The two guards had left early to prepare for their speedy return as he remained behind, scanning the battlefield from his vantage point.

The French struggled to force a final blow. Napoleon's invincible Imperial Guards were dispatched.

But Rothworth soon noticed a tremendous amount of movement from the east and far behind the French lines, the Prussians, perhaps. Even though none of them had stayed till the bitter end, the outcome was pretty clear to them.

While Rothworth sounded as confident as possible, his employer had become quiet. He was analyzing every word. What was the percentage of error, Rothschild wondered?

Footsteps could be heard around the house. The morning light slowly filled the room. Today would be a big day.

Rothschild stood, looked at Rothworth, and said, "You have done well, my friend. I knew I could count on you. Please come here at ten this evening, and bring your companions, for it would be a pleasure to meet them. Till then, be good and stay out of sight. I need to maintain the utmost secrecy. Thank you." The two shook hands and parted ways.

Rothworth and his two companions had been the first to deliver the critical news. Gold would be forthcoming. Keeping quiet and out of sight for a day or two would be the easiest part of their mission. He stepped out of the grand living room and woke Goodwyn, who led him out of the house.

At six in the morning, the house was still somewhat quiet. Rothschild kissed his sleeping wife, Hannah, who stirred and immediately returned to sleep. Nathan Mayer Rothschild had dressed all in black, as he often did. But this morning, he selected a dull black fabric. *Nothing shiny or reflective*, he thought. Rothschild skipped on the perfume and looked through Hannah's makeup to apply a touch of the light white powder she sometimes used. He laughed at himself and the entire scheme.

Rothworth knew the outcome of the battle of Waterloo, and he, Nathan Rothschild, was about to earn an immense profit from it. "Let's play," he said in a low voice, and left the house.

Nathan Mayer Rothschild was a gentle man. Never rude nor mean, he was very generous, though he preferred to share his wealth discreetly. Vanity had never taken root within him. He had an easy smile, and what remained of his light brown hair was cut short. He carried a few extra pounds, but who would not, when working fourteen to sixteen hours a day and only eating the most delicious food? The people who liked him knew him as a joyful and brilliant businessman. They often admired his incredible wit. Envious people who could see no further than the tips of their noses often did not like Nathan Rothschild and were led to those feelings by jealousy.

Goodwyn had gone to fetch Nathan Rothschild's assistant, James Talbot. The two soon returned.

"Mr. Talbot, I need you to collect a few of the bank staff immediately. Here is the list," Rothschild said.

Talbot, who always remained calm, immediately jumped into action. He knew each of the men on the list. Most were senior employees, agents, and associates. Talbot was in his late teens, of average size, with dark hair, brown eyes, and a pale complexion. The young man immediately sent each man a single message: "Come at once." In the meantime, Rothschild and Goodwyn settled in the warehouse office. The sizable space would easily accommodate a large group. Soon, Talbot joined them.

"Mr. Talbot," Nathan Rothschild said. "Today, the two of us will only speak in low voices. We will look somber, tired, and gravely concerned. Once I take my position, you will remain two feet behind me. If I wave to you, come closer. I will give you either a spoken or written trade order. Pass it to the recorder of trades. Once it has been recorded and announced, return to your position by my side. Understood?"

Talbot, who sensed the importance of the moment, nodded in agreement. Goodwyn, the gentle brute, would be tasked to check on his employer every hour, on the hour, and to remain quiet.

"To protect you from the madness which may ensue, only leave to place the order I request. It will most likely be to sell. If you need to break for the bathroom, wait for Goodwyn. He will accompany you and make sure you are not bothered," said Rothschild.

Tea and pastries arrived and were laid on a large table by the entry. Most of the employees who had been called upon moved around the room, eating sweets, and drinking warm tea. Everyone enjoyed a moment of peace.

Meanwhile, at the end of the warehouse, Rothschild conversed deeply with three men.

James, the warehouse secretary, had led the men through the side door straight to Rothschild a few minutes earlier.

Strangers to Talbot, the three men were dressed in formal black suits and stood at attention. They were men of importance who, Talbot assumed, would play a crucial role in the day to come. They faced Nathan Rothschild and listened attentively. After a few minutes, the men shuffled around, bowed, and left quietly.

The curtain was about to rise, and every actor needed to take his place.

Nathan Mayer Rothschild rose from his seat. He described everyone's duty throughout the day with a surprisingly powerful voice.

"Though you are my trusted employees," he continued, "I must emphasize how critical your discretion will be today. I have selected to undertake a series of decisive actions. These actions will forever change the N.M. Rothschild Bank, its role in the British and world economy will grow in power if my plan is effective."

None of the men before him knew Rothschild's messenger had arrived from Waterloo or what Rothschild had learned. To them, it all seemed like a grand scheme under the direction of their mysterious employer.

"Our success can only be achieved if you trust me. I want to thank you in advance for the important role each one of you will play." Rothschild looked at the many anxious faces staring back at him and waved Talbot to come over. He hurried to follow Rothschild out of the building.

Goodwyn trailed a few feet behind, and within minutes the warehouse was empty.

The London Stock Exchange was a short walk from New Court on Swithin. No one could predict that by the end of the week, the N.M. Rothschild Bank would become the most powerful financial company in the world.

At precisely four minutes past nine, on Tuesday, June 20th, 1815, a ghostly-looking Nathan Rothschild entered the hall of the London Stock Exchange and slowly climbed the stairs to the main trading room. He gestured weakly to the usual greetings offered, seemingly too troubled to raise his eyes to the crowd. The white powder from Hannah's makeup box had been reapplied.

"Are you all right, my dear Nathan?" Inquired Sir Dingham, surprised to see his friend so pale.

There was no response.

The fat, ugly man immediately deduced something was wrong and marched over to a group of traders stationed to the left of the hall. The small group included Sir Alexander Adams, a tall, scrawny, and unfriendly-looking individual who controlled the ports and the prices of commodities. With him was Christopher Watkins, a handsome Irishman who preyed on the richest of London's widows to finance his reckless trading habits. The third man was Mark Whitemoore, an attractive and somewhat trustworthy man who served trade unions and a few upper-class society families. These three men were the most active and influential traders on the exchange floor.

However, all eyes were set on the ghostly Nathan Mayer Rothschild. Upon seeing him, the cheerful traders became worried.

Trading would start in a few minutes, and through the hall, only one thing mattered; What was going on with Nathan Mayer Rothschild?

The stage was set.

At twenty minutes past nine, James Talbot was sent to place an order to sell.

Ferdinand Wooster, the principal recorder of trades, sat behind a tall desk. Wooster was a lanky, grayish man with deep, dark circles under his eyes. He was polite but often cantankerous. To Ferdinand Wooster, orders were orders. After twelve years in this tedious position, he cared little for what was sold or purchased. He fulfilled his function: he read the orders, checked the numbers of government securities, commodities, stocks, or bonds to be sold, and entered the information in his trade book. Once logged into the official ledger, the orders were passed to Philip, the exchange official trader, who, in a booming voice, announced the trade for all to hear. The transaction was, upon its official acknowledgment, complete.

Wooster glanced at the order James Talbot had just handed him. The number was too substantial to ignore, and the main recorder of trades froze briefly. He scrutinized the order once more and paused. His lips moved as he read it again and again. Finally, he inhaled deeply, stared at Talbot, turned to the register before him, and entered the order. But before passing the order to Philip, he looked at the young man and said, "This is going to be a long day."

Talbot, who knew better than to express any emotion, or respond in any way, just turned to rejoin his post alongside his employer. *If you only knew*, James Talbot thought. *A very long day it will be.*

The order was announced. A hush went through the room, with every trader stunned by the magnitude of the order. 70% of the Rothschild's British Government Bonds were to be sold. It was an enormous amount and would drastically lower the value of the bonds.

In the blink of an eye, a single man had set panic around the Exchange.

At first, men were confused, then worried, and started to look for answers where none could be found.

Sir Dingham frowned in disgust.

The group he had joined was arguing about what next steps to undertake.

Talbot now understood what Nathan Rothschild had said on their way to the London Stock Exchange: "When panic sets, reason departs. It leads men to reckless acts. Today, you will witness such behavior. Don't concern yourself with any of it. Too often, life is just like theater. We are all actors playing a particular role in a surreal play of our designs."

It all made sense now. Rothschild's first trade had been followed by a hush and a dreadful silence. This order transformed the Exchange into a deafening scene of chaos. Traders with panicked faces analyzed the order. Why would Rothschild sell this amount of British Government bonds? It was soon agreed there could be only one reason: The Duke of Wellington had failed, and Rothschild knew it.

For the last few days, around London, rumors had spread that Napoleon had defeated the Coalitions Forces.

"Rothschild must have received insights from his network of messengers." said Alexander Adams, who was worried about the plummeting prices of commodities.

"Traitors," said Christopher Watkins, the Irishman whose investment had suddenly shrunk in value, "No one has heard from the Duke of Wellington, but we know the Rothschilds have their network of messengers and spies."

The conversation between the traders became heated. Decisions needed to be made quickly. The value of every stock would soon plummet uncontrollably. The loss would be tremendous. It was only a little before eleven, and already the Exchange was in an uproar. Traders lined up before Ferdinand Wooster, who recorded order after order to sell.

Philip, who announced the trades incessantly, was losing his voice.

Around one, Rothschild moved a bit, and Talbot understood it was his clue to come closer.

Talbot leaned forward, listened to the order, wrote it in his logbook, and moved toward the end of the line.

The other traders invited him to cut the line.

Talbot looked at all the desperate faces staring at him. Nervous, the young man wondered if he could cut the line.

"Yes, you can cut in," one of the traders said. He was immediately the second in line. A few minutes later, he handed the order to Ferdinand Wooster. The British Government Bonds were down by more than half and still moving lower.

Now, Rothschild was aiming at various precious metals and stocks. The order listed six of the major English stocks. It was a well-calculated order. If the Duke of Wellington had failed, the price of steel would go down.

Talbot waited for the order to be announced. Another chill went through the hall.

Thankfully, Goodwyn had arrived and led Talbot to the restroom, where everyone harassed him.

"What is your boss doing?" Someone yelled.

"He has been informed Wellington was beaten, correct? We know it." Talbot was distressed when a voice boomed behind him. It was Goodwyn's.

"Back off, Gentlemen. Let the poor men use the latrine in peace."

All went quiet.

He had been nervous about being alone with this crowd, but for a moment, he relaxed, knowing Goodwyn would protect him.

The market was close to crashing. Some stocks had lost almost 70% of their value. The British Government Bonds were down 62%. Rothschild had placed a few more orders in the afternoon, and everyone else had immediately followed. Panic had set in, and reason no longer ruled.

The intensity of the day had tired the young assistant, who was dozing off when a door opened with a loud creak. It startled him out of his lethargy. Talbot turned and noticed one of the three men he had seen earlier in the morning. The gentleman entered through the side door. Sir

George Hennessy, one of the exchange managers, accompanied him. The two sauntered toward the dark corner of the hall and sat at a large table behind Ferdinand Wooster. Two floor officers followed them and stood by the table. It was 4:30 in the afternoon, with thirty minutes left to the trading day.

Goodwyn, the absent-minded witness, checked on his employer, who waved him off but nodded in Talbot's direction. This time, Goodwyn did not leave the room and took position next to the young man. The day was about to end.

Nathan Rothschild was almost in a trance. His eyes were fixed on the two men in the back of the room. At fifteen minutes before five, Talbot was given his last order. Unlike the prior orders, it appeared more formal and was enclosed in an envelope with the wax seal of the N.M. Rothschild Bank.

"Mr. Talbot, I want you to walk over to the table behind Ferdinand. Please, pass this note to the gentleman you saw in my office this morning, then come back here immediately. Thank you."

Sir George Hennessy, the exchange manager, read the letter at the desk. The mysterious gentleman stood beside him and pointed at the bottom of the page. The traders could only wonder about the meaning of this turn of events. Sir Hennessy placed the letter on the desk, picked up the quill pen, dipped its point into the small ink bottle, and signed Rothschild's letter, making it an official document.

The closing bell rang.

Trading the way Rothschild had done had lowered most bonds, commodities, and stock value on the English market. Their prices had hit rock bottom.

The traders who had been able to follow Rothschild's every step hoped for a positive outcome. The others had lost fortunes, their future uncertain, their search for answers unfulfilled.

As planned, thirty minutes before closing, Rothschild's agent poured enormous amounts of money to purchase all the available British Government Bonds and various stocks sold throughout the day, but at a tiny percentage of their value on the morning of June 20th, 1815.

The next day, on June 21st, 1815, at eleven in the evening, Major Henry Percy, a Duke of Wellington envoy, arrived at the War Office in London. He delivered the Duke's report: Napoleon had been crushed in a bitter, eight-hour battle. The French had lost approximately 20,000 men. The Duke of Wellington and the Coalition forces had been victorious.

Within a few days, the fortune of the N.M. Rothschild & Sons Bank became unlike any other. Nathan Rothschild had fooled the entire London Stock Exchange. The Bank had earned an estimated 20 to 1 return. This fortune allowed the Rothschilds to acquire complete control of the British economy and the Bank of England.

Talbot worked another eighteen months for Nathan Rothschild. He was 21 by then and had been able to save a fair amount of money. His employment provided him with room and board and allowed him to invest every penny he made into trades. The young secretary had followed his employer's every move, and his investment had grown substantially.

Talbot had considered remaining on the job and settling in London forever, but homesick and with enough money saved to open a small store in his hometown, he gave his notice.

As Talbot sat across from Nathan Rothschild on his last day of work, he reminded his employer he would be leaving for home tomorrow.

Rothschild stopped and looked at his assistant. "You have been an outstanding employee and an exemplary young man. Your family should be proud of you. Throughout the years, you have never doubted me nor been insolent or out of line. I greatly appreciate these qualities."

Talbot blushed a bit.

"Dear young man, I am so happy for you. Please know the N.M. Rothschild Bank would be happy to provide any loan you may need," Nathan Rothschild said.

"Thank you, Sir. It has been an honor. Can you believe the two of us fooled all the accomplished traders at the stock exchange?"

A rare laugh burst from his employer who, behind the insensible mask he projected, possessed a childish and warm personality.

Talbot smiled and said, "Well, the three of us. You, I, and the clueless

Goodwyn." They laughed a little harder.

"You did well, Talbot. I have been waiting for the right moment to show. my appreciation. I know your portfolio has prospered as you followed my every trade, but you may still need a little more money." Slowly Rothschild reached inside his desk drawer and pulled out a purse full of coins, which he handed to Talbot.

"Please, accept this as a small token of my appreciation," Rothschild said, standing. "Thank you, Talbot. I wish you all the success. Sadly, I must return to work. Please make sure you see Goodwyn. He would be heartbroken if you were to leave without saying goodbye."

As Talbot climbed the stairs to see Goodwyn, he noticed the line of people gathered to meet with Rothschild. There were men in tears, probably on the edge of bankruptcy. He also knew about the Princes and Ambassadors, who entered through a side door, and waited in a gilded salon. These beggars, who acted like men of importance, were kept away from the prying eyes of the commoners.

Talbot was relieved he would no longer be the recipient of their ire. He said goodbye to Goodwyn and prepared to leave.

A few months passed before Talbot returned to London. There to attend to his finances, he managed to find himself close to New Court in St Swithin's Lane. He decided to visit the tavern where he had spent so much time with colleagues and friends. There was a time when everyone paid attention to his every step. He had been Rothschild's protégé. No one would have dared to cross him. Today, no one paid him any attention. He preferred it this way.

Talbot entered the tavern and was greeted by the enormous Sir Williams, who owned the tavern and recognized him instantly. Thankful to have survived the owner's bear hug, Talbot moved into the dining area when he noticed Von Neiman, who had taken over Talbot's duties with Nathan Rothschild and started a few weeks before he left. While the two had often conversed, their discussions focused on work.

Von Neiman, who recognized Talbot, waved him over and insisted Talbot join him.

Talbot, glad to be received so warmly, felt welcome and sat at the table with his successor. They shared banalities for a while. Von Neiman said he was excited about an upcoming trip to France with Nathan Mayer Rothschild. Though, in truth, a little nervousness could be felt in his speech. He shared the difficulties he encountered following Talbot's footsteps. Goodwyn had been difficult with him at first.

"Oh, I had to do everything just the way you did. You would think someone may have shared the methods you used?" said Von Neiman.

The two laughed but grew serious when they discussed the rude visitors. Von Neiman broached the subject of the fateful day at the London Stock Exchange. "Well, my dear Talbot, I should return to work before I am too drunk to fulfill my duties. Forgive me for asking, but would you tell me what happened on that marvelous day?"

Talbot initially declined. "Nothing special happened." But Von Neiman begged to hear the story he vaguely knew. So, with just enough ale, Talbot soon relented. He had never shared the day's events, and somehow it felt good to free himself.

"Rothschild and I fooled the toughest businessmen in London," he said. "It was a wonderful day, Von Neiman. The Master was splendid. Dreadful and impenetrable. Still as a stone. Goodwyn was stoic. What a day." He continued, recounting every hour.

"Slow down, my young friend. I need details, every one of them."

So, Talbot described every moment. Somehow, it felt like he was reliving every breath he had taken on June 20th, 1815. The inquiring faces. The concerned looks. The frantic calls to sell, the voices full of uncertainty.

"How I wished I had been you then," Von Neiman said.

"Knowledge is power, Von Neiman, for it allows you to control every aspect of a situation." Talbot said as Von Neiman, who, after warm goodbyes, left the tavern.

Alone at the table, Talbot looked out the window and saw a flux of people hurrying. *The foolishness of it all*. He thought.

Out of the blue, Talbot remembered a day in 1814. It had been a typical day, on the quiet side, actually, when in the early afternoon, a courier sent by the Earl of Liverpool, England's First Lord of the Treasury, appeared at Swithin's Lane. From the Treasury, the messenger carried a letter for Nathan Rothschild.

The man was asked to wait while Talbot delivered the message to his employer. When Talbot entered the large living room, he informed Rothschild of the guest. His employer was distracted with other matters, so he asked Talbot to read the message. The note read,

Dear Sir,

I am writing to inquire about a private meeting with you, at Apsley House, at 10 in the morning tomorrow. Your attendance would be greatly appreciated. Please inform my courier of your decision.

Gratefully yours,
Sir Earl of Liverpool, First Lord of the Treasury

Nathan Rothschild directed Talbot to respond affirmatively, and Talbot hurried back to the courier.

The next day, they met at Apsley House was the London residence of the Duke of Wellington. It was located on the southeast corner of Hyde Park. The house was a proper and discreet place for the two to convene.

Robert Jenkinson, "Lord Liverpool," as he was commonly referred to, arrived a little before ten in the morning and appeared with two of his subordinates.

Lord Liverpool and Nathan Mayer Rothschild sat in the Piccadilly Drawing Room for hours. At three in the afternoon, it was agreed, the N.M. Rothschild Bank would provide funding to the Bank of England to support its troops and defeat Napoleon on the battlefield.

Talbot had the strange realization that England, unable to finance its affairs, needed the support of the Rothschild's international financial network.

The N.M. Rothschild & Sons Bank would procure resources the Bank of England, the country's national Bank, could not.

In the tavern, Talbot woke from his daydream as Sir Williams brought more ale. Talbot disregarded the pint, left a generous tip, and departed.

Over the years, Talbot grew his business using all the tools he had acquired from the man who had kindly mentored him. He followed the N.M. Rothschild & Sons Bank, and the events surrounding the five brothers.

In 1826, the Bank of England was at the edge of a liquidity crisis. The Bank was rescued by the Rothschilds, who supplied enough coins to avert such a crisis. Their financial dealings grew on and on. They agreed to provide a loan to the Holy See for £400,000 in 1832. Then a £5 million loan to the Prussian government.

Talbot's genuine fascination was with the unimaginable power the family had gained over the years. Grateful governments had showered honors and decorations upon them. In 1822, Francis I, the Emperor of Austria, bestowed on the five Rothschild brothers the title of Barons.

Upon learning he had worked under Nathan Rothschild, friends and acquaintances would implore him to explain how the house of Rothschild amassed such untold wealth. Talbot always responded in a kind manner.

"The Rothschilds, I knew, while prudent and perseverant, understood the power of knowledge and how to use the information they acquired to forward their goal. During the time I worked for Sir Rothschild, the family never flaunted their wealth. They were loyal, honest, but above all generous, extending their kindness to all, regardless of what class they belonged."

Though all of it was true, Talbot never mentioned the Royals, Ministers, and Lords who came begging at Nathan Mayer Rothschild's door. Nor did he disclose the deals the bank extracted from the very people it aimed to serve. But as clear as if it were yesterday, he remembered the day Nathan Rothschild said, *"I care not what puppet is placed on the throne of England to rule the Empire. The man who controls Britain's money supply controls the British Empire, and I control the British money supply."*

Talbot never spoke of the secret only a few knew—that the world was not controlled by fools who inhabited golden castles, but rather by the men who, in the shadows, led them. Hidden from the prying eyes, they were the true financial rulers of nations.

CHAPTER 5

THE FIVE ARROWS

When a government is dependent for money upon the bankers, they and not the leaders of the government control the situation, since the hand that gives is above the hand that takes ... financiers are without patriotism and without decency...

— Napoleon Bonaparte

BERLIN, 2017

Rosalie Feinhof sat in one of the dreary offices of the German Federal Intelligence Office. Greenish light, a gray desk, gray chair, and a monotonous panorama of a city she disliked. Her contact, Herr Friedrich Schmidt, a German spy with lovely blue eyes, a pale complexion, and a receding hairline, sat beside her, eyes fixed on a computer screen. She gazed at his suit and knew it had been purchased at a discount store by his unloving wife, who had not given a damn about the size, the color, or the man.

Rosalie had once found Schmidt attractive. But that was long ago. She turned her gaze toward the two-hundred-year-old document before her.

"Schmidt, I need coffee," said Rosalie. "8 a.m. in Berlin feels like 8 p.m. I'm already exhausted."

"I am at your service, Herr Rosalie Feinhof, Expert Paleographer," he said teasingly. "Let me guess; two lattes?"

"Thanks," said Rosalie, amused by the formality.

Thirty-five, with dark black hair, bright blue eyes, and a trim body, it would have been hard to imagine Rosalie was a bookworm. But eight hours a day, five days a week, the beautiful, lively, and forever joyful woman sat in her tiny office and transcribed historical manuscripts. An

Expert paleographer from Zurich, Rosalie had been referred to the German Intelligence Agency by Inspector Klaus Watzels of the Swiss Intelligence Services. Rosalie would jump on an early flight to Berlin on the first Monday of the month for over a year now. From the airport, an Uber would drive her to the massive building of the German Federal Intelligence.

Upon her arrival, she invariably found Schmidt waiting for her by the security desk. He escorted her to a nondescript floor, in a nondescript area of the building, where none could be seen nor heard.

"Here is the laptop you'll be using today," Schmidt said. "This manuscript is from 1815."

"How boring is this one going to be?" Asked Rosalie.

"Not sure, but there is a brief description," Schmidt said, pointing at the stack of paper. "Why don't you review it while I go get coffee?"

"Sounds good. Thanks." Rosalie reached for the description.

On July 20, 1785, in the small town of Regensburg, thirty kilometers northeast of Zurich, a man, later identified as Jakob Lanze, was struck by lightning. The powerful electrical charge killed him and the horse he was riding instantly. Bavarian officials, curious about the deceased's identity, examined the contents of his saddlebags. To their great surprise, the documents the man transported were signed by Adam Weishaupt, leader of a secret group called the Order of the Illuminati.

May not be boring after all, Rosalie thought.

Their search uncovered detailed plans for an upcoming French Revolution. Alarmed by their discovery and hoping to get to the bottom of the nefarious discovery, Bavarian officials arrested all known members of the Illuminati they could find. Unfortunately, Adam Weishaupt, their leader, had vanished.

Warnings about the possibility of an impending revolution were immediately sent to the French King. The pompous monarch, incredulous, ignored them. When the events listed in the nefarious document unfolded as described, the gravity of their discovery grew more alarming. The French King lost his head. France became a republic. The fearful Bavarian officials launched one of their longest investigations into the Illuminati. This document relates to one of these inquiries.

As Schmidt returned, Rosalie leaned back into her chair.

"Is this about the Illuminati?" She asked him.

"No, I think the Rothschilds. I guess the Bavarian authorities suspected them of being members of the group," he said as he placed the coffee on the table before her and smiled. "But the sooner you transcribe this document, the sooner we'll know." Along with two Lattes, Schmidt had brought a couple of delicious-looking pastries. She ignored the sarcasm.

Rosalie removed the pink leaf of paper covering the Bavarian document. The old cover page was intricate and beautiful. The page was filled with elaborate signatures, stamps in red and black ink, and a Bavarian blazon. The two-hundred-year-old document started formally:

On the order of the Director of the King's Special Services, I, Otto Kierke Heinegard, requested three Bavarian agents: Herr Karl Funsderbad, Nicolo Adventi, and Markus Klein, to investigate the events which took place between 6 October and 12 October 1815, at the Chateau de Rilly, located south of the city of Reims, in France.

Suspecting a possible meeting of members of the Order of the Illuminati, I was asked to investigate and report all findings in the quickest of manners. Said meeting was to include the descendants of Mayer Amschel Rothschild, a presumed supporter of Adam Weishaupt, the founder of the Order of the Illuminati.

She went on for a while in silence. At one point, the handwriting looked different, more rushed. Rosalie pulled a magnifier from her backpack and reached out for her headphones. She scanned her iPhone and found Dmitri Shostakovich's 24 Preludes and Fugues by Keith Jarrett, selected Prelude and Fugue No. 5 in D Major, and pushed play. She returned to the manuscript. An hour later, the monotony caught up with her. "Herr Schmidt, I need more coffee."

"No problem, I'll be right back," he said.

"No, no, no... I need to get out of here."

"Sure," he responded with a smile. "Boring manuscript?"

"It's quite interesting, but this office is suffocating."

They sauntered to a large cafeteria with bright green and white walls and sat by a window. The place was empty. Schmidt politely inquired about the manuscript.

"Well," she said. "I learned there were five Rothschild brothers."

"Yes, the Five Arrows, Amschel Mayer Rothschild, from Frankfurt, Salomon Mayer Rothschild, based in Vienna, Nathan Mayer Rothschild, in London, Jakob Mayer Rothschild who resided in Paris, and Calmann Mayer Rothschild, in Italy. They were all bankers in their places of residence, all representing the Rothschild Banking empire under various names," he said.

"The Five Arrows?"

"The Rothschild's coat of arms includes a hand holding five arrows to symbolize the five brothers," Schmidt said.

"But their financial power is barely referred to in the document," she said.

"The fact the Rothschilds once ruled and may still rule the financial world is rarely mentioned, Fraulein Feinhof. Everyone knows about the Medici, but as far as the Rothschilds go, little is known. I believe secrecy was one of their most important principles."

"Well, so far, it appears these bankers cared very little about the Illuminati and a lot more about money and power. As you mentioned, the Rothschilds controlled five of the most powerful Banking centers: Frankfurt, Vienna, London, Naples, and Paris, and it seemed their biggest scheme was setting up Central Banks. But the investigation was only focused on whether these men were members of the Illuminati or not."

She explained the three spies assigned to uncover the truth were sent to the Chateau de Rilly in France but could not enter it. "But agents had been placed inside the chateau and informed them that the English banker's secretary had attended and recorded every meeting. The three spies returned to London where they kidnapped Oliver Von Neiman, the secretary mentioned, and interrogated him." She paused.

Schmidt did not seem too interested. But after a moment of suspended silence, he finally asked, "And…?"

"King Frederick VI of Denmark had received generous support from the Rothschilds," she continued. "Now, he was prepared to approve a plan to create a National Bank called the Danmarks Nationalbank. Built in the mold of the Bank of England and The First Bank of the United States, it would be secretly managed by the Rothschilds."

Schmidt did not respond. Instead, he turned to look out the window. She reached out for her coffee, took a sip, and relaxed. Her phone indicated numerous incoming texts and messages, but instead of reviewing them, she typed "Danmarks Nationalbank." The first link was useless. She clicked on another link. It led her to a Bloomberg page:

Danmarks Nationalbank operates as the central bank of Denmark. It issues banknotes and coins; conducts monetary and exchange-rate policies to ensure the stability of the krone vis-a-vis the Euro; it holds assets comprising the foreign-exchange reserves and a stock of gold; and functions as a banker to the banks and mortgage-credit institutes, and central government… engages in maintaining the stability of the financial system, by assessing financial stability, overseeing payment systems, compiling financial statistics, and managing the central government's borrowing and debt…

Rosalie fine-tuned her search: "Is the Danmarks Nationalbank privately owned?" She scanned down the search page results and clicked. Google took a few seconds to answer.

By the ruling of King Frederick VI, Denmark's national banking system was first put into action on August 1, 1818, as a private institution and was given sole responsibility for issuing currency and controlling the money supply. By 1914 the bank had become governmentally controlled, before becoming fully independent in 1936 as a traditional central bank.

"Coffee to go?" Asked Schmidt.

"Please." Their eyes met. In his eyes, she could see sadness and the heavy burden of an unfulfilled life. In hers, he could see love, tenderness, and joy. He turned away and walked toward the counter to order their coffees.

She returned to the document. The handwriting was rushed, and her progress was slow. Adventi, the Bavarian spy, was leading the interrogation. They transcribed the dialogue.

Adventi: What are you talking about? Danmarks Nationalbank, we do not care about this. These men are members of the Order of the Illuminati. We know it, have proof, and want you to tell us the truth—no more stories about bankers.

Von Neiman: Sir, I beg you not to strike me. You asked that I tell the truth, and I have done so. I have never heard of the Illuminati. My employer and his brothers are bankers who want a stable World and European Order. While Kings and paupers came to boast at the Congress of Vienna, these bankers manipulated every aspect of the final treaty to be signed in Paris. It will provide stability, peace, and a chance for countries to flourish.

Adventi: Ok, this was Saturday. So, what happened next?

Von Neiman: What happened next was information, Sir; the sharing and acquiring of knowledge. Most bankers are ignorant. Their only objective is how much money they can make for themselves. The bankers I work for are geniuses with a broad view of the world.

Adventi: Continue.

Von Neiman: Our initial meeting covered technology: Development in iron, coal, and mechanical engineering, especially in the areas of textile manufacturing, medicine, and chemistry. The next day we launched into politics. First, with a report from Friedrich Gentz, Metternich's assistant secretly collected certain information at the Congress of Vienna. The N.M. Rothschild and its various affiliates lend these Kings money to stabilize their economies. But their wealth is often spent on foolish things—wars, palaces, and useless jewelry for the women they desire. In the meantime, their people starve. On Wednesday afternoon, each assistant was assigned a list of actions to be taken upon returning to their home office.

Adventi: What action were you to take?

Von Neiman: I was to create a series of symposiums on the growth of technology and its effect on the economy. My task included a search for the most prominent experts in four areas. Each area had been identified as a possible driver of a future economy. They were Textile, Steel, Chemical, and Medical. The experts would present discoveries and developments in specific industries to a panel of economists, who would try to calculate financial costs and benefits, and the possible return on investments.

Rosalie continued transcribing the document until she turned to a page full of signatures. The handwriting changed once again. It was Heinegard. She looked away from the document, stretched her neck and back, and glanced at her watch. It was 2 p.m., and once again, she needed a break.

Herr Schmidt sat beside her, locked into the laptop before him. Sensing her stare, he said, "Fraulein Feinhof, how are you?"

"Shall we take our lunch break, Inspector?"

The two ate in a massive dining room. Their eyes did not lock, and they ignored discussing the 200-year-old document. Instead, they chatted about their own lives, Zurich, his daughter, and an upcoming art show in Berlin.

Rosalie paused for a moment. "Herr Friedrich Schmidt of the German Federal Intelligence Service, what is so secret about this document? There doesn't seem to be any secrets worth anyone's time. The Bavarian authorities are the only ones to mention the Illuminati."

"These are old stories, Fraulein Feinhof. I read your transcription and did not find anything strange but remember these events may have been important then."

"If you ask me, these bankers were too smart for their own time."

Schmidt loved her voice and the emotion in her speech. He looked down at his suit and wondered whether it was gray or brown and if perhaps it had a touch of green. He hated wearing it; the fabric was cheap, and it did not seem to fit him. But it was clean, and who cared what he wore anyway? He stood, indicating it was time to return to their task. They walked silently back to their dreary office.

The page before Rosalie appeared to be the final review of the investigation. It was dated 18 December 1815:

I, Otto Kirk Heinegard, requested agents in Copenhagen to investigate the relationship between the N.M. Rothschild & Sons Bank and the Danish government. Their inquiry confirmed the statements made by Von Neiman about the possibility of a privately owned National Bank, similar in design to the Bank of England, the former First Bank of the United States, and many more. All but a formal Royal decree has been agreed to in principle. Everyone believed the development of a central bank was inevitable, a year away or more into the future. Neither our investigation nor Von Neiman's interrogation generated any leads into the Illuminati. A second group of agents placed and acting as servants within the Chateau de Rilly recorded the following speech by one of the brothers. The speech certainly indicated a strict focus on finance and demonstrated their strong interest in developing an international Central Banking system.

Kings and Emperors alike are sick with greed. Their thirst for blood and gold to pay for their failures is insatiable. While they continue waging wars, their people's lives are wrecked by poverty and famine.

Have you ever known Britain at peace? In recent years it has been in battle with the French, the Irish, the Polish, the Danish, the Regency of Algiers, the Kingdom of Mysore, the Maratha Empire, and the War of the Third Coalition. I could go on, but really, when will it stop? These monarchs are heartless creatures from whom we must remove control of all monetary matters.

Kings should be men of honor, their life dedicated to fulfilling the sacred duty bestowed upon them and working for the good of their people, the fortunate and unfortunate alike.

Our goal in Vienna was to create 'stability': economic, social and moral stability. The stability we proposed can only be implemented by developing and controlling a central banking system. Our economic principles have worked.

The Rothschild Banks will, therefore, continue its efforts to establish central banks in various parts of the World. We are a year away from success in Denmark and months away in Austria. The De Nederlandsche Bank in Amsterdam is flourishing fast. We will be forever grateful to King William I for his support.

And just as Napoleon predicted when he stated: *"Whether a monarchy or a republic, when a government abdicates the control of its money, it abdicates the control of its government."* Soon we will control these governments." The speech ended.

Rosalie had never known of this system of central banks and the control they exerted. Further, the document described the strict conditions under which a system of central banks must be implemented.

Again, she turned to Google to find more information:

The bank operated under three conditions; first, a royal or national decree to charter the establishment and management of a central bank for a period of at least 25 years. Second, the exclusive rights to issue bank notes, and finally, the central bank management will be controlled by governors, directors, and shareholders. Though deceivingly named as if they were national institutions, these central banks were to remain private banks whose main priority was profit for its shareholders.

She returned to the document and discovered the Rothschilds were furious with the entire situation in America. Their vitriol was aimed at Madison, and the US Congress and the deceased Robert Morris and Alexander Hamilton. But the focus of their fury aimed straight at the "dreadful Vice President," George Clinton, who, voted against granting a renewal of the charter of the First Bank of the United States. His vote broke the tie on the Senate floor, and the bank's charter thus expired in 1811. For the bank, the losses were unacceptable.

The Rothschilds seemed to rejoice when the War of 1812 had nearly bankrupted the United States Federal Government. Nathan Rothschild proudly shared a report describing the United States' total public debt, which had grown from $45.2 million on January 1sr, 1812, to $119.2 million as of September 30th, 1815. In closing, he said, *"... teach these impudent Americans a lesson."*

The document came to an end. Otto Kierke Heinegard formally expressed his failure to prove any association between the Rothschilds and the Illuminati. Signatures and stamps followed. She looked at the 200-year-old document in front of her in amazement. She thought of the men sitting by the light of a candle in a basement, interrogating Von Neiman. Otto Kirk Heinegard who secretly recorded every word of their final speech with his spies inside the Chateau de Rilly.

Herr Schmidt entered the room.

"I just completed the document," she said.

He walked over to his computer and typed a few strokes. Schmidt skimmed the document. He scrolled back to the top of the Word document and repeated his steps. "Fraulein Feinhof, you are a genius. Thank you," he said, smiling.

"Inspector, may I ask you a question?"

"Sure," he said while packing both laptops.

"In the document, Otto Kierke Heinegard raises a few concerns. They did not seem to alarm you."

"Fraulein, I studied economy before becoming a spy. This is an old document. We know what role the bankers played throughout Europe and in America. It has been analyzed and reported for years. Bankers do rule the world and control all critical areas of most governments. To think otherwise is plain naiveté. These bankers believed control could only be achieved through financial stability, which can only be achieved through financial control. If I lend you one Euro, your stability isn't my concern, for my loss, were you to fail on your repayment, is minimal. Change this single Euro into one billion Euros, and now let me ask you; should your stability be my concern?" Schmidt paused for effect.

"The English National Debt by the end of the Napoleonic Wars in 1815 was estimated at £850 million—an enormous sum for the time. Were I the lender of such a sum, the borrower's stability to repay would certainly be my concern. The Central Banking System evolved rapidly during the early part of the 19th century. The Netherlands Bank was created in 1814, the Austrian National Bank in 1816, the Bank of Finland in 1819, the Second Bank of the United States in 1816, the Banque de France in 1800, and the Bank of Denmark in 1818. All of these were privately run central banks and were given legal monopoly status."

Schmidt continued and explained no politician besides Andrew Jackson had the power or the courage to fight such a powerful financial institution. "The information is available for the citizens of the World to clearly understand the evil machination of this system; a system which, unbeknownst to most, controls our governments."

Schmidt reached out for his iPhone and typed. "Here is a quote from William Lyon Mackenzie King, who served as Prime Minister of Canada from 1921 to 1948: *'Until the control of the issue of currency and credit is restored to government and recognized as its most conspicuous and sacred responsibility, all talks of the sovereignty of Parliament and of democracy is idle and futile... Once a nation parts with the control of its credit, it matters not who makes the laws . . . Usury, once in control, will destroy a nation."*

Schmidt typed a few more words and continued: "This quote is from *Tragedy and Hope: A History of The World in Our Time* by Professor Carroll Quigley of Georgetown University. *'The powers of financial capitalism had another far-reaching aim; nothing less than to create a world system of financial control in private hands able to dominate the political system of each country and the economy of the world as a whole. This system was to be controlled in a feudalist fashion by the central banks of the world acting in concert, by secret agreements, arrived at in frequent private meetings and conferences.'* Quigley was quite famous in academic circles. Unfortunately, we have ignored the many warnings we were given," said Schmidt. He placed the document into a case, laid the pink leaf of paper on top, and closed it.

"So, is this about government control through financial control?" Asked Rosalie.

Schmidt liked her fiery attitude, a woman of conviction. "No, it's about governments controlled by a small financial elite intent on increasing their wealth; kings hidden behind a veil of secrecy."

Schmidt asked if she understood the GDP or Gross Domestic Product. She did.

He returned to his iPhone screen and typed. After a brief pause, he went on; "Here is the National Debt to GDP ratios for a few countries—what is owed against what is produced. Japan: 234%, Greece; 181%, Italy; 127%, United States; 109%. I could continue, but you understand how fragile a country is when its debt exceeds the total it produces. United States Federal debt is currently at..." more typing, "approximately $21 Trillion. Incredible." Schmidt scanned his screen once more. "The Federal Reserve, America's central bank, reported an estimated net income for 2017 of $80.7 billion... this information is straight from the Federal Reserve Bank website. These are staggering numbers."

Rosalie felt a little overwhelmed and not sure how to respond.

"This is from Louis Thomas McFadden," said Schmidt. "He was a Republican Congressman from Pennsylvania in the 1930s and a banker by trade: '... *one of the most corrupt institutions the World has ever known. I refer to the Federal Reserve Board and the Federal Reserve Bank.*' The message could not be clearer." Schmidt paused and looked at Rosalie. He was ready to leave.

Rosalie collected the few items she had used. They left the dreary office in the nondescript area no one seemed to use and made their way out of the building. Schmidt extended his hand.

She took it. "Thank you for the crash course, Herr Schmidt. I'll see you in a month."

He looked at her tenderly, smiled, and said, "Rosalie, please remember—ignorance is bliss."

CHAPTER 6

YOUR KINGDOM OR YOUR WEALTH

The real menace of our republic is the invisible government which, like a giant octopus, sprawls its slimy legs over our city, state, and nation. At the head is a small group of banking houses generally referred to as "international bankers." This little coterie of powerful international bankers virtually runs our government for their own selfish ends.
— John F. Hylan, Mayor of New York City, March 26, 1922

Secrecy is the freedom tyrants dream of.
— Bill Moyers

LONDON, 1816

"Which would you rather lose, my King, your kingdom, or your wealth?" The King did not respond to his advisor's question. Silence ensued.

"Prince Senars, Son of Arthis, the third Ruler of the Kingdom of Lath and protector of the Gold Mountain, had sailed into the harbor earlier in the day.

The King of Lath, his father, had been killed, he had informed the King. "The kingdom of Lath is no more." Prince Senars murmured.

"Troubled, the King had summoned his Wise Man and, upon his arrival, ordered the court to leave. The Wise Man could sense fear in the old King, whose eyes were fixed on the magnificent landscape before him.

"Your questions are as follows, my King: How has the Kingdom of Lath fallen to a popular uprising? Could a similar insurrection threaten your Kingdom? And what steps should be taken to avoid such an unfortunate destiny?" The tall and lanky man waited, not expecting a prompt response from his King, he continued. "The Kingdom of Lath is no more because their King failed. He indulged the few but ignored the many. He embraced ephemeral pleasures while squandering his nation's wealth— the wealth of his people.

"Though the markets were full in the Kingdom of Lath, most could not afford its offerings. Yes, its people danced all night, but it was to forget the misery which consumed the life they once cherished." Said the Wise Man as he joined the King at the edge of the terrace.

Before them was an infinite panorama, the coast, with its magnificent cliffs, and the rich blue sea. Far on the horizon, at the edge of the world, a body of land could be seen on this clear morning: The Kingdom of Lath. At its center was the Gold Mountain, known for its vast quantities of minerals.

"While the malcontent man stirs, the desperate man fights," the Wise man said. "In the Kingdom of Lath, the malcontents became desperate. They fought for their survival, for the crumb left behind by some wealthy members of the Kingdom's privileged few. The malcontent man, my King, rejoices at what little he owns, but the desperate man has nothing for which to rejoice and nothing to lose. As the number of destitute souls grew, their anger transformed into folly, and soon the culprit would pay for their unbearable misery. The King of Lath was the obvious choice.

"Their fury soon led to destruction. The fearful King escaped, and the people searched high and low to find him; first, throughout the palace, then through the city, ultimately scouring the entire Kingdom. Eventually, the King of Lath was captured, and no mercy had been shown."

"Should you be worried, my King? Unless changes take place, violence will grow, and soon your Kingdom will cease to be. I will pray the gods look kindly over you." The Wise Man paused. He walked closer to the King and turned toward the setting sun.

"Finally, to your last question; What steps may be taken to avoid such a future? My answer is this: Which would you rather lose my King, your Kingdom, or your wealth?"

"Aren't my Kingdom and my wealth one and the same?" The King responded, a touch of frustration in his voice.

To the King's surprise, his Wise Man launched into a discourse on governance, economy, and finances. A surprising dialogue ensued. The idea presented was shocking in its simplicity and fascinating in its ingenuity. The two paced around the terrace incessantly now.

Up until now, the storms had remained far and away, distant sightings in an overall peaceful kingdom, thought the King. Last night, however, far below the palace, in the dingy bowels of the lower city, revolts had erupted. The disturbances, while small and quickly foiled, had ushered in dark clouds.

"While the malcontent man stirs, the desperate man fights," he heard his Wise Man repeat once more.

The King knew a weak foundation would cause even the strongest structure to collapse. He sat on the wall at the edge of the terrace. The sea was a dark shade of blue, and the air mild.

Tea and sweets were brought in. Wine followed, with bread, cheese, and olives. More tea arrived as the sun rose over the golden sea. Hours later, the King and his Wise Man finally sketched out a plan for the future of the kingdom. This plan would change everything."

Von Neiman paused to assess his audience. He had completed the first part of his presentation. If the group appeared impatient, he would offer a brief overview of the rest of the story and stop there. But the group before him seemed intrigued.

While frightening, the events that had taken place upon his return from France were long gone memories. Against his kidnappers' advice, Von Neiman had shared the tale of his capture and beating. Nathan Rothschild immediately requested tighter security.

It had taken a week for the pain to subside. His family had returned, and all had soon been forgotten. At the Chateau de Rilly, Von Neiman had been tasked with creating a series of research papers on the possible financial growth in various fields of science. In London, the project quickly produced astonishing financial results. Researchers and inventors with brilliant ideas but lacking money could now access funding.

A few months ago, Von Neiman was offered the position of director of research and development for the N.M. Rothschild's new private investment branch. The Bank's main areas of interest were in the field of science, though at times, his research also focused on society, economy, and philosophy.

Von Neiman was about to carry on with the reading when a gentleman in a dark green outfit, red hair, and a crooked nose interrupted him.

"Dear Von Neiman, would you remind us how this story came about."

"Certainly, my Lord, thank you." Said Von Neiman.

The gentleman had arrived late and had not been given a copy of the handwritten program which described the subject of his reading.

"As you know, we present our experts with one specific subject of interest every month. It may be about a new medicine or a new method of textile fabrication. Our medical, financial, and industrial experts review the same problem but from their own vantage points. We collect these reports, search for cost estimates, review their effects on society. Finally, with your help, the Bank deducts the most fruitful answer to our query and creates a plan of action." Von Neiman walked over to his desk and picked up one of the handwritten programs.

"While this may help," he said, handing the program to the inquiring guest, "I'll finish responding to our inquiry. After the French Revolution, the future of monarchies appeared very much in question. The King's ability, or inability, to repay the massive loans that the N.M Rothschild Bank extended to them, could threaten the long-term health and stability of our institution. While the reports we receive from our brilliant experts are extremely useful, they are always over-analyzed, tedious, and include infinite details to support their opinions. Monarchs all over Europe have seen their legitimacy questioned. We were intrigued and wanted to understand the reasons behind such changes. Were these changes economic or social? Finally, we wondered, what is a King to do in order to survive such changes? This month, our question was, 'Success, failure, and the future of Kings.'"

"Out of curiosity, and as a challenge, we presented the same question to the senior class at one of London's most illustrious universities. A young man named John Wallsmith authored the essay I am reading. It was, for me, the ray of sunshine amongst the dread. While creative in its approach, it provided a clear and simple solution to our question; 'Success, failure, and the future of Kings.' If you permit me, I will now complete my reading. Thank you." Von Neiman cleared his throat, straightened, and read:

The news traveled like wildfire throughout the lower city. Announcements were posted on the trunk of exotic trees, on wooden doors, and on public sites. Ten days from now, on the third Sunday of the month, the King would give an address to the citizens of his Kingdom.

The disturbances, the anger temporarily tamed. The markets, whose merchants had been ordered to discount all essential items, such as milk, vegetables, and bread, saw the crowds of shoppers increase daily. Families in need and older citizens were offered further discounted prices. Upon the market closing, soldiers purchased all unsold produce and distributed it to the unfortunate—those too poor to afford anything. The merchants, who made less on each item but sold more, quickly grew prosperous.

On the third Sunday of the month, the King walked down the one hundred steps between the immaculate white palace to the bridge connecting it to the lower city. A large crowd had gathered.

Flanked by his Wise Man and followed by guards, the King appeared strong and majestic in a formal royal blue and foot-length tunic. As his Wise Man raised his hands to request silence, the King contemplated the landscape of people before him. He straightened and breathed in deeply.

"Dear Citizens, I have come before you with humility and great happiness in my heart. While I rejoice at the splendor of our great city, I would be irresponsible to ignore the ever-growing clouds of dissatisfaction that have appeared across our land. Sadly, while timid at first, these clouds have grown strong and menacing. Today, our Kingdom is under threat, and for this, I ask your forgiveness."

"For the last ten days, working alongside my most trusted advisors and with the generous participation of a select group of citizens, I have begun to devise a plan; not a plan to save my Kingdom or me, but a plan to transform this Kingdom into a prosperous community, led by you, my fellow citizens."

A low rumble of voices was heard. The apprehensive crowd fell silent. They sensed an imminent proclamation.

"After much deliberation, dismay, and sadness," the King continued, "I have come to realize time has slowly diminished my capabilities. This development has rendered me unable to fulfill my duties as I wish I could. Therefore, I have decided to surrender my role as your King, a role I have proudly and honorably fulfilled for the past thirty years. This Kingdom I love above all else must become its own community, its own nation."

The King continued, telling the spellbound crowd that over the next months, he would proceed with selecting four representatives of the people. The four would control finances, social welfare, the rule of law, and the protection of the new nation's territories.

"Any man or woman of respectable reputation is encouraged to apply for these honorable posts," the King declared. "Selection will be made in the fairest manner."

The crowd applauded loudly. The hope for a better future had been restored. The men and women of the Kingdom screamed, "Long live the King!"

Over the next few weeks, trepidation and joy reigned in the lower city. Each morning, applicants for the four leading positions lined up on the bridge. First, candidates were required to present their cases and explain why they felt honorable and capable enough to fulfill such a position. The candidates deemed able to carry out the positions would then enter the palace. There, they sat with an advisor to discuss the

Kingdom's future. The lucky ones would meet with the Wise Man. A few even met the King. Finally, a selection of four people's representatives was completed. Two men and two women would govern the new nation.

A few days before the King's formal abdication and the introduction of the new government, an announcement was made in the town square. The King had, sadly, fallen ill and would not participate in the upcoming celebrations honoring him and the new leaders. Though chagrined, the people were so excited about the future that they quickly forgot the old King.

The White Palace was quiet. Most of the staff had been dismissed, and only a few guards remained. The King, who had decided to expedite his move to a deserted town he had quietly acquired, was at peace.

He heard footsteps approaching. It was the finance representative accompanied by his Wise Man. The King welcomed them. Soon the three discussed the current wealth of the Kingdom, its holdings in gold, and the prospected cost of running the nation.

The Wise Man informed the finance representative that if loans were needed, the King would be most happy to provide the necessary funds.

"Out of his personal wealth and from a strong desire for our community to succeed, of course," the Wise Man said with a touch of concern. "The development of this new nation will be costly."

Within six months, the old King had become the nation's banker. Within a year, he had transformed himself into the invisible Ruler, who secretly advised and directed this new government.

The error most make, the King learned, was to rule openly. A King, who appears to be above all, will become the one to blame during the inevitable hard times. The King in the White Palace had lost his Kingdom, but not his wealth. Though the former King never ceased to rule, he now did so behind a veil of secrecy.

Von Neiman lowered the document, straightened up, and raised his eyes to his audience. A tall, pale gentleman soon broke a moment of quiet; "Rule in the shadow, and your crimes will forever go unnoticed," said the man proudly, "and as a result, these crimes will go forever unpunished."

The group cheered joyfully. The Kings' failures were the fruits of greed and folly, but these bankers were better, wiser, and more inclined to become the rulers. Von Neiman stood and clapped his hands together to get everyone's attention. The group quieted down and turned toward their host.

"May we withdraw behind a veil of secrecy and become the puppet masters who, in the shadows, will be the invisible rulers, the unknown masters," Von Neiman said. "To a new World Order!"

CHAPTER 7

I KILLED THE BANK

It is to be regretted that the rich and powerful too often bend the acts of government to their selfish purposes.
— President Andrew Jackson in his "Veto Message," 1832

The powers of financial capitalism had another far-reaching aim, nothing less than to create a world system of financial control in private hands able to dominate the political system of each country and the economy of the world as a whole...
— Professor Carroll Quigley -Tragedy and Hope, 1966

ANDALUSIA, PA, 1843

A guilty conscience forced him to look at the meal before him. *Putrid,* William thought, and ignored the food. Across from him was the beautiful Mary, shoulders straight, hair pulled tight in a bun. She smiled carelessly at the headmistress, a homely woman who seemed to be perpetually ranting about someone. Today, the victim of her tirade was an old cousin who had dared ask for a bit of money.

For the last few minutes, Mary's real focus had been on a more important matter. Unbeknownst to the headmistress, Mary's slender foot had patiently climbed the length of the charming boy's leg under the table. She had quietly wiggled her way to his upper thigh, and the poor William now struggled to contain himself. This time, Mary turned and smiled at him, victorious. She had found her way to his most sensitive part and pushed forcefully. He almost screamed.

"Well, I must make my rounds to the master's room," said the stiff woman. "Please, see to it that the kitchen is cleaned up." Mrs. Dawson, the headmistress, was a distinguished woman with defined features, a straight nose, and a pleasant complexion. Her light blue eyes lightened her pale face. She walked out of the kitchen, and within moments, footsteps could be heard climbing the stairs.

The young man cared little to think about the headmistress and her looks. Mary was his prey. He knew Mrs. Dawson would disappear for at least thirty minutes. No time to waste.

Mary, who had already grabbed his hand, was pulling him into the pantry, where she immediately kissed him. For the last two days, this had been their mid-day ritual.

He had not once touched his meal and just waited for the opportunity to lose himself in Mary's delicate and glorious body. They were tender and quiet, but ravenous.

Sadly, a stir was soon heard overhead. Without a word, the two separated. It was time to cease their carnal activities and return to their mundane task.

They kissed one last time, William returned to the library, and Mary straightened the kitchen.

Five days earlier, the young William Nostrand had left Philadelphia. He had been fetched by a formal but unpleasant and somber servant.

The man had arrived mid-morning on a lazy Sunday in late September. He wore black clothing, a black hat, and a grayish shirt that may have once been white. The brim of the man's hat was pushed low over his eyes, giving him a nefarious look.

William decided to ignore the man and turned to his mother, who seemed a little sad.

She hated to see him go and tried to cheer him up. "This is a good opportunity for you, dear William." His mother as she laid her hand on his gentle face, hugged him one last time, and they parted.

Mrs. Nostrand had been everything to William; an attentive mother who supported his interests and pushed him to attend college. Today, because of his studies, he was leaving home to fulfill the position of secretary.

William knew he owed it all to her. As the carriage rolled down the cobblestone streets of his home in Philadelphia, he was unsure when they would see each other again. He waved goodbye.

Their destination was an estate called Andalusia in Bensalem Township, north of the city, the country home of one Nicholas Biddle. A man of importance, he had been told. It was his first job, and he cared little who his employer was.

It was September 16, 1843, and at eighteen years of age, William Nostrand was taking his first steps into adulthood and was grateful for the opportunity. William had felt a little threatened by the man who had picked him up. He judged him to be grumpy and rude and decided to ignore the man, assuming it was the safest option. Within half an hour, he dozed off.

The man called him a little while later. "An hour to go, young lad. Hungry?" He asked.

William answered he was.

The carriage pulled to the side of the road, parked under a tree and along a sturdy stone wall on which they sat. The man placed a basket of food between them and said, "My name is Martin."

William detected a strong accent and soon learned Martin was French.

"I am from Auvergne," he said proudly. "Do you know where it is, William?"

The young man did not.

Feeling suddenly at ease with the Frenchman, William decided to join him up front to their destination.

The old Frenchman informed him he was most often embarrassed by his poor English and thick accent and preferred to remain silent.

William soon discovered that Martin was a happy soul who loved to share the many stories he experienced. Were you to be patient enough to decipher his speech, you would have been transported to the central mountains of France, where myths, legends, and tales of bravery were numerous. William was patient and found Martin's stories fascinating.

"This is it. Nice house, eh?" Proclaimed Martin as a stately home appeared in the distance.

"Magnificent is the correct word," he informed the Frenchman.

Martin pulled into the stable and led William to the house. They entered the house through the side door and met a stern but polite woman who introduced herself as Mrs. Dawson, the headmistress. Martin quickly disappeared and Mrs. Dawson took him on a tour of the house.

She introduced him to Mary. "This is Mary. She tends to the many needs of the house. She is a wonder."

William agreed but did not mention it. The curves of the young woman's body, her piercing green eyes, and delicate features made his heart tremble.

Mary smiled warmly.

The headmistress was a bore, thought William.

Nonetheless, he followed her through the house and nodded as she indicated the various rooms.

They entered a dark, wood-paneled room, walked through it, and into a small study in the back left corner.

"This will be your temporary office, Mr. Nostrand," said Mrs. Dawson. He looked at her. Blue eyes and dark hair, five feet, five inches of height, and very thin. She wore a dark and plain dress much too large for her small frame.

"Mr. Nostrand?" She startled him out of the reverie in which she was his subject. He smiled, and they soon returned to the kitchen. Dinner would be served at seven sharp. William was shown to his room, where she left him alone to settle in.

"Meanwhile, you are welcome to explore the property. Were you to need Martin, he can be found in the stable or possibly in the greenhouse around the building. It was a pleasure to have made your acquaintance, Mr. Nostrand." Mrs. Dawson turned and left, not expecting a response from the shy, young man, who had, up to this point, remained silent.

Alone, William took his boots off and laid on the bed. Within a few minutes, the young man fell asleep. At first, the day's events replayed at various speeds, but soon he fell into a deep slumber.

Andalusia was a grand residence for a most notable man, a paradise. Upon its discovery, most would have taken the opportunity to explore its many rooms, gardens, and surrounding woods.

But the young man slept the afternoon away, ignorant of the treasures he had missed. A knock was heard. He jumped off the bed and opened the door.

Mary was about to say something but realized the young man was shirtless. She blushed momentarily but stared, nonetheless.

William possessed a muscular and extremely well-shaped body, each muscle clearly defined. Mary's eyes slowly returned to his face.

She instantly found his deep blue eyes, long wavy blond hair, a perfectly symmetrical face with high cheekbones, and full lips irresistible. She would have been delighted to spend the next hour discovering the rest of his body, but instead, she informed him dinner was served and immediately turned away, walking briskly back down the stairs.

A few minutes later, he joined Mrs. Dawson, Martin, and the lovely Mary for supper.

Mary sat across from him.

"The Master would like for you to be in the library tomorrow at 9 a.m. sharp. If you need them, supplies can be found in the left drawer of the desk in the study. Please be prompt, Mr. Nostrand," said the Head Mistress.

He smiled at Mary but immediately realized he had been spoken to. Turning toward Mrs. Dawson, he smiled again and confirmed he was looking forward to meeting Mr. Biddle.

The group was quiet, which made William uncomfortable. The four soon retired for the evening.

William was a man at peace, a quiet but discernible peace, within and without. Though he was young, he was an old soul. A simple man who woke early, enjoyed nature, and had few needs.

"Early to bed and early to rise makes a man healthy, wealthy, and wise," his mother had so often repeated. "William. I hope you'll follow Benjamin Franklin's advice, for you will prosper, my son."

Each morning, he woke before the sun rose, often took a short walk, and started his day fully grateful for his blessings.

He woke up at 5:30 the next morning. He dressed and decided to explore the garden. He walked down the stairs to the kitchen, where he found a silent Martin sitting at the table. The Frenchman pointed at the teapot on the counter. William poured himself a cup of tea, picked one of the warm, blueberry scones, and walked outside.

It was a glorious morning, so he decided to sit on the steps of the patio. A light mist rising from the Delaware River battled the warm rays of the rising sun. He thought of Keats' poem "Ode on a Grecian Urn" and remembered this line:

"Beauty is truth, truth beauty—that is all ye know on Earth, and all ye need to know."

William Nostrand spent the next hour walking quietly along the river's shore. He discovered that, from this point of view, the house took on a different appearance. With its six massive Doric columns, the house resembled a Greek temple. Its majestic side proudly faced the Delaware River. He found the gaming house discreetly emerging from the trees. The building was a simple, two-story house.

Following the path along the edge of the Delaware River, listening to the birds chirping and the flowing water nearby, he may have found himself enchanted by such a magical place.

A small stone house soon appeared by the shore. The house faced the river and was surrounded by trees. Its enclosed yard was full of magnificent and colorful flowers. The house looked like a humble stone country farmhouse. He learned later it was the private home of Mrs. Biddle.

William entered the library at around 8:30 a.m. In the study, he checked for the supplies he might need and found them exactly where Mrs. Dawson had informed him, they would be. He heard footsteps in the library.

William exited the study but was a little surprised to find himself in the presence of a lovely woman.

"Hello, Mr. Nostrand. It is a pleasure to meet you," Mrs. Biddle introduced herself and explained her husband would arrive momentarily.

William politely bowed.

She had hoped to meet him. The two exchanged niceties, and she soon parted.

The young man, instantly bored, decided to pick a book. He reached for the one laying on the coffee table in front of him, *Inquiry into the Nature and Causes of the Wealth of Nations*. He started reading but was soon interrupted.

It was Martin. "Young lad, Mr. Biddle would like you to meet him on the patio." William thanked Martin, who quickly disappeared.

William was a little nervous but, upon seeing Mr. Nicholas Biddle, offered a strong and polite greeting.

"Good morning to you, Mr. Nostrand," responded his employer. The two chatted, and once again, William found himself exchanging polite but meaningless words.

"Sit with me, young man," Biddle said.

William sat.

"Mr. Nostrand, my request for your services was born from the sincere reflection upon events known as the 'Bank War.' Are you familiar with these events?"

"No, Sir," said William.

"I was the president of the Second Bank of the United States," said Biddle. "Its twenty-year charter was about to expire when I embarked on a mission to have its charter renewed and I succeeded. But Andrew Jackson, who disapproved of the Bank, declared war against the Bank, its allies, and me. Thus, its name; 'The Bank War'. Sadly, this event left me reeling, my reputation tarnished, and the Bank I so cherished in ruins." Biddle stopped. Lost in a momentary dream, he paused. "What do you know about me?" He finally asked.

William expressed regrets for his ignorance.

"No apologies needed, Mr. Nostrand. I prefer it so. When men fall, the smallest of their errors nullifies the greatest of their deeds. With your help, I intend to properly record these events for posterity, for I cannot allow history to be misled into creating a monster out of me." Biddle turned toward the river, contemplating the beauty before him.

"What sights. Aren't we lucky?"

William hesitated but courageously said, "There I sat this fine morning. It may have been six at the latest, and as you just now expressed, was also touched by the splendor I witnessed." He repeated the lines of Keats 'poem. *"Beauty is truth, truth beauty, —that is all ye know on Earth, and all ye need to know."*

"Well done," said Biddle, who continued. "Mr. Nostrand, over the next few months, I hope you will be able to transcribe my notes on the aforementioned events. My health, of late, has deprived me of the energy I once possessed. It has, quite frankly, almost pushed me to insanity, but time is the master of all, regardless of rank or status.

"Let me ask you; If I were to dictate my recollection of these momentous events, might I assume you would be able to correctly record them in writing?" Biddle paused, but as William remained silent, he continued. "Do you believe this to be a feasible task? It could be something we explore as we get to know each other." Biddle stood. "Well, let's plan to meet in my study an hour from now, Mr. Nostrand."

William was glad to see Mrs. Biddle arrive.

Upon being offered the position at Andalusia, William had been informed that his employer was one Nicholas Biddle. But very little information had been shared besides that he had been a banker, a politician, and once collaborated with Lewis and Clark on the report they published of their expedition to the West. William, who at the time was unconcerned with the fine details, had now become quite intrigued. He found himself in the kitchen, where the beautiful Mary seemed busy with many chores.

"Hello, Mr. Nostrand," she said with a beautiful smile.

How beautiful is she? He wondered. "Please, call me William." He answered.

Her smile grew wider.

"Well, William, you are most welcome to call me Mary."

Mrs. Dawson entered the room, and he told her how grateful he was to see her.

"I am to be in Mr. Biddle's study in an hour but have no clue as to its location. I surely would not want to be wandering around the house unattended."

The firm and unresponsive face of the headmistress offered no indication as to whether a response was forthcoming. He waited silently, unsure how to proceed.

"I can take you there," said Mary.

But Mrs. Dawson, sensing his nervousness, assured him he would be there on time.

"May we sit and have some tea, Mr. Nostrand? I would like to discuss our house rules."

The two sat around the kitchen table as Mary brought a teapot, a couple of lovely China cups, and the few remaining pastries.

"It appears you possess a rare quality in men your age. I noticed you start your day early."

The poor William felt as if he were being reprimanded.

She assured him he was not. "Were you to be favorable to the idea, I may move you to another room. It is smaller but will be able to enter and exit quietly without disturbing anyone."

He instantly accepted the offer.

She continued by discussing other boring but essential details.

He was glad for her calm and patient manner.

She clarified many important facts; when he would receive his pay, where to place his laundry, and other matters he would have ignored.

"Well, Mr. Nostrand, if you are ready, let me take you to Mr. Biddle's study."

William followed Mrs. Dawson up the main stairs. They passed the library on their left to the last door, in front of which she stopped and knocked. Hearing no response, she entered.

"Please do not touch or move anything," she said in a stern voice.

The room was narrow and long. Nicholas Biddle's study was an ornate room whose walls were a royal blue and accented by decorative wood molding that had been painted gold. Many windows covered the outside wall and allowed the glorious fall light to enter the study, forming shapes and patterns of gold around the room.

William sat and waited for his employer to arrive.

But it was Mrs. Biddle who arrived in his stead.

"My dear Mr. Nostrand, I must apologize on my husband's behalf, for he is not feeling well." She walked past him toward the desk. After a quick search, she remembered that the documents she was looking for were on top of the bureau, behind the desk. "There they are," she happily announced.

"Dear Mr. Nostrand, would you mind going through this document? Please get acquainted with the information it contains. Lunch will be served at 12:30 p.m. Return to this room after lunch and continue your reading. Mr. Biddle will join you sometime this afternoon. Any question?" Mrs. Biddle had a kind and considerate demeanor.

He had no questions, so she returned to her husband.

William looked around the room and noticed the small desk facing the window. He decided to make it his desk. After collecting the document, he pulled up a chair and sat, eager to finally get to work. The first page was titled "A Banker's perspective on the War against the Second Bank of the United States." William pulled the chair closer to the desk, turned the first page, and read.

The Second Bank of The United States.

To believe in guilt, one must also believe in innocence, for no condemnation can prove its worth unless the heinous is balanced with the good, and the shameful with the respectable. It is with the lens of fairness I ask the reader to weigh the villainous actions the Bank was accused of with the worthy functions it provided our young Nation.

Rechartered in February 1816 under President James Madison, the Second Bank of the United States became the third bank of its kind in our Nation's history. A central bank is designed to manage the affairs of the Government. In its various forms, the Bank performed its duty honorably, but did, throughout its history, retain a suspicious image I believe it did not deserve.

The purpose of a central bank is to act as an agent of the government. It creates and destroys the circulating media or notes, known as currency or money and it is the lender of last resort.

When created, the Second Bank of the United States received a twenty-year charter. It raised its capital stock to $35 million, four-fifths or 80% owned privately and one-fifth, or 20% owned by the government. It was authorized to create branch banks and approved to issue banknotes in denominations no smaller than five dollars.

The Second Bank of the United States offered a $1.5 million bonus to the government. These payments would be paid in three installments. Finally, the bank served as a depository for the Treasury and was subject to Treasury inspection.

The Second Bank of the United States, some believe, was granted its charter only because of the resurgence in our national debt and an increased need for capital. The growth in our national debt was the result of massive loans required to manage our country's affairs.

The enormous expenses incurred during the War of 1812 with Great Britain contributed to the rise in our national debt. During the period between 1812 to 1816, the Nation's coffers had been critically and repeatedly low. Had the United States not gone to war, the national debt in 1812 would have likely been paid off by 1815. However, the United States spent an estimated $158 million on the war.

A financial catastrophe had been avoided because the United States government was, by November of 1814, essentially bankrupt. The Nation could only afford to pay a minuscule portion of this enormous expense. As a result, the debt ballooned to $127 million. Loans were impossible to obtain. Wary of an unstructured, unmanaged, inefficient financial system, creditors pushed for a Central Bank.

William heard footsteps getting closer. He paused and turned to see Mary enter the room. She came closer, raised her index finger over her mouth, signaling him to remain quiet, leaned over, and kissed him. A tender kiss, at first, it soon became passionate. She straightened.

"I was asked to fetch you. Lunch is ready." Mary turned around and left him.

He wandered down the stairs thinking of the beautiful young lady who had just kissed him. He found Mrs. Dawson, Martin, and Mary in the kitchen. The three sat around the table, quietly staring at what looked like a pitiful plate of food.

Martin stood, walked to the counter where he broke a piece of bread, cut a morsel of cheese, and left.

Mrs. Dawson quietly watched Mary in disbelief.

The beautiful maid was voraciously eating her meal.

Mrs. Dawson attempted a spoonful of what looked like a stew. She immediately put her spoon down and calmly stated she would be touring the upstairs to check on Mr. and Mrs. Biddle.

Mary wiped her plate with a piece of bread. Her shin rising toward him, she smiled. "You are a good kisser, William." She stood and walked over to him.

Unsure of how to proceed, he lowered his eyes to her breasts.

She approached him, took his hand in hers, and laid it on her breasts. She held his other hand and pulled him toward her.

For the next twenty minutes, the young man lost himself in lust and discovery.

She suddenly froze, pushed him gently away, and straightened herself. William left the kitchen quietly and tried to go back to work. It was difficult. He returned to the document.

For the record, I, Nicholas Biddle, was named the President of the Second Bank of the United States on January 7, 1823. I was the third President of the Bank and ought to state the following: The first President of the Second Bank of the United States was Captain William Jones. He had been Madison's political choice. It was neither an educated choice nor a brilliant one, in my view. I trust finding a more crooked and incompetent character to lead the Second Bank of the United States would have been a futile exercise. His actions nearly ruined the Second Bank of the United States. Captain Jones offered his resignation and was replaced in 1819 by Langdon Cheves.

Images of Mary suddenly returned. He soon forgot the document before him. The poor William found it impossible to concentrate while Mary's breasts and kisses remained in his mind. He wondered how long he would have to sit here reading a boring account of the Second Bank of the United States.

He strategized on his next move, how he would kiss her next time, how he would let his hand slide down her leg, slowly rising back up, but this time under her dress. He could no longer wait. He stood, and as he did, he heard footsteps, he quickly returned to the document.

Langdon Cheves, the second President of the Bank, was a good and honest man whose error, I believe, was in his lack of expertise in the proper functioning of a Central Bank. He most certainly understood its basic function, but I believe lacked a clear understanding of its subtleties. In attempting to repair the Bank and return it to financial soundness, Cheves implemented a course of actions resulting in a nationwide depression. A depression which quickly spread worldwide. William H. Crawford, Secretary of the Treasury, clearly described the situation; *"All the evils which the community in particular parts of the country has suffered from the sudden decrease of currency, as well as from its depreciation have been ascribed to the Bank of the United States."* The national discontent with the Second Bank of the United States was growing rapidly.

Andrew Jackson became a more popular contender for the presidency because he vehemently voiced his dissatisfaction with the Second Bank of the United States.

"Hello, Mr. Nostrand." It was Mrs. Biddle.

"I have come to offer a reprieve from the boring document you are reading. Nicholas…" she started, but realizing her mistake, corrected herself and continued. "My apologies. Mr. Biddle is resting; I may be of help, answering questions you may have." She sat across from him, turned toward the small table beside her, picked up the bell, and shook it vigorously.

"Tea?" She asked him. She smiled, but he could detect sadness in her eyes as if she had recently cried.

"Mr. Nostrand, it may be that the document you are studying reflects a dark period in my husband's glorious life, as I fear this could be his last accomplishment. I hope your testimony goes beyond just documenting the Bank War in which he was deeply involved. May this be a testament to the kind and honorable man I shared my life with."

Mrs. Dawson entered.

"Elizabeth, would you be kind enough to bring us tea?" Mrs. Biddle demanded.

The headmistress nodded and exited the room.

"Mr. Nostrand, would you please fetch something to write on?" Mrs. Biddle asked.

He collected a stack of blank paper and quickly returned.

She immediately continued, "Forgive me, but I am going to assume your first question would be the following: 'Who is Mr. Biddle?'" She paused as William, who had remained silent until now, sat with the loose leaves of paper on his lap. He set the ink on the low table and looked up at Mrs. Biddle.

"Mr. Nostrand, I know silence is often a helpful shield, but I must request your voice be heard."

He straightened. "Please forgive my youth and timidity, Mrs. Biddle. I am new here and still learning which steps are deemed proper and which are not. We may begin."

Mrs. Biddle smiled.

Mary arrived with the tea. The lusty young man could barely keep his eyes off her. The curves he impatiently waited to discover, the breasts he desired to touch once more.

"Mr. Nostrand."

William almost jumped out of his chair.

"Don't you think you may be more comfortable at the desk?

Mary, please put a cup of tea and a scone on the desk. Thank you."

Mary did and left.

"Nicholas…" She stopped briefly. "I am sorry, I did it again. Would you forgive me if I called my husband by his first name again?"

He would, and she continued.

"Nicholas was born on January 8, 1786, in Philadelphia. His father, Charles Biddle, was an affluent Philadelphia merchant. My husband's father distinguished himself during the Revolution and became Vice President of the Supreme Executive Council of Pennsylvania. He was a good father, and Nicholas was a brilliant young man."

"Nicholas entered the University of Pennsylvania when he was ten. Within three years, he had completed all the requirements for a degree. Sadly, the school declined to grant him his diploma because of his young age. So, he entered Princeton, where he received his baccalaureate at 15, as valedictorian.

"He visited Europe, traveled, and fell in love with Greece, and upon his return resided in London, where he served as temporary secretary to James Monroe, who at the time held the position of American Minister to Great Britain.

"Nicholas returned to the United States in 1807, I believe, and practiced law. The Pennsylvania legislature was next in 1810. We met around then and soon married. I must stress my husband is a good man. John Quincy Adams once said Nicholas was a man *'of eminent ability, of a highly cultivated mind, of an equable and placid temper, and in every other relation of life, of integrity irreproachable and unreproached...'* These were kind words from such a bitter man," she offered with a smile.

They had not heard Nicholas Biddle's footsteps, and the two were surprised when he entered the room.

"My dear Jane, you are my biggest advocate," he said, smiling as he had heard part of their conversation. Biddle walked with the aid of a cane. He made a few slow steps and sat across from his wife on the couch.

The husband and wife exchanged pleasantries, and one could easily sense their care and love for each other. William looked at Nicholas Biddle, whose life had just been described to him minutes before. He could see the aristocrat who once may have been handsome. Indeed, the man appeared to be sensitive, intelligent, and honest.

"My dear young man, I hope my wife has not bored you with inconsequential facts," Biddle said as he turned toward William, expecting a response.

"This has been the most informative afternoon, sir. I did explore the documents on the Second Bank of the United States. I have found them most fascinating."

Biddle smiled. A proud smile, an aristocratic smile. "I would be pleased to answer any question, Mr. Nostrand," Biddle said.

William was unsure whether he should be frank or complimentary. He opted for diplomacy. "Sir, I do not feel fluent in either of the subjects I am to cover. It is my belief that the Second Bank of the United States undertook certain actions deemed, later on, unpopular—'villainous,' I believe, is the word used to describe them. My only question, if I may, is who was the author of such characterization?"

Mrs. Biddle shifted uncomfortably.

Had he asked the wrong question?

Mr. Biddle, facing away from William, turned slightly toward him but paused for a long, painful moment. "President Andrew Jackson was the culprit of such characterization."

William asked whether Mr. Biddle had met President Jackson.

"To my great chagrin, I can say that I did. Many a time. Do you know what I think of Jackson?"

But before William had a chance to answer, Biddle continued.

"Jackson was a poisonous leader, with a thirst for power, who, regardless of consequences, forced his way into destroying the Second Bank of the United States. He was a sentimental westerner whose badge of honor was he had killed Indians. Jackson was an uneducated orphan who became a roughneck, then miraculously won the presidency of the United States." Biddle paused. "I am sorry, young man. Jackson was the President, and I owe him respect. I do, however, find myself a little bitter, angry sometimes, for he and I were two adversaries in a long and difficult battle." He paused once again.

A redness appeared on Mr. Biddle's face.

His wife stood and came to her husband's side.

He needed to rest, she said.

William helped him up, and the two walked out of the room.

Alarmed and unsure of what to do next, he returned to the desk and his notes. A few minutes later, Mrs. Biddle re-entered the room, apologizing for the incident. He was asked to continue reading the document for a little while.

"The two of you will meet again in the morning," Mrs. Biddle said. She was a very sweet woman who repeatedly apologized.

William insisted that he was happy to help Mr. Biddle in any way. "It is an honor for me, Mrs. Biddle, a great honor. You mustn't apologize."

She left, and he returned to the document.

In 1820, there existed throughout the Nation grave concerns and hate for the Second Bank of the United States. When I was offered to become the Bank's new President and knew its challenges, President Monroe called on my patriotic sense, and I accepted the position. I hesitated. However, on January 7, 1823, I took it upon myself to straighten the bank's problem. During my tenure on the board of directors, I developed a strong interest in understanding the Bank's functions. This curiosity led me to study the various central bank models used. Of course, the Bank of England was well documented and provided me with the knowledge and understanding of the Bank's intricate functions. This inquiry was mainly focused on the successes and failures experienced by such a complicated central banking system.

I believed this study would help me offer educated counsel. Between 1823 to 1829, the Second Bank of the United States regained its health and grew in popularity, especially throughout the Nation's banking industry. Sadly, it was often portrayed as an enemy of the regular citizens, an extension of the powerful and wealthy money lenders. The bank had found a growing enemy in Andrew Jackson, who repeatedly attacked it. The board of directors grew concerned. I must stress that the bank, under my supervision, fulfilled its duty properly. It was a solid pillar of our young Nation. I had taken it upon myself to rectify its deficiencies and had, I believe, brought it back to excellence."

William paused and realized the house was very quiet. He estimated the time to be around 5 p.m. and decided to call it a day. William's mind was racing, so he opted for a walk along the edge of the river. He found Martin sitting on the steps outside the kitchen.

Martin recommended he walk up the river for a mile. "The land rises from the river forming a small hill. It has a great overview. I like it there. It is beautiful," the Frenchman said excitedly.

The air was warm, and the country was peaceful. He took a few deep breaths and immediately relaxed. William had sensed a feeling of confusion rising within him.

Mary had stolen every bit of concentration he possessed. She was all he could think about. He wanted her. Did he love her? How could he? Barely a few words had been exchanged between them. Nonetheless, her incessant presence in his thoughts indicated he might love her. He wondered if his feelings were purely physical.

Then there was Mrs. Biddle, who touched him deeply. Her poor husband appeared to be suffering so much. Wounded physically, he had been terribly affected by the loss of the Second Bank of the United States.

Biddle despised President Jackson.

William realized Biddle would never be capable of honestly telling his story. Hatred had forever blurred the events in which he had played such a role.

To William, Jackson had been a hero. The young man had found himself most touched by Biddle's demeaning words aimed at Jackson, the man he was proud to call his President.

With these thoughts in mind, he arrived atop the small hill and sat under a maple tree. The view was glorious indeed. The sun was low over the horizon; a fireball burning all it touched with sparks of gold. He leaned on the tree and peacefully dozed off. Half an hour later, he woke up and strolled back to the house. He was starving. Besides a couple of scones, he had not eaten anything else the entire day. As he approached the house, he saw Martin burst out of the kitchen, looking upset.

"Martin, merci. Your suggestion was ideal. It was a perfect spot."

The French man waved in approval; his hands full with a large piece of bread in one hand and a cup in the other.

William entered the kitchen to find Mrs. Dawson at the stove. But he ignored her once more to focus on Mary, who was sitting at the kitchen table, appearing content to be eating alone.

The air was tense.

William could feel it. He quickly looked at the food on the table and decided to ignore it. He climbed the stairs to the study and scribbled a few ideas.

To fulfill his task and write Mr. Biddle's manuscript, William felt he needed a plan of action, so he drew a chapter list. It would first include a description of the Second Bank of the United States, its inception and purpose, its leaders, and the Bank's effect on the economy; then Mr. Biddle, the third President of the Bank, his leadership, work, successes, and failures; and finally, the Bank War. He continued for a while until he heard footsteps. They were followed by a door opening and immediately closing.

William blew out the candle, gingerly returned to an empty kitchen, and found his room. Sleep took him over in no time. He dreamed of Philadelphia and his mother.

An hour later, William was abruptly woken up when his bed covers were pulled away from him.

A lit candle laid on the bureau. Confused, he turned and saw Mary.

Her hair was down, her eyes fixed on his. She smiled and slowly pulled her nightgown over her head. Her naked body, in all its glory, slowly moved closer. She climbed over him.

They made love frantically, keeping as quiet as possible. He kissed her, held her against his warm body, and slowly caressed her hair. To his chagrin, Mary suddenly stood, threw the nightgown over her glistening body, and left his bedroom. His heart still racing, he wondered if they had exchanged a word. They had not. Sleep returned, but now, his dreams took on a more mature theme.

He woke to the smell of bacon and eggs. William prayed for a good breakfast. In the kitchen, Martin welcomed him. "Bonjour, William," said the Frenchman, quite pleasantly.

William was handed a plate covered with scrambled eggs, bacon, and a large slice of bread covered with jelly. The young man was ravenous and immediately devoured his food. Looking through the window, he saw Mary in the yard. She was accompanied by a stranger. The two were walking toward a carriage.

Mrs. Dawson entered and loudly announced, "Well, we closed this chapter amicably, I would say."

Martin, I am famished. Please, could I have breakfast?" Martin obliged and set a plate of food in front of her.

"Mary's husband came to fetch her, Mr. Nostrand. I must apologize for the commotion. We all believed we were going to die of starvation. The poor woman could not cook at all."

William agreed but remained silent. His thoughts were on the previous night, and Mary's incredibly warm, delicate body.

The plate in front of him was empty. Martin refilled it.

When finished with breakfast, he decided to take a short walk. Once done, he headed to his study, excited to get to work. He was, however, disturbed by the fact Mary was married. To his surprise, he found Mr. and Mrs. Biddle sitting in the library. They were waiting for him and needed to discuss a certain matter.

His heart sank. Had he been caught? Had he and Mary made too much noise the previous night, he wondered.

Mrs. Biddle said, "Mary will no longer be working for us. We have decided, in the interim, to allow Martin to try out as our main cook. We love Martin, for he has been with us for many years—always kind and reliable. We do have a slight concern, however. One, which we believe, could be easily corrected. We were wondering if you would be kind enough to support him with the kitchen's finances; offer guidance and teach him how to keep up the books, work within an assigned budget and record his spending in the expense book?"

The young man was delighted the matter had nothing to do with Mary. "I would be more than happy to help Martin," he responded.

Mrs. Biddle presented the ledger they used for their bookkeeping. She sat next to him, pointing at dates, various entries, and costs. She discussed the weekly household budget for food.

"Of course, it may vary, but if so, Martin should inform them of any variations and their costs." She concluded by saying, "It would be nice for Martin to become our full-time cook. He is getting older. The work on the grounds and the stable is becoming harder for him."

William agreed and stated his willingness to help as much as he could.

Though he had not uttered a word, Mr. Biddle appeared in good health this morning. He asked William how far he'd gotten in the document. The young man informed his employer he was at the part of the document when Mr. Biddle had taken over the reins as President of the Bank.

"I would find it easier to answer questions that may be more specific to your inquiry," Nicholas Biddle said.

William agreed. He asked if Mr. Biddle could describe the actions he undertook upon joining the bank.

"As President of the bank," Biddle answered, "I sponsored policies restraining the supply of credit to the country's banks. We tried and succeeded in stabilizing investment, money, and discount markets. I led the Bank to regulate the money supply and safeguarded government deposits. The Bank, I believe, flourished. Unlike my predecessors, I recognized the central bank's responsibilities and carefully implemented them. I did so as consciously as the British had done for the Bank of England, which was the model we followed." He paused and looked outside the window. It was a glorious day. The leaves had started to change in color. "I collected many documents related to the Bank War. They are stored in this bureau. Please look there, in the left drawers. I hope you find them enriching."

William walked over to the bureau Biddle had pointed to and opened the drawers. Each was filled with various papers.

Nicholas Biddle noticed the young man was unsure where to start. "Open the bottom drawer. In it, you will find a transcript of Jackson's veto message. Maybe we should start with the end. What do you think, Mr. Nostrand?"

William, scanning the page in his hand, could hardly believe this was a copy of the full Veto speech President Jackson had delivered.

Nicholas Biddle shifted in his chair.

"Sir, an interesting concept would be to review the veto speech and have you rebut various highlighted paragraphs," he said, looking at the old banker.

"I find the idea quite fascinating, young man. If you do not have any questions, I may return to my room." He turned to face William.

"I have found your written document quite enlightening," William said. "The information offers enough details and has given me the necessary knowledge about the state of the bank. However, if I dared to ask, I would find it extremely beneficial to understand the person you battled—the man whom you called an "uneducated roughneck." It would seem proper for me to have an honest idea of the man you faced."

Biddle crossed his legs and turned toward William. "I find your concern a reasonable one. It is my wish you forgive my prior angry and improper burst. Andrew Jackson was a good man, certainly an honest one. He had campaigned as the hero of the people. A powerful general, he appealed to the masses. He and I met early on. I found him loyal to those close to him and forgiving to those closer. But he was menacing to those who disagreed with him and threatening to those who dared oppose him. Andrew Jackson believed the Second Bank of the United States was a "monster," a *"hydra-headed" monster,"* he called it, an evildoer. He accused the Bank of having corrupted our statesmen, to have tarnished the morals of our people. *"The Bank has bought up members of Congress by the dozens."* Jackson had proclaimed. The populace loved it, for it had conclusively found its enemy; the Second Bank of the United States." Biddle stopped for a moment, and William took the opportunity to speak.

"Sir, if I may, how would you respond to these accusations?"

Biddle, the banker, seemed momentarily annoyed. He straightened and responded, "Was the bank a monster? A hydra-headed Monster? These are the words of an astute politician hoping to incite anger within his constituency. A Central Bank is designed to perform its functions as the representative of the government it serves." Once again, Nicholas Biddle appeared angry. His face had become reddish. He continued. "Yes, it is a private, for-profit institution, but without malice. Of the honorable statesmen whose morals may have been tarnished, rest assured, all were money-grubbing, power-hungry men. All were fighting for their survival, but above all, for their accumulated personal wealth. None could be corrupted, for they were all corrupt to start with. Did we try to influence their opinion? Did we purchase members of Congress? Well, of course. We would be fools otherwise. The Second Bank of the United States was, after all, being attacked on all sides; not for its performance, but for what one may call its dubious actions, whatever they may be, and regardless of the tremendous stability it brought to a nation in its infancy."

The young secretary dared not say a word.

Biddle, sensing the tension rise within his body, slowed, breathed in deeply, and smiled at William. "Mr. Nostrand, let's meet again tomorrow." At the same instant, Mrs. Biddle magically appeared at the door and whisked her husband away. William found himself alone in the library, confused about whom he should believe. The words of Nicholas Biddle came back to him, and the gentle warning with which he started his document.

To believe in guilt, one must also believe in innocence, for no condemnation can prove its worth unless the heinous is balanced with the good, and the shameful with the respectable. It is with the lens of fairness I ask the reader to weigh the villainous actions the Bank was accused of with the worthy functions it provided our young Nation.

It took a day for Mr. Biddle to recover, but the weekend arrived. An invitation was received, and the family accepted it and departed for Philadelphia. They would be away for four days. Mrs. Dawson, William, and Martin were the only guests remaining at Andalusia, the Biddle's magnificent home. Most of the workers were journeymen. They would arrive in the morning and leave upon completing their tasks. Martin seemed to enjoy his new position.

William missed Mary but surely appreciated the great food the Frenchman served daily. He also enjoyed helping him figure out how to work within the assigned budget. On a Tuesday, having read and re-read most of the documents Mr. Biddle had collected, he decided to go for a walk.

William walked toward the game house and up the river. Soon he found himself close to Mrs. Biddle's private house. To his surprise, he heard someone singing. He approached the house, curious as to who it may be.

It was Mrs. Dawson. Hearing his footsteps, she turned and saw him. "Hello, Mr. Nostrand."

William stopped and waved.

"Would you care to join me?" She asked.

This time he answered and climbed over the stone wall.

"There is a gate, you know. Right here." She pointed, and they laughed.

He joined Mrs. Dawson at the table.

She looked much younger. Her long, light brown, and wavy hair were loose over her shoulders. The oversized outfit she usually wore had been replaced by a tight-knit shirt, accentuating her breasts. She offered him a drink and he readily accepted.

Mrs. Dawson stood and went inside the house to get his drink.

William could sense a certain tension within his body which he quickly recognized from when he was close to Mary.

She returned with two glasses of brandy. It was strong, and within an hour, the two were laughing, sharing stories of their youth, of the places where they had lived. She was charming. Her beautiful smile was sweet and kind. Accidentally his eyes rested on her chest a moment too long. He was caught.

"Mr. Nostrand. Are you looking at my breasts?" She asked him.

It took only a second for the blood in his entire body to rise to his face. He turned a bright shade of red. Embarrassed, he looked into her eyes apologetically. Their stare, which seemed to last an eternity, ended when she smiled. "Forgive me, Mr. Nostrand. Rare are the moments when I feel like a woman. While certainly surprised, I appreciate the compliment." She smiled again. "Let me close the house. We can stroll back to the house. It is almost dinner time." The headmistress disappeared for a few minutes. She returned with a shawl over her shoulders and stood before him. She looked up at him and softly spoke, "Mr. Nostrand, would you be kind enough to hold me in your arms?"

Without hesitation, he approached her and wrapped his arms tightly around Mrs. Dawson.

She smelled so sweet, and he loved the softness of her hair against his face. *But something was wrong*, he thought.

Sensing she was crying, he patiently waited for a signal before releasing her.

"I have not been held by a man in years. Thank you for your kindness, Mr. Nostrand."

William gently let go of her, and the two walked back toward the house. They decided it would not be proper for them to be seen together strolling from the woods, so she left him by the river where he sat, throwing pebbles at the water.

A light drizzle woke him from a daydream in which he argued both sides, Biddle's and Jackson's. Each in their respective position was correct. He was a lawyer defending the accused and accuser. Nicholas Biddle, on the one hand, performed his duty as the bank's President honorably. He transformed the Second Bank of the United States into a healthy and successful institution promoting a strong and stable economy. Yes, it had been a private Bank, but it was James Madison who, in 1816, had signed and approved the Bank's twenty-year charter. Neither the bank nor its President should be blamed for carrying out its mandate. This would be inconceivable.

President Jackson presented a different point of view, however. The Second Bank of the United States, a private entity, enjoyed enormous power—a power it used to unjustly insert itself into the nation's affairs. Jackson believed the bank dictated legislations, influenced elections, and manipulated the government's operation to reach its goal—profit. All in all, the very actions and existence of the Second Bank of the United States were unconstitutional, the President believed.

How could one reconcile the fact the Bank, which had been granted a virtual monopoly, could exercise such influence over all matters dear to the well-being of the people of the United States but remain independent of presidential, congressional, or popular oversight?

These questions remained as William found himself in front of the glorious Greek facade of Andalusia, its stunning columns wrapped in the golden light of the setting sun.

No one was in the kitchen. He noticed a plate had been saved for him. A napkin covered it, an attempt to protect it from the many flies.

Famished, William discovered ham, cheese, bread, a sliced tomato, roasted beets, and potatoes. The young man remembered his mother and how happy she would be to see him so grown up. He took in a deep breath, closed his eyes, and prayed for her welfare.

"Hello, Lad. How is everything?" Martin said as he sat across from him. The two chatted for a little while. The cranky and impolite Frenchmen he had met had now become his dear friend.

"Please, put away your plate and shut all the candles once you are done, William. I am exhausted and going to bed." Martin left for his room above the stables. His new position as the cook offered him the opportunity to stay in the house, but he was happy where he was.

William finished his meal, cleaned up, and headed to bed.

Mrs. Dawson, who had escaped his mind, seemed to have disappeared somewhere in the house.

He had enjoyed their conversation, and while a little surprised by her comment when she caught him looking at her breasts, he sensed she was an extremely lonely woman.

William laid on his bed and picked up the book he had borrowed from the library when he heard a knock on the door. He stood a little surprised and opened the door to see Mrs. Dawson standing there, a chamber stick in her slightly trembling hand. She remained quiet and looked nervous.

"Are you hoping to continue the marvelous conversation we started this afternoon?" He said, moving out of the way to open the door wide.

"Forgive me, Mr. Nostrand, for, while I long for your touch, I fear my ineptitude in the matters of love will anger you," she said timidly.

"May your heart be as beautiful as it is gentle, for I may lose myself in it. It is all I require, Elizabeth." He responded. The two held each other tenderly all night. Over the next few days, the two discreetly engaged in a tender and loving romance.

Elizabeth learned to love without fear.

William discovered she was a gentle soul. He continued to study the events known as the "Bank War." William learned an important fact.

Nicholas Biddle, hoping to guarantee the Bank's survival, had pushed to recharter the bank before its expiration. The re-charter of the bank was soon approved by the legislature. But William found some of Nicholas Biddle's statements troubling: *"This worthy President thinks that because he has scalped Indians and imprisoned Judges, he is to have his way with the Bank. He is mistaken."*

Or the following about the threat posed on the Bank, which brought grave concerns to William; "Nothing but widespread suffering will produce any effect on Congress.... *Our only safety is in pursuing a steady course of firm restriction – and I have no doubt that such a course will ultimately lead to restoration of the currency and the recharter of the Bank."* Biddle had written.

This was a direct threat against our Nation; *"widespread suffering," "Firm restriction"*? These seemed like formal warnings sent to an enemy.

The Bank, he had learned, managed, and controlled all aspects of the nation's economy. It could therefore manipulate America's affair in any way it pleased. It controlled the country's rise and fall.

Maybe Jackson was correct in his judgment; the Bank had little concern for the Nation and only cared for its own profit.

William, in Biddle's writing, had found an arrogant man who could be obstinate, impatient, and subject to tantrums.

Jackson's many statements against the Bank, on the other hand, exposed a fierce disdain for the institution. His many statements against the bank were certainly much more entertaining:

"You are a den of vipers. I intend to rout you out, and by eternal God, I will rout you."

President Andrew Jackson was a general, an astute politician who understood a battle was won one little step at a time.

William learned Jackson had employed a well-thought-out campaign of misinformation against the Second Bank of the United States. He had directed his staff: *"to attack incessantly, assail at all points, display the evil of the institutions, rouse the people, and prepare them to sustain the veto."*

The President was combatting a man whose only tool was money. It had been a powerful tool indeed, but one necessitating extreme discretion. The Bank War destroyed any chance at hiding the profits from these nefarious back-door deals.

The Biddle family returned on a Saturday morning.

William had been there for three weeks now. His first steps into adulthood had been promising. He had certainly been successful in the affairs of the heart and loved the work he had accomplished for Mr. Biddle. Of all the reading he had done, William kept returning to Andrew Jackson's veto speech.

Upon the family's return, Mrs. Dawson became distant, unwilling to jeopardize her position with the Biddles.

He understood.

Late Saturday, when Mr. and Mrs. Biddle had moved to their little country house paradise and the rest of the house quiet, Elizabeth entered his room without knocking.

She quietly stepped into the bed and murmured in his ear she had missed him.

William did not get to see Mr. Biddle till late Monday. He was a little anxious but felt he had worked hard and was ready to complete his task. He sat in the study and heard Mr. and Mrs. Biddle chatting and sounding joyous.

They entered the library, and she rang the bell.

William, who was in the study, joined them.

Mrs. Biddle was kind and sweet and welcomed him warmly.

Mr. Biddle was the victim of a privileged upbringing. Little had been refused to him. The banker was a good man caught in the wrong place at the wrong time. "Well, how are you, Mr. Nostrand?" The banker asked.

William shared the progress he had made.

Biddle could sense the excitement in the young man's voice.

"I followed your advice and studied the Veto speech. Accordingly, I outlined a few parts I feel it would be beneficial to hear your response," said William.

Nicholas Biddle seemed rested and unconcerned. They decided to first enjoy a little tea and some freshly baked scones. The three spoke of Philadelphia.

Fifteen minutes later, Mrs. Biddle excused herself, and the two were finally ready to converse.

"Upon my research, a few questions arose. I would be extremely grateful, Sir, were I able to explore your answers before dealing with the Veto speech," William said.

Biddle was agreeable.

It appeared odd to William that a request for the renewal of the Bank's charter had been presented to Congress years before its actual expiration. What precipitated such a motion? He wondered.

"This is an excellent question, Mr. Nostrand. Certain actions, while initially assumed to be wise, turn out, in retrospect, detrimental and misguided. However wise, the decision to renew the Bank's charter prior to its expiration may have appeared to be at the time, once the process had started, it was impossible to change direction. It must not be ignored that I was the Bank's President, not its owner, and had to respond to the shareholders. However, as its representative, I take full responsibility for it."

William was taking notes.

"Let's return to the question you posed last time we met, Mr. Nostrand. If I am not mistaken, it was related to whether we had tried to influence certain Congressmen. The board of the bank, its major stockholder, and I strongly felt we would win the Bank recharter in Congress. Senators Henry Clay of Kentucky and Daniel Webster of Massachusetts decided to make rechartering a referendum on the legitimacy of the Bank in the 1832 elections.

"However, we had been correct. The Senate, on June 11, 1832, voted 28-20 to reauthorize the Bank's charter. Not long after, on July 3, the House voted by a margin of 107-85 to reauthorize the Bank's charter. We had played our cards right and succeeded. Upon learning of the favorable votes, the furious Jackson stated, *'The Bank, Mr. Van Buren, is trying to kill me, but I shall kill it.'*"

William was impressed by the honest response. He wondered if the President was really opposed to a central bank.

"Young man, to imply Andrew Jackson may have, in any way, been supportive of a central bank is to imply he detested my bank so much he was willing to destroy our Nation's economy to prevail."

William raised his hand.

Biddle stopped.

"Is it not what his veto speech presents? A strong dissatisfaction with the act he was presented with on July 4th and titled, *'An act to incorporate the subscribers to the Bank of the United States.'* In his speech, Jackson clearly outlines his specific concerns." William hoped he was not about to upset Mr. Biddle.

"It may be so, Mr. Nostrand. The act had been reauthorized by both houses. The economy was strong. Jackson had used his veto power more than all previous presidents together. We believed he would accept the will of the people and move on." Nicholas Biddle reached for the bell.

They remained quiet until Mrs. Dawson appeared. She was trying to avoid eye contact with William at all costs.

"Elizabeth, would you be kind enough to ask Martin to prepare a light meal for Mr. Nostrand and me? We will eat here."

Elizabeth disappeared. She returned a few minutes later to clear the table in the corner of the library.

"Let's continue, if you please," said Mr. Biddle.

William offered to present the parts of Jackson's Veto Speech he had outlined.

His employer agreed, and William read: *"A bank of the United States is, in many respects, convenient for the Government and useful to the people. Entertaining this opinion, and deeply impressed with the belief that some of the powers and privileges possessed by the existing bank are unauthorized by the Constitution, subversive of the rights of the States, and dangerous to the liberties of the people."*

"In my humble view," Nicholas Biddle started, "it is a foolish and ignorant statement for one simple reason: the Bank was chartered by President Madison in 1816. It was not chartered by a group of private investors. The Bank followed agreed-upon guidelines to help our young nation prosper."

William decided to continue and read the next line of the Veto Speech: *"It (the Bank) enjoys an exclusive privilege of banking under the authority of the General Government, a monopoly of its favor and support, and, as a necessary consequence, almost a monopoly of the foreign and domestic exchange. The powers, privileges, and favors bestowed upon it in the original charter, by increasing the value of the stock far above its par value, operated as a gratuity of many millions to the stockholders."*

"Is Jackson correct in his statement regarding, first, the powers and privileges and then of the monopoly?" Asked William.

Mrs. Dawson, accompanied by Martin, arrived, each carrying a tray. They set them on the table and left.

"Once again, Mr. Nostrand, the "powers and privileges" President Jackson refers to are the tools we had been legally provided with. As a private institution, growth and profit guided each and every one of our actions. As far as a monopoly is concerned, I can only offer the same answer; What had been given in its charter had been given legally."

They sat around a beautiful tray of food.

"Thank God for Martin," said Biddle. "He has been a delight in the kitchen. Also, thanks to you for helping him see through the managing of the budget."

William shared that he loved Martin. "I did not eat but a couple of scones for the first three days I was at Andalusia."

They laughed and enjoyed their meal. The conversation brought back the memory of the beautiful Mary.

"Let's look at this statement," William said: *"If our Government must sell monopolies, it would seem to be its duty to take nothing less than their full value, and if gratuities must be made once in fifteen or twenty years, let them not be bestowed on the subjects of a foreign government nor upon a designated and favored class of men in our own country."*

Nicholas Biddle laid down his fork and responded. "It is true a large number of foreigners are stockholders in the bank. But an educated critic would be cognizant of the fact that 70% of all central banks are owned by foreigners. The same critic would certainly be aware that Great Britain is the primary source of capital.

"Of the wealthiest bankers in Great Britain, only one possesses enough wealth to finance a government; the Rothschilds. In this charade, young man, there are only willing participants. None of this information was hidden or protected from Madison or the Congress he led. The tide changed, and it became convenient to accuse foreigners of abuse."

The two spent the next couple of hours going back and forth.

At 3:30 p.m., Biddle took his leave.

William spent the next few hours transcribing the extensive notes he had taken.

Somewhat frustrated by the one-sided point of view he had been offered, William decided to ignore his feelings and focus on the task.

A bell rang in the distance, announcing that dinner was ready. William left the study, ate quietly, and decided to take a walk. He returned to the hill Martin had recommended. There he sat under the same tree, but he was somewhat troubled this time. The day replayed itself.

Mr. Biddle's defense repeatedly relied on the fact the bank had been chartered by James Madison. Therefore, the Bank's actions, while seeming nefarious, had followed the charter by which it had been created and therefore were legal.

William sided with President Jackson in believing the bank had promoted profit and control to manipulate the entire governmental system. It had thus succeeded in total dominance of the market and the country. Its power had grown immensely. The Second Bank of the United States could threaten the Nation and, in the words of Biddle, create; *"widespread suffering will produce any effect on Congress"* in order to lead the government to recharter the bank.

Mr. Biddle seemed to accept bribes as an established means of influence. The bank had poured fortunes into the pockets of the men whose duty was to serve and protect our population.

Jackson, William believed, was correct when he said; *"It is to be regretted that the rich and powerful too often bend the acts of government to their selfish purposes."*

The sun set over the horizon in a burst of glorious reds, gold, and deep blues. The stars appeared in the night sky.

The young Nostrand could hardly offer an ounce of agreement in defense of his employer. William doubted the Second Bank of the United States had been chartered to exploit our nation. Paying off its Congressman, infiltrating itself in the many facets governing the Nation, and leading politicians to exercise the will of the Bank: *"The bold effort the present bank had made to control the Government, the distress it had wantonly produced ... are but premonitions of the fate that awaits the American people should they be deluded into a perpetuation of this institution, or the establishment of another like it,"* Jackson had stated in his speech.

He had properly done so, William believed. He suddenly remembered that a few days earlier, upon looking for a book to read during his stay, a note had fallen from a book as he pulled it from the shelf. The loose paper was tightly folded. Upon examination, William discovered it was a printed page torn from a newspaper.

Unfolding it, he read the article, which contained the following line:

"'Our whole banking system I ever abhorred, I continue to abhor, and I shall die abhorring...' John Adams, 1811."

Over the next week, William did not meet with Mr. Biddle for any length of time. They would have tea on the porch, maybe, while enjoying a glorious morning. A few times, Mr. Biddle had entered the library to inquire about William's progress. Once, they took a short walk to the edge of the river while clarifying events described in the documents.

On a beautiful Tuesday in the middle of October, Martin came to fetch William.

However, due to the Frenchman's strong accent, William had not really understood why. But he trusted Martin and assumed he needed him, so he descended the stairs behind the Frenchman.

In the salon, they found Mrs. Dawson, a few of the workers, and Mrs. Biddle.

Mrs. Biddle welcomed everyone. "Mr. Biddle and I will be traveling to Philadelphia this afternoon," she said. "We will remain there for a week or so. Martin, we would like you to join us. I request you hire someone to join you. The cold seems a little premature. Wood will need to be cut for the fire, and the house in Philadelphia prepared for winter. Please hire someone strong, as you will need a lot of help.

"Mrs. Dawson, I need you to stay and manage the house while we are away. I would prefer you would join us, but we need you here. Gardeners, I need to review the preparation for winter. I hope this can be accomplished while we are away. I will meet with you and go over this in detail once this meeting is over.

"Mr. Nostrand, how are you doing with your project?" Her voice felt sharp. He responded that all was going well.

Mrs. Biddle cut him off. "Please, meet my husband in the library in 15 minutes. You may present your work for his review. Thank you. Does anyone have any questions?" As no response came forward, she informed the gardeners to meet her in half of an hour by the garden.

"Elizabeth, will you be kind enough to see that Mr. Nostrand is looked after? You will oversee the house." They left.

William found Mr. Biddle in the library.

He was looking awful, pale, and swollen. The poor old banker could barely move.

William told him he would love for him to read the document he had been working on.

Biddle nodded in approval, but within minutes, appeared to have fallen asleep. The poor man was not well, and a strong odor had permeated the room. The banker woke up, startled.

He saw William and said, "You are a nice young man, Mr. Nostrand. You have a lot of talent. I have really enjoyed the work you completed thus far."

Tommy, a young but muscular farm hand, appeared in the doorway.

"William. Got to get the Master. How is he?" Said the handsome brute.

Thankfully, Martin entered, followed by Mrs. Biddle.

William was relieved. For a minute, he thought Tommy was about to place Mr. Biddle on his shoulder and carry him to the carriage.

They sent Tommy to fetch the suitcase while Mrs. Biddle and Martin tried to carry Mr. Biddle down to the wagon.

"Please, Mrs. Biddle, let me help, please," said William.

Silently, she withdrew and left in search of Tommy.

It took Martin and William ten minutes to guide their employer down to the wagon. They covered him with a blanket.

"Is he okay?" asked William.

Martin shook his head.

Within a half hour, the house was empty. The gardeners dispersed about the property and left upon completion of their duties.

For the first time, William wondered how futile writing this document may be. Nicholas Biddle needed peace, not the turmoil of having to relive the Bank War. He walked to the library and collected his notes. Nicholas Biddle's absence had suddenly become a reminder of the insurmountable pain the banker had lived through.

William heard light footsteps approach the library.

Elizabeth appeared in the doorway, a candle in her hand.

William had not realized night had fallen.

She entered and lit a few of the candles around the room.

He had grown very fond of Mrs. Dawson. She was a delicate soul willing to withdraw herself to help others. She was gentle, patient, and a good listener.

"How are you, Mr. Nostrand?"

He smiled at her. "Delightful, Elizabeth. Thank you," he said, somewhat disingenuously. There were papers scattered everywhere. He had been troubled with the work he had produced so far.

She was sitting on the couch.

He approached and sat on the floor next to her, leaning on the couch.

"In all truth, I am extremely frustrated," he said, explaining that a few weeks earlier, he and Mr. Biddle had spent a lot of time working on collecting information and clarifying a multitude of important events. William felt that his report could not be completed. "I would have loved to hear Mr. Biddle's response to this statement: *'Suspicions are entertained and charges are made of gross abuse and violation of its charter...'* You see, Elizabeth, I believe honesty may have been disguised. The Bank, led by our dear employer, too often engaged in unlawful actions to preserve, and grow its own wealth, not the wealth of the country it was meant to serve. Listen to this quote by Andrew Jackson."

Once again, he read aloud, *'There are no necessary evils in government. Its evils exist only in its abuses.'"*

She raised her hand, signaling him to stop. "You scare me, William," said Elizabeth softly.

William, who had risen to his feet to collect another note, raced to her.

"My Dear, I am so sorry," he said, kneeling by her side. But his consolation did not help.

She burst into tears.

Surprised, he silently held her hands and wrapped his arms around her. William waited patiently for Elizabeth to calm down, intrigued by what had triggered such an outburst. On the couch, he sat next to her patiently.

Soon, she no longer sobbed uncontrollably. Elizabeth reached for her handkerchief to wipe her eyes.

"I am sorry, William," she said. "I am heartbroken to see what has come upon this family. They have been so good to me." Elizabeth leaned on his shoulder.

"Did you know the Master has been indicted for fraud and theft?" She continued. "Such injustice. I have worked with the family for the last ten years, and never have I seen them treat anyone unfairly."

William noticed tears were, once again, swelling in her eyes. He remained silent.

"I hate the Bank War you speak of. Accusations aimed at the poor Mr. Biddle, who has been so sick ever since he left the bank." She paused and looked into his eyes. "Please do not share this with anyone, but a year ago, upon the collapse of the Bank, I overheard a conversation between Mr. and Mrs. Biddle and a guest—a visitor from Washington; an old friend, I'd guess. The three were discussing the collapse of the Bank."

"'I am sorry, Nicholas, but the Bank has taken it all. Your fortune has evaporated,' the visitor said to Mr. Biddle. I was about to enter the room, but upon hearing this, I stopped. I was shocked and returned to the kitchen. The bell rang a few minutes later. It was Mrs. Biddle who requested some tea. The man from Washington had left. Mr. Biddle was in a daze. His wife was repeatedly telling him not to worry. They ignored me. I knew then that poor Mr. Biddle would never be the same. Thank God, the mistress is a woman of means."

William waited for her to finish and, after a few minutes, thanked her for sharing. "Fortunes and misfortunes are the evils that lead us to despair, for neither is eternal," he said. "You should know, my Dear, the words I have written do not accuse Mr. Biddle of any wrongdoing. I promise."

She hugged him. The two lovers spent the night in each other's arms.

The next morning, William set his mind to work. At the desk by the window, he decided to adopt an impartial look at the collapse of the Second Bank of the United States. Ignoring his feelings toward the Bank allowed him, in a way, to free himself from the inner battles he suffered while writing. The process instantly became easier, and he made great progress.

A week later, on a gray morning, Martin appeared in the driveway. The Frenchman had traveled to fetch Elizabeth, whom the family needed in Philadelphia.

"Mr. Biddle isn't well, my Lad. It is very sad to witness. His health is failing him so quickly. After a brief pause, Martin changed the conversation. He was in a hurry to get back on the road.

"I stopped at the Rockwell Farm. They will send provisions with Little Pat, the gardener. You will be the only guest here. If this is not acceptable, then you can accompany us back to Philadelphia."

William decided to stay and assured him he would be fine. It was now late October, and the countryside was magnificent. He would enjoy the solitude.

"I must request that you perform certain duties while you are here alone," said Martin, who explained which doors to lock and emphasized the danger of candles. The request mostly covered the safety of the property. Within an hour, Mrs. Dawson was climbing beside Martin for their long ride back to the city.

"The plan is to be back here in four days. Please be safe," said Martin.

Elizabeth remained quiet and politely waved goodbye.

William returned to his small desk. Over the next few days, the document he had been drafting was completed. The young man had tempered his emotion toward the bank and produced a document he felt would provide a detailed account of the event while remaining impartial. It did, of course, portray Mr. Biddle as an honest steward of the Second Bank of the United States.

William omitted many troubling facts. For instance, the bank's one-year profit during the 1830s equaled around $3.5 Million. This was an enormous sum. He neglected to mention taxes on the profit of the bank's stock would be levied on our nation's citizens but not on the foreign stockholders, exacting a greater burden on the public. This, William knew, bothered Jackson, and he agreed. He also had grave concerns the bank was controlled and influenced by foreigners he distrusted as this quote from Jackson's Veto Speech demonstrated.

"Is there no danger to our liberty and independence in a bank that in its nature has so little to bind it to our country?"

Jackson continued further into his speech.

"If we must have a bank with private stockholders, every consideration of sound policy and every impulse of American feeling admonishes that it should be purely American."

The Second Bank of the United States possessed inconceivable powers. Jackson believed these powers influenced areas the bank had no business exploiting.

"Controlling our currency, receiving our public moneys, and holding thousands of our citizens in dependence, it would be more formidable and dangerous than the naval and military power of the enemy."

The sun was wrapping its golden hues on the landscape before him. William stood and organized his desk. He put away the many stacks of paper he had read. The study was now clear, the library immaculate. He decided to make himself some tea—a simple but well-deserved celebration. As he left for the kitchen, the young man felt odd. While he found great satisfaction in his accomplishment, he had betrayed his principles to complete his task. It bothered him. Andrew Jackson had been a hero to him—a president who had been entrusted to fight for and protect the nation's citizens.

William walked down the stairs thinking of Nicholas Biddle—a man of importance who had fallen from grace and had lost his fortune, his old friends who had deserted him, and the Bank he so cherished.

Elizabeth came to his mind, replacing the unfortunate banker. A much more pleasant interruption, he concluded.

Sitting on the porch, surrounded by the massive columns, he heard noises from the road. The family was returning from Philadelphia. William rejoiced, and within minutes he and Martin unloaded the carriage.

Tommy, the strong farm hand, called on William to help with Mr. Biddle.

He gladly helped Tommy.

The two of them, under Mrs. Biddle's guidance, carried the poor man to his room. He appeared half asleep. The next few days became a blur of activities.

Mrs. Dawson had returned to her cold and distant behavior.

Martin was overwhelmed by the amount of work to be done besides his kitchen duties, so William offered to help.

The family had quietly withdrawn to their quarters.

Soon everyone was settled.

On a beautiful morning, William was sitting in the kitchen having breakfast when Mrs. Dawson cheerfully entered the room. She sat right next to William and offered a warm smile.

Martin served her breakfast and excused himself. "I must go and collect a few more eggs. I'll be right back."

As he left, Elizabeth laid her hand on his. "I have missed you, William." Her words warmed his heart.

Footsteps were heard coming down the stairs. It was Mrs. Biddle who also seemed in a pleasant mood.

Martin entered at the same time as she was inquiring about his absence.

Mrs. Biddle kindly requested breakfast to be served in the library.

"Please, Martin; eggs, bacon, muffin, a piece of cheese, bread, jelly, and a pitcher of coffee. Elizabeth, would you bring the breakfast and set the table in the library?"

Mrs. Dawson replied affirmatively and stood to prepare.

Martin cooked more eggs and collected the other items he would need.

"William, it would be wonderful if you could join us. Mr. Biddle would love to hear about the work you have completed," said Mrs. Biddle.

William responded he would meet them in the library at once. Little did William know he would find Mr. Biddle sitting at the table, reading. The morning light was glorious and enveloped the superb furniture. The young man was welcomed warmly and was asked to sit. He complied and offered a brief report on the completion of the document.

Mr. Biddle asked William if he wouldn't mind reading part of it.

William, who had been here at Andalusia for over two months now, had worked extremely hard, and was excited to present the fruits of his labor.

He started to collect the documents and was immediately interrupted by Mrs. Biddle. She was accompanied by Mrs. Dawson and Martin. The food smelled delicious.

William took the opportunity to explain he had kept most of the introductory text Mr. Biddle had authored.

"Fine, young man. I am grateful you approved of the writing."

The commotion ended when Mrs. Biddle asked her husband if it would be satisfactory for her to leave and check on the garden.

"Of course, my dear. I am in good hands." He turned to William and, with a wave of the hand, informed him it was time to read.

"The Second Bank of The United States," By Nicholas Biddle, November 1, 1843

To believe in guilt, one must also believe in innocence, for no condemnation can prove its worth unless the heinous is balanced with the good, the shameful with the respectable. It is with the lens of fairness I ask the reader to weigh the villainous actions the Bank was accused of with the worthy functions it provided our young Nation."

William Nostrand read on. He knew he had succeeded, for not a word was expressed. Yet, at times he could hear a spoon stir the tea that had just been poured or a bite taken out of a warm scone. It was almost noon when

Mrs. Biddle stopped at the threshold of the library. William finished his paragraph and paused.

"Thank you so much, Mr. Nostrand," Mrs. Biddle said and walked to her husband. She rested a hand on his shoulder.

"Dear," he said to his wife. "Could I take my lunch here?"

She agreed and disappeared.

William took a break and followed her to the kitchen, where he devoured his lunch. He helped Elizabeth bring the tray of food.

The afternoon continued uninterrupted.

William was getting tired when suddenly, he turned to the last page. He took a deep breath to read one of Biddle's quotes; *"...Yes, sir, in the sweeping ruin which will overwhelm humble and useful industry in the general submersion of small traders, the only beings who will be seen floating on the wreck are these very 'monied aristocrats,' whom the resolutions denounce with such indignation..."*

The young man took in the moment. Once again, he inhaled and looked at Mr. Biddle. Speechless, the poor man had tears in his eyes.

"I appreciate you ending with my comments on the possible bank closure. A dreadful warning. You have done a splendid job, Mr. Nostrand. I am indebted to you forever," he said, grabbing the bell to call his wife.

Mrs. Dawson appeared in her stead.

He sent her to fetch his wife.

William decided to take a walk. The world he had entered, he was about to leave. His duties had been completed. He was no longer needed. Late in the evening, knowing Martin would be in his room above the stables, he stopped by to say hello.

Martin congratulated him on his accomplishment. "The Master was very happy with you, Lad," the Frenchman said. They spoke for a little while, and soon he left William.

The kitchen was quiet. Once again, he found a plate had been prepared for him, so he sat and enjoyed one of the last meals he would have here at

Andalusia. He ate quietly, hoping to see Elizabeth enter the kitchen, but she did not.

A few hours later, she entered his room. Over the next day, the two spent a good amount of time together, discreetly chatting, kissing, and planning for an uncertain future.

Two days after presenting his document to Mr. Biddle, he was asked to present himself in the library.

Mrs. Biddle, alone, welcomed him. "I had hoped Nicholas... excuse me, Mr. Biddle hoped he would have been able to say goodbye, but he is unwell. I am sorry." She presented him with a note.

"Please present this note to Mr. Rutherford in Philadelphia. The address is listed in the letter. Martin will drive you back. He knows where Mr. Rutherford's office is located. Make sure to stop by on your way back. Here are three copies of a letter of recommendation Mr. Biddle dictated and signed. You may use them at your own discretion. Also included is a list of names; old friends and associates with whom you may inquire for a position." She handed him a book and said,

"This is a personal present from my husband to you, Mr. Nostrand. It is one of the first copies of *The Journals of Lewis and Clark: Excerpts from the History of the Lewis and Clark Expedition.* Nicholas worked on editing their tale when he was young. It contains a personal note from Clarke, who had given it to him. On the back is a note to you from my husband."

William stopped her. "Mrs. Biddle, I cannot leave without saying goodbye. I must insist." He could see her heart was broken.

"Follow me," she said sternly.

William found Nicholas Biddle in his bed, barely conscious. His face was red and swollen, his lips chapped and trembling slightly. William looked into the banker's eyes, but they remained fixed on a mysterious point on the ceiling. The young man reached out and held the dying man's hand in his. He could feel a slight squeeze but was uncertain whether the man had any strength left. "May your days blossom endlessly here in Andalusia. I must leave you now but hope to see you better soon. It has been an honor to serve you, Mr. Biddle." William said. He stood and left, heartbroken at the sight of Nicholas Biddle, whom he believed was a good man, a warm husband, and a loving father.

The young Nostrand rose early the next morning. He and Elizabeth had spent one last night together. He dared not wake her, for he feared a sad goodbye. He placed a handwritten note on the side table, stopped, and looked once more over the beautiful Mrs. Dawson, and left. He joined Martin in the stable.

The Frenchman was impatient to start their journey to Philadelphia, so the two immediately departed. The young man turned to look at Andalusia as it slowly disappeared in the distance. Wrapped in the early morning fog, it stood out like a ghost. A ray of sun fought through the mist to brighten the columns of Andalusia. The house looked majestic. It slowly disappeared.

The Saturday morning markets were closing, and the city was bustling with activities as they entered Philadelphia.

Mrs. Nostrand was surprised but extremely happy to see her son. She invited the Frenchman to lunch, and he gladly accepted.

Within an hour, Martin was heading back to Andalusia.

William was now back home, with his mother, without a job, and away from the woman he had become attached to. He loved his life at Andalusia, where he had enjoyed working for Mr. Biddle, who hopefully would soon regain his strength.

A few days later, the young Nostrand proudly presented his letter of recommendation from Nicholas Biddle to Mr. MacHenry, a former banker who was looking for help with some of his records. He was tall and boney, with long, greasy black hair, and suffered from a terrible skin condition. He spoke in a low, unhurried manner.

The two discussed the task in need of completion, and after agreeing on compensation, William was hired. He would start the following Monday.

Over the next few weeks, life returned to normal for the young Nostrand. He only saw Elizabeth once, during her brief stay in Philadelphia. The family had returned to the city to celebrate the Holidays.

Mrs. Dawson had explained that Mr. Biddle had recently felt better, but the toll of the many relapses had left its mark. The 58-year-old man now walked with a cane and was always under the supervision of an aide. Usually, the role was assigned to Martin, who, unfortunately, was also getting older.

Tommy had traveled to join the family. "It has been difficult for all of us to see the poor Mr. Biddle failing so rapidly. His arms and legs were most often swollen. Martin is heartbroken over the master's suffering," said Elizabeth.

William was ecstatic to see her. Sadly, immediately after the Biddle's arrival in Philadelphia, creditors had come knocking on his door.

A day later, new indictments had been announced, accusing Nicholas Biddle of more fraud and theft. The family decided to return to Andalusia. Their journey back was difficult. Attempts at staying warm were fruitless.

The horses were slower.

Mr. Biddle, who could no longer sit still, laid across the main bench.

Mrs. Biddle, Elizabeth, and Tommy shared the front seat of the carriage, sharing one of the remaining blankets. The other three blankets covered Nicholas Biddle's shivering body.

They arrived late in the evening.

It was a bleak and cold February afternoon when Charles Whitmore visited William. The two had grown up in the same neighborhood, attended the same schools, and in their teens, had been inseparable. While their paths led them to different universities and areas of study, their friendship had only grown stronger.

Mr. Whitmore, who worked in Washington, had returned to Philadelphia to attend to some personal business. They headed to a small tavern at the corner of High Street and Seventh.

Charles was an intellectual, William believed, with a rare, analytical mind and a keen intellect. "Tell me about Mr. Biddle, William," he said.

"Personally, I admire President Jackson. His actions were fearless, calculated, and, in my view, conceived to benefit the citizens of this country." William paused. "However, I opted to write a tale embellishing my employer's actions and disregarded unfavorable facts. It pleased Mr. Biddle, whom I had grown fond of. The poor man had lost his personal fortune in the Bank War; a war in which, I believe, there had been no winners."

"How was Jackson able to take the bank down?" Charles asked.

"Willpower? Foolishness? Who knows? I truly believe the Bank had acquired too much power in many areas it had no business with. But the Bank did provide a tremendous service and the financial stability our young country needed. Had the bank been restrained in its influence, power, and its greed, it could have continued to flourish." William paused once again and took a sip of ale. "Biddle had dared a fearless redneck General to act, and Jackson lifted his gun and coldly shot the bank in the heart. The President stopped all deposits of government funds from going to the Second Bank of the United States, cutting the bank's cash flow."

On April 4, 1834, the full house voted to deny the recharter of the Second Bank of the United States. Worst of all, it voted overwhelmingly to authorize the creation of a committee to investigate the bank's affairs and its involvement in the recent financial panic. Checkmate! A year later, Andrew Jackson, the Seventh President of the United States of America, proudly paid off the final installment of the national debt. He was the first American President to do so.

"This is one of my favorite quotes by Andrew Jackson," said William; *"The bold effort the present bank had made to control the Government, the distress it had wantonly produced ... are but premonitions of the fate that awaits the American people should they be deluded into a perpetuation of this institution, or the establishment of another like it."*

The two were interrupted by a short fat man, whose name was Morton; a simple-minded local whom they had known forever. Distracted by the interruption, they decided to leave, promising to stay in touch.

The news came to William on February 28th, 1844. The previous day, Nicholas Biddle had succumbed to bronchitis complicated by dropsy.

Saddened by the news, William took a long walk. He stopped by the Biddle's house in Philadelphia, but the house was empty. He reminisced on the weeks he spent with Nicholas Biddle.

Blindly walking the streets of Philadelphia, he found himself on Church Street. He turned onto 2nd Street, where he knew he would find the magnificent Christ Church. He entered the church to offer a prayer for Mr. Biddle, his sweet wife, and their extended family. He thought of Martin and Elizabeth. William lit a candle, prayed silently, and walked out of the church.

Stepping onto the sidewalk, he crossed paths with a strange man. He was tall and extremely thin, with white hair and piercing, light blue eyes. Initially, William ignored the feeling within him, but suddenly he wondered. Was the man he had just seen Andrew Jackson? He certainly looked like the former President.

William turned to check. As he wondered if he had crossed paths with Jackson, the tall man facing away from him suddenly turned to his right and disappeared. The man certainly bore a strong resemblance.

Instantly, a faded memory came back to him. It had been early during his stay at Andalusia. He could clearly picture the scene before him. It had been a long day reviewing various documents and old newspaper articles when he found a folded newspaper. He unfolded it and read the title: "President Jackson's Proudest Moment." It was an interview with the now retired President.

The reporter, a certain Mortimer Wilson, had asked Jackson, "which, of your many accomplishments, was the most important?"

William could still remember holding the newspaper in his hands. He could see each printed word as if he held the note in his hand.

Jackson's response had been, *"I killed the Bank."*

CHAPTER 8

MORE DESPOTIC THAN A MONARCHY

The modern theory of the perpetuation of debt has drenched the earth with blood, and crushed its inhabitants under burdens ever accumulating.
— Thomas Jefferson

MANHATTAN, NY, 2012

As he walked away from the school building and down Broadway toward W. 65th Street, questions surfaced in David's mind, unwelcome guests in an already irritated subject. He now doubted the path that had led him to practice the cello a minimum of five hours a day and still not be good enough. Business school had once been considered, but music had appeared a more righteous path at the time. Puzzled, he continued his journey toward the train station.

David had grown to despise New York City, its dirty streets, and the dismal lifestyle its inhabitants accepted as normal. These men, women, and children survived this incomprehensible petri dish of violence fueled by mental illness, of untold wealth and utter poverty, of failed dreams and servitude.

And then there were the incomprehensible piles of trash left to feed the massive rat population. How could a city so rich fail to manage its trash.

David passed by a Thai restaurant; a cruel reminder of the miserable condition New Yorkers endured. The sidewalks smelled rancid.

However, what troubled David was the unexpected new program the school had decided to implement randomly. Its glorious title was "Cross Platform synergy." The program made no sense to him. He could not see the reason why he would have to waste time on this.

"Synergy," the plump, middle-aged woman had proudly announced before the class, "is the interaction or cooperation of two or more organizations, substances, or other agents." Miss something from the drama department continued, but she had already lost David. The "Miss," he assumed, stated the obvious; She was an old maid, probably owned a cat or two, and her sex life was a long-gone memory.

David reflected on the assignment as he walked down the Columbus Circle station stairs; "Which piece of music, from Sonata to Symphony, would most evoke the story of the Civil War—our story?"

David first selected the "Duet for Two Cellos, Präludium" by Dmitri Shostakovich. It was touching but too short. He needed a different piece, Barber's Adagio for Strings, maybe.

David mentally replayed the piece in his mind. It was magnificent. But Camille Saint- Saëns' "The Swan" entered his mind, perhaps his "Dance Macabre." Yes, David decided, the "Dance Macabre" it is! He reached for his phone to search the Spotify library.

The train arrived.

David scrambled to find a seat with enough room to stand his cello by his side. He was lucky, found one, and sat, ignorant of his surroundings. He continued his search; "Meditation" from the Opera "Thaïs" by the French composer Jules Massenet played on his phone. He loved it. It was magnificent.

But sadly, he began to sense stress rising within him.

David had known the signs and decided to pause his search. He took a deep breath and tried to relax.

As David looked up, he saw a pretty woman beside him. She was speaking to him.

"I beg your pardon," he said as he fumbled nervously to lower the volume on his phone. The two smiled, and their eyes lingered on each other, Massenet's music still resounding in his ears. Its longing tore him apart.

Could I just lean over and kiss this beautiful stranger? He wondered.

"Is this a Guitarrón Mexicano?" She asked. Her eyes were dark, and her long, black, and straight hair fell far below her breasts. She reminded

David of an Aztec goddess, of the woman depicted in Diego Rivera's "Tenochtitlan Marketplace;" the proud, inquiring, and mysterious woman at the bottom right of the painting he had seen long ago on a family trip to Mexico.

"No, it is a cello," he responded. "My name is David."

David extended his hand, white, sterile; a white arm floating between two strangers. Dismembered from time and reality, it awaits, but this time, on a New York City train, not in a painting by Diego Rivera.

She reached out. "Nice to meet you, Mr. David. My name is Adelina."

The stops came and went in a noisy rumble of metal hitting metal. Click, clack, click, clack.

They spoke and smiled at each other.

David heard her words, but it was her lips he devoured, her eyes in which he immersed himself.

Adelina stood. Her stop was next.

"Méditation" played delicately and unendingly in the young man's mind. Following the "Méditation" Thaïs tells Athanaël she will follow him to the desert. David looked up at Adelina.

I am Thaïs, he thought and stood.

"I will follow you to the desert," David blurted out. The tender and delicate melody still flowed through his mind.

Adelina looked at him inquisitively and exited the train.

As David hurried behind her, his cello bumped into an unpleasant-looking man who grunted some insult and pushed him. He tried to ignore the man. The doors were about to close. The alarm rang loudly. He rushed out.

The platform was packed. David looked around for Adelina. *I hate New York City*, he thought.

David believed he saw her in the distance and rushed forward, but his cello was a burden in the crowd. *She will wait for me.*

David climbed the stairs two at a time. There were people everywhere. He could not see her.

The sign above him said 161st Street Exit. He realized the enormous crowd was moving toward Yankee Stadium.

I will never find Adelina.

Resigned, David turned around and went back down the flight of stairs, fighting an incoming mass of people. Luckily, the platform leaving the station was empty. He sat disappointed at losing Adelina.

David's Phone rang.

It was his dad. His father was kind, patient, and a good listener.

David shared his frustration at the city he did not want to live in, at the school, and at himself for doing something he loved but always required more from him. He wondered if the passion music had demanded had escaped him. But David did not share the last part. Instead, he described the "Cross Platform Synergy" assignment.

"How about "Fanfare for the Common Man" by Aaron Copeland?" His father said.

"Interesting choice, Dad."

"Call your uncle George. He was an expert on Lincoln and the Civil War."

"Sounds good. Dad, the train is coming. I'll call you back soon."

The four stops to the 125th St. Station went by quickly. By the time he exited the train, David was even more upset with himself for losing Adelina. He kept replaying the moment he last saw her face.

His Phone rang once again.

"Yes." He answered nonchalantly.

"David, It's uncle George. How are you?"

"I am good. How about you, Uncle George?"

"I'll be better when I see you. How about I treat you to dinner tonight?"

Uncle George was very wealthy, and David knew he'd have the best dinner, so why not?

"Sounds good."

"I am sending an Uber to pick you up. Claremont Avenue, right?"

"Have the Uber pick me up at the corner of Claremont Avenue and La Salle Street. I am just getting there, so … twenty minutes?"

"Great. Looking forward to seeing you, David."

Unlike most of his family members, Uncle George had opted for the big bucks.

Though David was unsure what his uncle did, he knew he worked in the field of finance.

The Uber driver picked him up and drove him to the Upper East Side. Their destination was Antonucci, on 81st Street.

Uncle George was tall, with broad shoulders, long, wavy Chestnut hair, and bright blue eyes. A pleasant man, happy to offer a warm hug, to listen and get to know people. His uncle traveled all over the world, slept in the best hotels, ate in the best restaurants, and always had great stories to share.

They chatted at the bar.

"I hear you have an interesting assignment?" Uncle George said.

"Yes, but the school is driving me crazy. How can this help me play my instrument better? Cross Platform Synergy. I initially liked the idea. But it quickly became overwhelming. There are too many options."

"I hear you," his uncle said—a careful, gentle response.

"My father told me you were an expert on Lincoln and the Civil War."

"I'm not sure about being an expert, but I wrote a paper on the Civil War, well, not exactly on Lincoln himself. I studied the economic effects, costs, and creative steps the Secretary of the Treasury took to borrow the enormous sum it took to pay for the Civil War."

The food arrived, but Uncle George seemed more interested in chatting about the Civil War.

"By 1861, weeks upon taking office, seven Southern states had already seceded and formed the Confederate States of America. Lincoln, whose life had been under constant threat of assassination, now prepared for War. Sadly, the president was unaware and naive about the cost of War. Every day, the cost estimates of the war grew larger and larger.

"There was a Congressman from New York who declared: *'War is not a question of valor, but a question of money... It is not regulated by the laws of honor, but by the laws of trade... The practical problem to be solved in crushing the rebellion of despotism against representative government is; who can throw the most projectiles? Who can afford the most iron or lead?"*

"Roscoe Conkling was his name, I think. The War became about money—money the country did not have, but that it soon borrowed or created out of thin air. The cost of the War was tremendous." Uncle George paused and took a bite. He looked around the room. The food was delicious. The restaurant was crowded and loud, and he loved it.

"Have you ever heard of Jay Cooke? He and his brother Henry campaigned for Senator Salmon P. Chase to be the Republican nominee for president against Lincoln. When their effort failed, they figured out their best bet was to make Chase the Secretary of the Treasury. The brothers succeeded, and Jay Cooke was assured access to one of the most important men in the government, so he immediately set up his investment bank.

At that time, Jay Cooke said: '...*and that now is the time for making money, by honest contracts out of the government.*'

"Secretary Chase granted Jay Cooke and Company a total monopoly on the underwriting of public debt. It sounds like a boring subject until you realize Cooke's bond sales reached $1 million to $2 million a day. We are talking 1860's-dollar value. These were enormous sums of money."

The Maitre D' came to greet his uncle, and to David's surprise, the two conversed in fluent Italian.

Soon his uncle returned to his meal.

"I think this synergy program is good, David. In the end, it will greatly help your playing."

"I just think it's a distraction. I am so busy with every other class."

"The exercise, I believe, is for each student to think of a piece from the point of view of a writer, a fireman, a painter, or a historian. What does joy, sorrow, or misery sound like? The assignment is intended to add a new layer of emotion to your playing."

David could understand his point.

"Before leaving the house, I looked at some numbers," Uncle George said as he dug into his jacket pocket, pulled out a perfectly folded piece of paper, and read.

"Seven hundred thousand people died in the Civil War. Over 40% of the dead were never identified. Two out of three deaths occurred from disease rather than battle. Now, what if you were to close your eyes and imagine any of these scenarios—would your selection of music change?" He paused, giving David a chance to respond.

But David remained silent.

"As I said earlier, one must consider that War is a very profitable business, David. The fortunes made by the weapons suppliers and those who finance these wars are rarely discussed," Uncle George said. "Federal expenditures grew from approximately $66 million in 1861 to $1.3 billion four years later. The government borrowed, issued bonds, and used every possible scheme to create money. Men made fortunes financing the War, and from the profit of these fortunes, they chose to manipulate members of Congress to support their cause, whatever their cause may have been."

David realized how passionate his uncle was about finance. Never had he even considered the cost of War and the burden on the population. To his surprise, colors appeared in his mind—a rich royal blue, bloodied and muddied, moving in a forward motion. David could sense a heart beating behind the blue fabric, and fear. A musician must be like a painter who mixes emotion into various colors.

"Let me read you this statement by President Lincoln. I want you to listen and imagine which music you would select to support his words," Uncle George said.

David rested his silverware at the edge of the plate and listened.

His uncle read: *"The money powers prey upon the nation in times of peace and conspire against it in times of adversity. The banking powers are more despotic than a monarchy, more insolent than autocracy, more selfish than bureaucracy. They denounce as public enemies all who question their methods or throw light upon their crimes. I have two great enemies, the Southern Army in front of me and the bankers in the rear. Of the two, the one at my rear is my greatest foe. Corporations have been enthroned, and an era of corruption in high places will follow. The money power of the country will endeavor to prolong its reign by working upon the prejudices of the people until the wealth is aggregated in the hands of a few, and the Republic is destroyed."*

He paused, but to emphasize Lincoln's dire warning, he repeated, *"I have two great enemies, the Southern Army in front of me and the bankers in the rear. Of the two, the one at my rear is my greatest foe."*

The History books do not print such statements, David thought.

A gloomy picture appeared in his mind; away from the darkness of the battlefield, men gather; docile financiers claiming an honorable neutrality in the face of horror. Men, who, behind a veil of secrecy, guaranteed the loans, which soon inflated the public debt. In time, their profit soared while the blood of innocent souls spilled onto the battlefields.

"What do you do for work, Uncle George?" Asked David.

"I thought you would never ask. My official title is Senior Director of International Development," Uncle George paused. "Have you ever heard of John Perkins?"

David shook his head.

"In 2004, Perkins published a book called *Confessions of an Economic Hit Man*. It could be my informal title. Economic Hit Man. My function is to make the richest of people even richer."

They returned to their meal.

"Economic Hit Man," David finally repeated. "What does that mean?"

"I help the richest acquire what they desire. Let's assume my client discovers there is an enormous amount of lithium in a certain area of the world. On their behalf, I acquire the land, rights, and set up the companies their schemes require."

"Sounds like a strange job."

"No one really believes what I do, because, you see, men are only capable of accepting simple truths. Most people lack the imagination that a grand scheme involving the existence of a shadow government secretly manipulating all to satisfy its thirst for wealth and power is a reality. Because anyone thinking this way is automatically called a conspiracy theorist—a nut, essentially."

The waiter arrived cheerfully to clear their plates.

I should have taken notes. Thought David.

"Dessert?"

"Yes, two cappuccinos, and bring two of your favorite desserts," said Uncle George.

The waiter scuttled away.

A dark-looking credit card appeared on the table.

David turned to see a wad of banknotes being handed to him.

"Take this, please. Treat your girlfriend to a nice dinner."

As David reached out and took the money, he sheepishly responded he currently didn't have one. "Thank you, Uncle George, it's a lot of money."

"Don't worry about it. Can I pick you up this weekend? Let's do something fun."

"Great, Uncle George. This weekend is Memorial Day, and my school is closed. I would love it."

Uncle George took a sip of his Cappuccino and continued. "There has always been a battle between the government and the financial elite. On one side are those who believe that private interests should run the American financial system. On the other side, there are a few, like Andrew Jackson, who agree with the necessity for a robust financial system but disapprove of one managed by private interests."

"The period after Andrew Jackson was a period when State banks issued currency at will and during which the banking system had little Federal supervision. Lincoln cleverly started to organize a solid banking system. He issued a unified currency called the 'greenback' and passed a National Bank Act. These actions frightened International Bankers. The steps Lincoln took, would push them out of their most profitable scheme ever; the business of creating a central bank." Uncle George stopped and reached out for his cell phone.

"Here it is," he said after scanning his phone. "This is a statement by Otto Von Bismarck, the German Chancellor during the late 19th Century.

After Lincoln's assassination, he said the following:

"The death of Lincoln was a disaster for Christendom. There was no man in the United States great enough to wear his boots... I fear that foreign bankers with their craftiness and tortuous tricks will entirely

control the exuberant riches of America and use it to systematically corrupt civilization."

"Whoa, pretty intense," David said.

"Indeed, it is. You can't study America's financial and banking history without shock and outrage. From General Washington on, the battle for power has raged on. Well, until the Federal Reserve Act of 1913. Then, America lost!"

They continued chatting for a while and soon parted ways. It was ten. David decided to return to school, where he would borrow one of their instruments and practice a bit. Curious, he pulled out the wad of cash he had been given and counted—$600. His father would die to know his brother had nonchalantly handed him so much cash.

What is an 'Economic Hit Man'? David wondered.

The Uber pulled up in front of the school. He was about to enter the building when he heard a voice.

"Mr. David." Adelina rushed toward him, a big smile on her face. She told him she had noticed the sticker on his cello case, so upon deciding to look for him, she knew where to start.

The school was empty and the two quickly found an open practice room and kissed the night away.

David's phone pinged and woke him. Beside him, the beautiful Adelina slept quietly. A text appeared on his screen; "Great to see you, David. I'll call you Saturday morning. Consider Henryk Górecki's 'Third Symphony,' 'The Symphony of Sorrowful Songs,' for your assignment."

David typed a few keys on his phone and reached for his earbuds in his coat pocket. Górecki's Symphony No.3 played. The music was haunting and beautiful. Eyes closed, he pictured the score and the delicate emotion one would need to support the piece.

His finger returned to the phone and, after a brief search, discovered a BBC interview in which Gorecki speaks of his masterpiece while the music played in the background. *"I remember,"* Gorecki says. *"when I was twelve, we went on a school outing to Auschwitz. Auschwitz and Birkenau,"* said Gorecki. *"The human ashes had been used to fertilize the*

145

cabbages growing between the huts...But the paths themselves and this image has never left me. The paths were made of human bones... The only way to confront this horror was through music. Somehow, I had to take a stand, as a witness, and as a warning."

David closed his eyes once more—every note more powerful, more meaningful. The young man reached out, laid his hand on Adelina, and began to cry.

CHAPTER 9

FATHER OF THE FEDERAL RESERVE

Our financial system is a false one and a huge burden on the people . . .
This Act establishes the most gigantic trust on earth.
— Charles Augustus Lindbergh, Sr., Congressman (1907-1917)

If the American people ever allow private banks to control the issue of
their currency, first by inflation, then by deflation, the banks...will deprive
the people of all property until their children wake up homeless on the
continent their fathers conquered.... The issuing power should be taken
from the banks and restored to the people, to whom it properly belongs.
— Thomas Jefferson, in the debate over the re-charter of the Bank Bill (1809)

WASHINGTON D.C. 1918

Paul was not a powerful man, but he was a man of power. The powerful
man takes what he desires, for the world is his own; Women, money, and
properties are the fruits he deserves. The man of power gives in order to
receive. Max, his brother in Hamburg, was a powerful man. Paul was not.

Paul turned to smile at his other brother Felix, the ever "Bon Vivant,"
who was neither a powerful man nor a man of power and cared little about
being either. Long ago, the three brothers had learned to appreciate each
other for who they were. It had been a lesson their parents had enforced—
love each other and embrace your differences, for they are your strengths.
This understanding allowed their family to build a powerful, international
bank.

Miss Davenport, the gorgeous Swedish model dressed in a light pink
dress featuring her amazing curves, tenderly rested her delicate hand on
Felix's forearm. She laughed at his every word, inching her chair closer
with every smile.

Felix was dressed in a stunning silk suit from Bach, Werner & Sons, the most prestigious tailors in Hamburg. The suit, in royal blue, enhanced his warm skin tone. The touch of gray in his hair made him look distinguished. Felix was rich—very rich—and loved to show it. He was the kind of wealthy man who surrounded himself with beauty, the superficial kind most often, but beauty, nonetheless. He was undoubtedly a man of taste who loved the arts, music, and beautiful women.

Paul had already forgotten the name of the other young woman sitting next to Felix.

She seemed quiet, reserved, but of a striking beauty; delicate, fragile, almost angelic.

As a teenager, he had embraced the role of a playboy, and for a while had only cared about seducing the pretty girls in his neighborhood. But that was in the past, and what flirtatious skills he may have possessed, they had vanished long ago.

Women saw him as an overworked man, a bore with little to be excited about.

Paul did not care for their attention either. He preferred intellectual stimulation. It excited him much more and made him feel alive. In Nina, his wife, he had found the partner he desired; a quiet, responsible person with the same intellectual faculty.

Paul, however, had changed the world. He had commanded the attention of presidents and experts in the field of economy and finance. Unlike his brother Felix, Paul preferred to remain discreet about his wealth and his accomplishments.

Long ago, in the homes of the wealthy families in Hamburg, he had learned when to speak and when to stay silent. Tonight, was no exception, for he had yet to share the news with Felix.

What good would it do? Paul thought. *Why ruin such a pleasant evening?* He offered a tender smile in the direction of the three, but anger was burning from within.

The beautiful young woman by Felix's side smiled at him; a timid smile, he thought. Her gorgeous face was framed by delicate, curly, blond hair. He wondered what was hidden behind these mysterious, magnificently rich green eyes.

His arm locked around Miss Davenport, Felix raised his free hand to order more wine. He was happy.

Stone by stone and lies upon lies, Paul had quietly built the castle no one believed would ever be constructed. He had committed eleven years to this miserable task and had masterfully deluded his audience into trusting him. He had manipulated their reason, and soon these men appreciated and embraced the ideas he so clearly, so gently presented. His patience had grown to an unimaginable degree.

Today, however, the miserable Woodrow Wilson informed Paul he would not be reappointed as Vice Governor of the Board of the Federal Reserve, a post he cherished. To think of his achievement, of the many exhausting battles, the lies, and the years of scheming … and in a moment, it had all been taken away. Furious, he had returned to his office and had composed his letter of resignation.

Paul grabbed the glass of dark whiskey before him and turned toward the young lady across the table.

"Catherine," she said, leaning on her elbow and toward him, "my name is Catherine."

"Thank you, Catherine; I am quite distracted this evening and must apologize for my rudeness."

She offered a beautiful smile.

Could he just reach out and kiss her? Paul wondered.

"Catherine, tell me about you. Where are you from? Do you model with Miss Davenport?"

Catherine O'Reilly, as she finally introduced herself, had left Virginia and had recently arrived in Washington to study. With a bit of help from family, she was able to go to school and work a little bit as a model for fashion houses. "I hate modeling," she proudly announced.

Paul laughed, as if he understood what it was like to be one. The invisible currents driving the rise and fall of currency were more his area of expertise.

Dinner was served, and they broke off their conversation for a while.

The two women stood and left to refresh, and Felix immediately switched to their native German.

Felix had learned that Max, in Hamburg, was alarmed. The Warburg Bank was growing faster than he could manage on his own, and Felix wondered if Paul should go back to Hamburg.

Paul immediately dismissed the idea but quickly suggested a few solutions to his brother's concerns. Soon a conversation about the changes in German politics followed.

Hamburg, Paul thought. "It has not been on my mind in a long time." Staring into the candle at the center of the table, he listened to Felix describe the Bank's financial growth in real estate investment when someone touched his shoulder. Surprised, Paul turned around, thinking it was Catherine.

"Herr Warburg?" It was not Catherine. "I am Elsa Mueller."

Paul did not respond.

Realizing she may be mistaken, the young lady said. "Sir, I am sorry to have troubled you. I thought you were someone else."

Still, no response. She stepped back.

"I am Felix Warburg. This is Paul, my brother. Paul Warburg," Felix said in German. She smiled at Felix, and the two exchanged pleasantries. Suddenly, Paul rose to his feet and faced Elsa Mueller.

"Fraulein Mueller, we have met before, correct?"

She smiled, somewhat relieved.

"In New York, you worked for Senator Aldrich? No, I do remember now. We met at Professor Edwin Seligman's house," Paul said.

Misses Davenport and O'Reilley returned to the table, and all were introduced.

"Please join us, Fraulein Mueller," said an enthusiastic Paul.

"Oh no, I could not. I am waiting for someone. I am an economist and just wanted to take a moment to congratulate you on the amazing work you have done." Elsa smiled timidly and switched to English to say goodbye to Felix and the ladies. She turned to face Paul and said in German, "It was a pleasure to see you, Herr Warburg. An honor, I must confess. I look forward to the day we meet again."

Paul seemed nervous and shifted a bit as his body turned toward her. "The pleasure was mine, Fraulein Mueller. I wish you a wonderful evening."

She bowed slightly and walked away to her table.

To Paul's delight, Fraulein Mueller sat in his field of view.

As the evening progressed, Felix became a little louder, and the two charming ladies laughed a little harder.

Paul was distracted, and as the three grew noisier, he grew quieter. As gentle, witty, and modest as he was, he had lost a war; his post of Vice Governor of the Federal Reserve would simply not be renewed. A page had been turned, and no battle would come of it.

The summer heat was slowly dissipating over Washington.

Felix would cheer him up. His brother was the enthusiast away from his prison, away from New York City, where the jailers watched; his wife and the men who so often doubted him, happily filled that distasteful role. But tonight, Felix was free.

Paul turned slightly to see an older man approach Miss Mueller's table. She rose and they shook hands. He heard the lovely Catherine call his name. "Dear Sir, you have been touched."

Paul smiled at the gorgeous Virginian. Had he been younger, he might have just kissed her right there and then. But he did not.

"Paul, let's go to Harry's. We can do a little dancing. The girls want to have fun," Felix said.

Paul was in no mood to argue and the four stood to leave.

"I'll meet you in the lobby, Felix," Paul said and walked toward Miss Mueller's table. As Paul approached, he recognized Professor Langdon from Georgetown University, an old acquaintance with whom he shared a passion for math and economics. "Hello, Professor Langdon. Please forgive my intrusion, but I was about to leave but could not do so without saying hello. How are you?"

The Professor was in his early seventies and looked Irish from a mile away. He wore tightly trimmed hair and wired glasses. Langdon stood to greet Paul.

"Please forgive me, Fraulein Mueller. I had to say hello."

Elsa Mueller looked at Paul and smiled.

She is so beautiful, thought Paul.

"Well, the University is interviewing Miss Mueller for a teaching position at the University. Dr. Pratt is retiring, and we need a replacement. The two of us had a wonderful day on campus, but I felt a quiet place would be nicer to answer any concerns Miss Mueller may have. Moreover, I would not be a gentleman if I were to leave Miss Mueller all alone in this city," the Professor said.

"Paul, please join us for a drink. Miss Mueller is also an economist."

Paul would have loved to sit with them, but Felix was waiting. "I am afraid I cannot, but it is so good to see you, Dear Professor," Paul said and turned to Elsa. "Fraulein Mueller, we meet again. It has been a delight. Please, here is my card."

She looked down at the card, now in her hand. A big gold eagle was emblazoned across it. Paul Warburg, Vice Governor, Federal Reserve Bank.

"Please come visit me at the Treasury of the United States; the office of the Federal Reserve is located there, and I would be delighted to give you a tour. I will be in my office all day tomorrow." He smiled, a timid and unassuming smile, shook hands with Langdon, and left.

Felix, Miss Davenport, and Catherine were waiting outside when Paul exited the Willard Hotel. He immediately switched to German.

"Felix, today, President Wilson informed me he would not reappoint me to the Board of directors of the Federal Reserve. I sent my letter of resignation from the Board effective at the end of the week. I hope you will forgive me, but my heart is not into dancing tonight. You go along and enjoy yourself."

The weight of the event, which had taken place earlier in the afternoon, seemed to have finally come down upon him. He felt his legs tremble slightly.

"This is scandalous, Paul. Why would they do this?" Felix said, upset. The two chatted for a while.

Paul affirmed he was fine. "In the end, brother, in the making of the Federal Reserve, I succeeded in achieving the unachievable, and no one will ever be able to take this accomplishment away from me," Paul said as he waved to the ladies.

They smiled and waved back.

"Let's talk tomorrow at breakfast," Paul said.

Bring down a powerful man, and a fight breaks out. Bring down a man of power, and the slow winds of destiny will sweep you away.

A strategy had to be defined, thought Paul as he walked away from the Hotel.

Paul wondered what fault he may have committed, but he was rich and would never be in need of anything. He rounded the corner to the left, contemplating a path back into the Federal Reserve; the institution he, himself, had built. Quickly though, he wondered if this was really what he wanted.

I must call Nina at once, Paul thought.

He followed the sidewalk hurriedly and found himself back at the entrance of the Willard Hotel, entered the Hotel and marched toward the bar.

"Ernesto, could I have a dry martini and the phone, please?" Paul asked.

The bartender, a tall, thin, handsome Italian man in his mid-forties, grabbed the house phone and, gliding behind the bar, placed it right in front of Paul. "Of course, Mr. Warburg, here you are," he said in his accented English.

Paul looked at the rows of liquor bottles, the chandelier, the mirror, and finally, as he dialed his home, he noticed the clock. It was way past ten and too late to call Nina. He quickly hung up.

Paul did not know how to tame his anger. He had been instrumental in building the Federal Reserve and was deeply disturbed he would not be reappointed to its Board of Directors. He wondered if, being a German immigrant, with Hitler and the World War raging on in Europe, a slight appearance of bias toward Germany needed to be avoided. The truth was much different. Paul was a naturalized American citizen and no longer German. He daydreamed of revenge, punishments, and schemes when a hand softly touched his left arm. Startled, he turned.

"Fraulein Mueller," he said.

Her crystal-clear blue eyes pierced right through him.

"Sorry, I was lost in my thoughts."

She reminded him of the young girls he had grown up with. The blond, fair-skinned beauties with perfect lips and perfect curves. The strong and healthy German women he had so often dreamed of.

Fraulein Mueller surely must have been one of the disarmingly charming angels of his youth.

"Are you all right, Herr Warburg?" She asked in a tender voice.

He looked at her slowly; her lips a light but a rich shade of pink, her hair pulled back in a bun, her ears, her eyes. "Please forgive me, Fraulein Mueller. How did you do with the Professor?"

Elsa offered a warm smile. "The Professor is a wonderful man. Thank you." She inquired about the beautiful ladies.

Paul politely inquired a little more about the teaching position. He ordered coffee and cognac and led her to a table by the bar.

They had grown up only a few miles from each other. Both had loved the same areas of Hamburg; The Berliner Bahnhof, the enormous train station they both had visited in their youth.

"Das Zoologische Museum was my favorite," she exclaimed joyfully.

"Fraulein Mueller, what brought you to America?" Paul asked.

Elsa explained her family had immigrated from Hamburg, hoping for better days. Settling at first in Cleveland, the family had finally moved closer to relatives in upstate New York, the Albany area.

Paul looked at the bartender leaning against the wall, almost asleep. He turned to read the clock and realized it was now two in the morning. He had completely lost track of time.

"Fraulein Mueller, it is now so late. We should free the poor Ernesto."

She turned in search of the bartender and burst into a tender laugh.

"It has been a joy to spend time with you, and though we have just met, my heart trembles at the thought of separating," he said, looking into her eyes once more.

Elsa looked into his. She appeared at peace, unafraid, and strong.

Paul wondered what clue he might detect behind these gorgeous blue eyes. But Paul Warburg had been a bookish man, an intellectual who had ignored his sexual desires which had been dormant in some dark and unknown place for years.

"Out of a thunderous storm and the sailor's despair to survive another day, came the simple but striking beauty of a rose," Paul murmured in German.

Fraulein Mueller stepped back a little and fixed her gaze deeper into his. "I beg your pardon, Herr Warburg, could you repeat?"

She was so beautiful, he thought. *I wish I could be Max for an instant, take her gently in my arms and kiss her.*

"Out of a thunderous storm and the sailor's despair to survive another day, came the simple but striking beauty of a rose," he repeated.

She reached out and laid her hand on his.

"Herr Warburg, this is so beautiful." Her hand tightened around his.

Their eyes locked in an eternal moment. Two souls, long separated by the chaos of life, timidly finding each other again.

She slid her hand into his and held it there for a moment. "Herr Warburg, Friedrich Nietzsche once said: 'There is always some madness in love. But there is also always some reason in madness'." She kissed him on the cheek, stood, and walked away.

How could my world be turned upside down twice on the same day? Paul wondered, knowing deep in his heart, he had been touched.

From the despair of losing what he had so cherished was born the anger he had failed to temper all day. But this tremendous, bitter, and heinous feeling had been gently washed away by the beauty of an angel— an angel he suddenly feared he would lose.

Paul Warburg gently woke the bartender. "Ernesto...Ernesto."

The poor man immediately apologized. "Mr. Warburg, I so sorry."

Paul loved to hear the small mistakes immigrants, such as he, made when speaking English.

"Ernesto, can I pay my bill. I want you to go home to your family."

The bartender was only too happy to oblige.

Paul settled his bill, left a large tip, and walked away from the bar and toward the reception desk. He recognized the night manager, a Frenchman everyone called Monsieur Fernand.

"Monsieur Fernand, Comment allez-vous?" Said Paul.

The jovial Frenchman immediately smiled at Paul. "Well, Mr. Warburg, I must say I find myself particularly well tonight. Great news from home. I am going to be a father soon. It has warmed my heart so sweetly." The Frenchman raised his large reddish hand to his chest, laid it on his heart, and closed his eyes for a moment. "But how are you, my dear Mr. Warburg?"

Paul loved staying at the Willard Hotel. It was like a second home. "Monsieur, I was speaking with Miss Mueller at the bar. I am to deliver a series of important papers to her by morning, but I realized she forgot to tell me her room number."

Monsieur Fernand was no idiot. He knew even the most important of papers could easily be delivered to the front desk and, if necessary, stored in the hotel safe. But he liked Mr. Warburg, whom he believed was a good, respectable man who had always treated everyone fairly. But most of all, Monsieur Fernand knew Paul Warburg was a generous customer.

"Miss Mueller is in room 312, Mr. Warburg."

Paul pulled a five-dollar bill from his wallet, laid it on the counter, and thanked the night manager for his trouble.

"Merci Monsieur Warburg, you are too kind."

Paul took the elevator to his room on the top floor, knowing all too well Monsieur Fernand would be watching on which floor the elevator stopped. He was the night manager, after all, not a fool. It was his job and responsibility to know all the affairs of the Hotel.

The John Adams Suite Felix and Paul had rented was on the top floor. It had one large bedroom, a large living room with a corner desk, a dining room, and an optional smaller bedroom attached to the suite. Paul stayed in the smaller room. After pouring himself a small amount of whiskey, he took the glass and sat. The day was playing itself over and over in his mind. The anger had disappeared, and his madness subsided.

Elsa Mueller had won his heart.

"Out of a thunderous storm and the sailor's despair to survive another day, came the simple but striking beauty of a rose."

He waited thirty minutes and quietly walked downstairs to room 312. Though Paul was afraid, he gently knocked on the door once. The door slowly opened.

"It is true: There is always some madness in love," Elsa said as she opened the door wide to let him in.

He entered her room and held her in his arms. Their eyes locked on one another for what seemed an eternity. Silently, their souls asked each other, *Are you the one I have been looking for? Are you the treasure I had lost? Are you the mystery I aim to solve?*

The next morning, Paul awoke naked next to Elsa Mueller.

She was leaning on her elbow, smiling at him. "Herr Warburg, wake me up from this dream. Are you real? Let me kiss you. I want to make sure this is not a dream." Elsa kissed him so tenderly, so affectionately.

He reached for her shoulder and rested his hand on her soft, porcelain skin.

She leaned back on her pillow. "Paul, do you know I have read everything you ever wrote?"

He smiled but did not care. He loved her eyes and her kind smile. "Elsa," he said, kissing her. "I need to go to my room before the hotel is full of activity. What do you say we meet in the restaurant for breakfast fifteen minutes from now?"

Elsa kissed him on the cheek and stood, her naked body in full display. "Make it thirty minutes, Herr Warburg," she said, and walked into the bathroom.

Paul discreetly exited the room and climbed the steps to the top floor.

The hotel was still quiet.

He found Felix crashed on the couch. He walked over to his room and closed the door gently. Paul showered, slowly remembering every moment of the previous night: Elsa's gorgeous body, her soft skin, her blond hair, her smell. He dressed, and within minutes was strolling down the stairs to the dining room.

Paul took a seat by the window, far in the corner of the dining room, and while he had only slept a few hours, he felt incredibly alive. A cart covered with all kinds of fresh pastries, eggs, fruits, cheese, and meats was rolled over next to his table.

"Sir, may I serve you?" The waiter asked.

"Yes, please give me one of these muffins," he said, pointing toward the corner of the tray, "an apple Danish and a toast with jelly. I would also love some orange juice, and please bring a kettle of coffee. Thank you."

Monsieur Fernand appeared in the dining room but, upon seeing Paul, immediately retreated into the lobby, only to re-appear a minute later holding a stack of newspapers.

"Good morning, Mr. Warburg. Here are your newspapers. I hope your night was peaceful," he said with a smile and left.

Thank God, thought Paul, who was in no mood to expend energy in small talk with Monsieur Fernand. The waiter arrived with coffee. Paul looked at the young man and said, "Please, would you mind going to speak to the woman who just entered the dining room and ask her to join me? My name is Mr. Warburg."

The waiter reached Elsa, who acted surprised but soon walked over to his table. She wore a light salmon dress, tight at the waist and a brown suede belt, matched by brown suede heels. Her hair, in a tight bun, framed her delicate features.

He stood to welcome her.

"Good morning, Herr Warburg. Thank you for the invitation," she said.

The waiter disappeared, and the two smiled at each other.

"Newspaper?" He asked, but she declined.

"What is your day like? Are you still coming to visit me at the Federal Reserve?"

"I would love to witness the activities of the bank which controls America."

"I am not sure I would agree with the word 'control.' I would certainly agree with fuels, leads, directs, monetizes, and orchestrates. These verbs appear more appropriate, considering the Bank's function only applies to the economy, Elsa."

She turned toward the window and looked at the scene before her: the street merchant pulling his cart, the policeman, proud. She turned to him: "Paul, I am an economist. If I were a man, I could be your colleague. We both know since the inception of the Federal Reserve; the failures and successes of our nation hang in the hands of the Federal Reserve and a few creditors. Above all, the Federal Reserve, a fully private entity, is completely independent of government oversight." She paused and once again turned to look at the scene outside. "But it does not matter. I would love to see you this afternoon."

Paul smiled. "Elsa, you are so beautiful."

The fact Paul had ignored her statement disappointed her.

She felt cheated. Thankfully.

He continued. "You are correct. If you were a man, a higher position would be accessible to you. Yes, the Federal Reserve is a supreme entity in a way. It controls our nation's finances, and by law, it is allowed to control its credit, the interest it charges for the loans to the Government, and most importantly, has control of the printing and issuing of our country's currency. As you know, a national central bank creates stability in the markets and strengthens the nation's wealth."

The two quickly became animated and discussed the pros and cons of a central bank. Both agreed on its necessity. Her concerns resided in the ever-ballooning growth of the national debt.

"Paul, Wall Street has slowly become a casino where rich and poor alike invest at random and strictly for profit. I believe a tightening of credit is imminent. Banks will call in their loans and this could undo all the gains made over the last few years. The purpose of a nation's stock market is to strengthen and support the financial and health of existing or growing companies, not a place to bet one's revenues. I looked at certain numbers, and I feel a crash created by and to benefit certain financial institutions is inevitable."

Paul looked perplexed. He asked if he could see her research. They continued for a time. Elsa was extremely intelligent; brilliant, in fact, he thought.

"Good morning."

They both turned to see the handsome Felix smiling at them.

"You two seem to be bickering. May I bring peace?"

Paul was happy to see his brother. "Of course, Felix. Peace you must bring. You remember Fraulein Mueller?"

Felix bowed slightly. "It is a pleasure to see you, Miss Mueller. I must make a quick call and will return promptly. Paul, could you please ask the waiter for all the food in the world to be brought and a lot of very strong coffee." Felix walked away in the direction of the reception hall.

"Why couldn't we have met in Hamburg many years ago?" Asked Paul.

But Elsa ignored him. "Professor Langdon will be in the lobby at ten. I should get ready."

Paul set a time for them to meet in the afternoon. A car would be sent to pick her up at 2:30. She left before Felix returned.

The two brothers sipped coffee and discussed what had taken place the prior afternoon. Paul did not care anymore. The decision had been made by President Woodrow Wilson and would not be reversed. He was German by birth. The war had been raging on for almost four years now. The vice governorship of the Federal Reserve Bank of the United States was no place for a German Jew.

"I no longer care, Felix."

As planned, Elsa arrived at the United States Treasury building, where she was accompanied to Paul's office and thanked the secretary but remained formal.

"It is a pleasure to see you, Miss Mueller. Please sit." He picked up the phone and asked the person on the other end to join them in his office.

"My guest has arrived," she heard him say. He looked up and smiled.

"Elsa, Miss Dunbar will give you a guided tour of the building. When you come back, I should be done here. I'll take you to visit the burglar-proof vault." He paused and looked tenderly into her eyes. A knock on the door interrupted him.

Miss Dunbar entered the office and, in perfect German, welcomed Elsa Mueller. She was tall and strong, but with age, Miss Dunbar had acquired a few extra pounds around the waist.

Miss Dunbar, whose Maiden name was Folker, was quite pleasant, friendly, and extremely knowledgeable.

Elsa was a passionate learner whose appetite for new things to discover had never ceased to grow. She was pleased to hear about the history of the building, its architecture, and its mysteries. She rejoined Paul in his office an hour later and was ready to leave.

Paul agreed and decided to drive her back to the hotel.

For a moment, she hesitated. Paul was a married man. "No need for you to leave the office." She stopped as his hand rested on her forearm.

"Elsa, since I last saw you this morning, not a thought could eclipse your face for longer than an instant. I could not bear separating right now."

Her heart trembled. "We should leave now then," she said.

They rode back to the hotel in silence.

Paul never ceased to look at Elsa.

She could feel his gaze. When she finally turned to look at him, she noticed tears flowing down his cheeks. Elsa reached and held his hand.

They entered the hotel separately and within minutes of each other.

She walked to the reception to pick up her key.

He aimed for the bar. Seeing the French night manager, he asked whether Mr. Fernand had seen his brother Felix.

"Yes, Mr. Warburg, your brother arrived about half an hour ago." He paused. "Miss Davenport, I believe, was accompanying him." said Monsieur Fernand.

Paul thanked him and asked the bartender, whom he did not recognize, for the house phone. He dialed and waited. A soft feminine voice answered.

"Hello, Miss Davenport. This is Paul. Could I speak to Felix, please?" He heard her call for Felix and was immediately back on the phone. "How are you, Paul? Happy birthday. I hear we are going to celebrate together tonight. Felix has big plans." Before he could answer, Felix was on the phone.

"Paul, happy birthday, brother. I have made plans for us tonight. Let's meet in the lobby at 7:30."

Paul did not know how to answer. "Are you dressed, Felix? I'll need to change, and we are sharing a suite."

Felix burst out laughing. "Yes, of course, come on up."

Paul hung up and ordered a Martini. He was in no rush to make small talk with Miss Davenport. All he wanted was another night in Elsa's arms. He picked up the phone and called New York. He spoke to Nina, who, to his dismay, had been suffering from a strong bout of pain in her hips.

"Please, Nina, you need to rest. Do you need more help from a home nurse?" She did not respond and suggested he speak to his daughter, Bettina. Now eighteen, she was full of joy, having returned from a month's vacation in New England. She warmed his heart as she recounted her trip. She had learned to sail.

"I miss you, father," she said.

Paul suddenly felt teary. He ended the call, drank his Martini, and headed to his suite.

He and Felix shared the John Adams Suite at the Willard. Paul slept in the room attached to the suite. He found Felix at the desk, looking at documents.

"Paul, I have just received some bad news. The fools need more money for their never-ending war. It has been four years now," Felix said upon seeing him. "Germany had been in dire straits for a while now."

"Where is Miss Davenport? I just spoke to her." He learned she had gone to pick up some items at the local store.

"Cigarettes or something. Not sure exactly what she needed. My temper may have been the cause for this errand. She'll be back," Felix said.

Paul walked over to the heavy mahogany chest, on which was a tray

162

with glasses and a variety of bottles of liquors. He poured two glasses of Whiskey.

"Are you sure we should go out tonight?" Asked Paul.

Felix held Paul off as he finished reading the documents. He flipped back to the previous page and skimmed it from top to bottom to review it. Finally, he signed its last page and turned to Paul. "I am heading back to New York City soon. The follies of men may ruin our Bank in Hamburg. War, alarmingly, has reached a crescendo. I am upset with President Wilson. To dishonor you in such a manner, so ungrateful, such a shame. Paul, you are the father of the Federal Reserve—the only man able to save this country from an archaic banking system. You worked tirelessly to bring this system to fruition, and President Wilson dared discard you. But today is your birthday. Yes, we must celebrate." Felix looked down at the documents before him.

"I am tired, Paul," Felix continued. "What good is wealth if one cannot enjoy it? And I can't. If I were able to choose to do what I want, what do you think I would be doing right now, Paul?"

Paul knew it would be useless to answer and shrugged.

"I would certainly not return to New York. Most likely, I would disappear in the arms of the charming Miss Davenport, never to be seen again. I would enjoy my days one at a time, hour by hour, minute by minute." Felix stood and turned toward the window overlooking Washington. He pulled the curtain opened and stared into the distance.

"But tomorrow, I'll prepare to leave for New York City, a slave to my wealth and my role as the pleasant banker."

They heard the door open. Miss Davenport entered, radiant. She smiled and walked over to Felix and kissed him on the cheek.

"Gentlemen," she said. "Aren't we supposed to be leaving soon? We must be getting ready."

Paul agreed and left for his room. He called Elsa, but there was no answer. Over the next thirty minutes, he tried over and over again. But he was unsuccessful. It was now time to leave and celebrate, but he did not care about his birthday. He was furious to find himself in such a predicament. For an instant, he wondered if he should just go to Elsa's room to fetch her. He knew there was no point in it since she was not answering his many calls. He would most likely find her room unoccupied.

Paul heard a knock on his door and went to open it. No one was there. He realized the knock came from the suite. He turned, walked through his bedroom, and opened the door. "Hello, Miss Davenport."

Without asking, she entered his room. After a brief stop, she aimed for the armchair in the corner and sat.

"Paul, please call me Lara." Miss Davenport's striking beauty made her irresistible. She smiled and gently patted the armchair beside her.

Obediently he sat.

She reached for his arm. "Paul, I know you have little interest in joining Felix and me tonight, but nothing else would satisfy your brother more than to spend his last evening here with you." She tightened her grip on his arm. "I will miss him dearly."

Four souls who had been destined to be joined forever were about to part ways forever, he thought. *This should make for a fun evening.*

Elsa, the only person he cared for, was nowhere to be found. He reached out and held Lara's hand. "Fun, we must have," he said cheerfully. The reality was Paul was furious at his inability to reach Elsa. Miss Davenport's pleading was genuine. It had touched him deeply. She cared so much for Felix.

Miss Davenport knew Felix was about to leave her forever.

So, Paul would act as the crutch—the friend who silently understood one's sorrow.

In the hotel lobby, they waited for Felix.

Paul heard footsteps and turned.

It was Elsa walking toward them. She looked amazing in a light baby blue coat and a Cloche hat a darker shade of blue.

"I invited Miss Mueller to join us," said Lara. "I hope you won't mind."

Paul looked at her. "My dear Lara, I will forever be grateful." He kissed her on the cheek. "Thank you."

The limousine waited outside and took them to "Chez Pierre," a fancy restaurant a few blocks from the White House. They celebrated joyfully, ignorant of what they really were celebrating.

For Felix, was it his prompt return to a dreadful life in New York City, away from Lara?

For Lara was it the separation from the one she truly loved; the kind, handsome, generous man who had become her rock?

And Paul, was he celebrating loss or discovery? The achievement of a lifetime or the rose he had fallen for.

For the beautiful Elsa, who seemed so lonely, so reserved, so tender, lost amongst the rich, the powerful. What warmed her heart?

Love seemed to be the thread that held these four souls together on the night of August 10, 1918. Paul was turning fifty. They celebrated.

The Willard was quiet when they returned. Felix walked over to the reception desk and ordered coffee and pastries to be brought to the suite. It was two in the morning.

Monsieur Fernand, who was used to capricious demands, responded kindly.

The four settled in the parlor of the Adams Suite.

Elsa walked over to each of the windows and took in the magnificent views. She looked over 14th street, then moved to enjoy the sight of 'F' Street.

Happy to be together, they laughed, hoping the night would never end. The food arrived, delivered by a sleepy bell boy. They tipped him generously. The four were starving and devoured the fresh croissants, muffins, and Danishes in silence. Monsieur Fernand had been kind to send two coffee pots and a third full of Viennese chocolate that Lara savored.

Soon, Elsa tried it and helped herself to a cup. At 3:30, Felix was lying across the couch, half asleep.

Lara had excused herself to use the lady's room but had never returned. Paul and Elsa left the suite for her room. Sitting on her bed, they embraced for what seemed an eternity. She stood in front of him, holding his hands in hers. After releasing him, she undressed.

"Ich denke dein, wenn mir der Sonne Schimme Vom Meere strahlt;..."
she said, reciting "The Nearness of the Beloved," a poem by Goethe.

"I think of you when I watch the sunlight glimmer
Over the sea:
I think of you, when the moonbeams shimmer
Over the stream.
I see you there when the dust swirls high
On the far road,..."

They made love slowly, tenderly.

He woke hours later. She was in his arms. Once again, tears slowly rolled down his face. Tears of love, tears of joy, tears of sadness. He wiped his face, and the slight movement woke her.

Elsa drew closer to him. After resting her head on his chest, she went back to sleep. So did he.

At ten, the phone rang. She had just gotten up and picked up the phone.

"Yes, 11 a.m. Thank you for your call," he heard her say.

"Elsa, what is going on?"

She sat on the bed. "Herr Warburg, I must be going. The University made the reservation, and I must check out of my room by 11." She stood as to make herself busy.

"Elsa, what are we going to do?" He said. "I cannot imagine being separated from you."

She smiled, sat close to him, and laid her head on his shoulder, her lips inches from his. "It is a very good question, Herr Warburg. What are we going to do?" She raised her eyes to his and kissed him.

Paul called Felix, who was on his way to see his travel agent, his banking agent and attend to other appointments. He was to have lunch in Georgetown with the retired German Ambassador to discuss the developments in Germany. Felix was trying to wake Miss Davenport, who was supposed to have an appointment later...

"Paul, I should be back at 5 p.m. Let's meet then." Felix hung up.

"Elsa, I am going to take the day off. Let's spend it together." He paused, looked at her, and said, "Love is the untamable force that pushes us into madness."

They agreed to meet in his room in an hour.

"I will have a bell boy come by a little before eleven to pick up your suitcase and bring it to my room. Once you return the key, find a quiet seat in the Peacock Alley. I'll meet you there."

A car was waiting for them.

"Hungry?" He asked.

She smiled. "Starving."

They traveled to Cleveland Park, where they settled for a modest coffee shop advertising German Food.

"Herr Warburg..." she said, but he stopped her.

"You like calling me Herr Warburg. Why?"

Once again, she smiled. "Do you know a large part of my studies was about your speeches and ideas? I read every one of the articles you published in the *New York Times*. My thesis was on Central Banking, and frankly, I am still unsure whether this isn't a dream, Paul."

He reached out and held her hand.

"Paul, we met in 1906, when an American central bank was but a dream. I remember when Professor Seligman said, 'It's your duty to get your ideas before the country.' So, you did. 'Defects and Needs of our Banking System' was the first of your many articles published by the *Times*." Elsa reached out and held his hand. "However, there have been so many questionable reports on the development of this Central Bank, our Federal Reserve Bank. I must ask you, 'Mein Liebhaber' (my lover). You are, after all, one of the lead characters in this incredible story. You have been called the 'Father of the Federal Reserve'."

Paul had retreated to the quiet man he was known to be, calculating, somber. "Am I to understand you are not a supporter of the Federal Reserve Act? I thought from an economist's point of view, this would be the system of choice."

Their breakfast arrived, and they relaxed.

"I do not stand against a Central Bank and/or the Federal Reserve Bank System." She paused and smiled kindly. "I really like you, Herr

Warburg. I sincerely do."

A few hours before they met, Paul explained, he had learned he would not be reappointed to the Board of the Federal Reserve. Initially, he was devastated, mainly because he had worked so hard to achieve such a role. He blamed the recent rise in antisemitism, German bashing, and Wall Street haters for his demise. "But then," he said, "I met Fraulein Mueller, and none of it mattered any longer."

She smiled.

"The story of the Federal Reserve system and its birth is long. Looking back, I may say a dreadful one. I am afraid it will bore you."

It was then she reached and kissed him. "I could lie silent for days with you, Paul, and never be bored."

They finished breakfast and exited the coffee shop. The chauffeur was waiting inside the car.

"Here's ten dollars," Paul said to the driver. "Go enjoy a warm breakfast. We are going for a short walk."

The Irish-looking driver thanked him and stepped out of the car.

Paul and Elsa walked close to each other, and she put her arm around his.

"I miss Hamburg, but now with the war, I am not sure when I will return, if ever. How about you?" Paul asked.

"Since my family had left Germany, none had ever returned," she said, "as if a chapter had been closed forever." Elsa did have fond memories of her youth there and the brief time working for her studies. She loved the port.

He explained that the entire city had changed drastically in recent years.

"Maybe it is not Hamburg I miss but Germany." She drew closer. "If there is something I miss, it is to feel at home. I mean, it took such hard work to speak English properly and without an accent. So many things are different here. For the first few years in America, I only spent time with Germans. It was easier. I could speak freely and not feel ashamed of my inferior English skills. I guess it was difficult to be an immigrant."

They continued in silence.

Paul knew the pain she spoke of. He had just been dismissed for being an immigrant, even though he had been a naturalized citizen for a few years now. "What do you say we go back to the Willard?" He asked.

She looked at him. "Paul, I was just wondering the same thing." She stopped and turned to face him. "I want to make love and lie naked next to you for the rest of the day, Paul."

The driver was enjoying the last sip of his coffee when they got back to the car. He drove them back to the Willard.

Elsa wondered how successful he felt the Central Bank had been over the last four years. What emotions did he experience at being let go from the Board?

"Elsa, I was furious. I have never exploded into such a fit of rage in my life. The night we met, I worked so hard to make small talk with Miss ... I can't remember her name, and I hate small talk. It made me even madder. But then you tap me on the shoulder. It was as if I had been waiting fifty years for this moment. You looked into my eyes, and my heart was yours. In an instant, the anger disappeared."

She moved closer to him and laid her head on his shoulder. They remained quiet for the rest of the drive.

They entered the Willard through the Peacock Alley. Elsa headed to the suite while Paul collected the key and checked for messages. They entered the room and fell into each other's arms immediately. They made passionate love for hours.

Paul left to fetch a pack of cigarettes in the living room of the suite while Elsa lay naked on the bed. Her head rested softly on the pillow. She never hid her body from him.

She sat up and smoked with him.

Paul picked up the phone and ordered room service.

"I arrived in New York in 1902, Elsa," Paul said, seemingly ready to discuss his life and the Federal Reserve.

"As most would agree, America's financial system was archaic and the market volatile. The system did not use a uniform currency and needed a more elastic currency backed by gold. I took a position at Kuhn Loeb, and for the next few years, I spent six months here and six months in Hamburg, where I helped Max with our Bank, The M.M. Warburg. When I first arrived in America, my English was terrible, and frankly, I was homesick.

I became a witness to the fragility of the archaic American financial system, and I decided to draft a critique of its Banking System which I believed was insufficiently centralized. But, self-conscious, I kept this document tucked in a drawer of my desk."

Paul explained it was four years later when his employer asked to see it. By then, his children had grown fond of New York, and they had many friends. Nina, his wife, enjoyed knowing her family was close by. Her health was weak, and she needed help.

Paul had grown to enjoy himself, meeting men with similar interests. He liked the work at the firm, and his English had certainly improved, at least to the point where he could express his ideas clearly.

"It is probably around then we met at Professor Seligman's house. I was invited to a dinner party at his home. My knowledge of the Central Banking System was by far superior to most contemporary economists. The professor was very impressed by the views I presented. From then on, I became the leading expert in the field in America. Soon, I published 'Defects and Needs of Our Banking System' in the *New York Times*. I became the spokesman for the implementation of a Central Bank System. My employer, Jacob Schiff, thought a new modern banking system was an absolute necessity."

"A few of the Wall Street banks joined forces, supporting the creation of a central bank. Our goal was to replicate the systems which had been in place all over Europe for decades." Paul said.

Elsa reached out and laid her hands on his chest. "A privately owned banking system with the power to issue currency, control interests, and be the primary lender to the Government it serves. Similar to the Bank of England, Danmarks Nationalbank and the Reichsbank for example or the First and Second Bank of the United States," she said.

"Correct, Elsa. Similar, but with one crucial factor to account for; The enormous size of the system it would require. When the Panic of 1907 took place, with its many runs on banks, every financial institution believed a change was necessary. These panics could not continue. Plus, one must remember the San Francisco earthquake required $350 million for its reconstruction. These funds came from the New York Banks. It depleted their coffers. Though the banks were sound, there were massive problems with liquidity which soon affected credit. The Knickerbocker Trust Company failed. The crisis grew."

Paul believed the American system could appear a little temperamental, but he thought it was overall sound. From his vantage point, it was a failed attempt, an archaic system in a modern world. The Treasury was incapable of taking any decisive action, and he believed this role belonged in the hands of bankers.

"The following year, Senator Nelson W. Aldrich established and chaired a commission to investigate the 1907 Financial crisis and to propose solutions. In December of 1907, I was introduced to Senator Aldrich from Rhode Island. I believe Jacob Schiff recommended we meet. In me, the Senator found the expert who could help make sense of a complicated crisis. I soon became his closest advisor on financial matters. At the time, Aldrich was one of the most powerful Senators. He advised me to apply for the United States citizenship, and I did."

They heard a knock on the door.

"Food," Paul said. He jumped into some clothes quickly, and she moved to the bathroom.

Elsa heard Paul thank the server.

Paul was laying the tray of food on the bed.

Naked, Elsa entered the room and jumped in bed. She was ravenous and picked one of the small plates. She helped herself to everything.

Paul sat and kissed Elsa gently.

As they ate, the conversation turned to Senator Aldrich.

She had met him once and felt he was full of himself.

Paul smiled. "Humility is a quality rarely found in the men I rub shoulder with." He poured two cups of coffee. Paul turned toward Elsa and looked at her.

She was so beautiful. He loved her healthy body, her porcelain skin, and her bright blue eyes. Her blonde hair was down and fell a little past her shoulders. She had long, delicate, and beautiful fingers.

He leaned and put his head on her shoulder. "I love you, Elsa."

She turned and kissed him on the forehead. "Is there any truth to this mysterious meeting to create a plan for the Federal reserve?"

Paul laid back on the pillow and put his hand around her waist. "For over two years, we faced a strong opposition to a Central Bank. Actions had to be taken fast and decisively. We were losing steam, exhausted by the effort. It had been eight years since I arrived and started to educate people on the benefit of a Central Bank System. In time, a meeting was planned. Away from prying eyes and listening ears, away from the critics and doubters, from the judges and the executioners. It was a bit foolish, but in the end, we all agreed this matter required our full attention and time."

Elsa turned, leaned on her elbow, and laid her hand on his chest.

"We set up a meeting for November. Secrecy was paramount. Each one of us arrived separately at the train station in Hoboken, New Jersey. We all wore a disguise to look inconspicuous. Most of us were dressed as duck hunters. Only first names had to be used. We rode in J.P Morgan's private car to the Jekyll Island Club, which Morgan also owned. The group stayed in Georgia for nine days. Senator Aldrich and his secretary led the group. Ultimately, he would be the one to present this plan and enact it into law."

She stirred, and he stopped. She covered herself.

He smiled at her.

"Why such secrecy Paul? Wasn't the plan to benefit the country?" She pulled the sheet over him and snuggled a little closer.

"Our goal was to create a final draft for an American Central Bank Act to be presented to the Senate for a vote. It would not be just a Central Bank but a system of 12 Central Banks. Opposition to such a plan, while misguided, I believed, was extremely strong. Most thought such a system would only benefit the Banks, mainly the Wall Street Banks. I believe it was an archaic way of thinking. The adage, old and new, light and dark, good versus evil. We were not building a bank but a system of multiple central banks working together. Yes, profit would be created, vast profit. But debt would be controlled, the unending bank panics would disappear once and for all, and stability, under the guidance of finance experts, would reign." He took a sip of coffee and kissed her.

They went on to discuss currency, possible inflation, and the control of interest rates. She loved numbers, and so did he.

She moved a little closer. "So you love me, Herr Warburg?"

Paul did not respond but looked deeply into her eyes. The moment felt like an eternity.

They finally kissed and made love once more. The tray of food was revisited.

Paul called for more hot coffee and a bottle of Champagne.

Within minutes, the waiter arrived with their order.

"Tell me more about the Jekyll meeting, Paul."

He put a few pastries on a plate, took the two Champagne flutes, and joined her on the bed.

"None of us could have created this Act alone. It was an extremely complicated process. It had to be a law and written as such. It could not attract suspicion that we were its creators. Millions of details were discussed, analyzed, approved, or rejected. Its name needed to be logical and discreet. I thought the Federal Reserve Bank was a fantastic name because it implied a government-owned bank. But Senator Aldrich desired to have his name attached to such a bill." Paul stopped, asking why she suddenly looked concerned.

"Paul, it seems to me secrecy was a major concern. Every aspect of this Act had to be somewhat hidden from view. The name was misleading and suggestive of a government-run system. None of its actual creators had to be known, discovered, or even mentioned. To me, these actions represent a muddied water in which one may be looking for something but can't find it. It lacked transparency."

He straightened, feeling a little guilty. "Elsa, you must understand the participants in this secret meeting were not your regular bankers. Since 80% of the funds would be coming from private investors, we invited the most prominent bankers to join; first and foremost, J.P. Morgan. We were his guest at the Jekyll Island Hunt Club, and he had supplied the private train car. However, it would have been impossible for J.P. Morgan to join us, as he was constantly hounded by journalists. Henry P. Davison was present in his stead, Senator Nelson Aldrich and Arthur Shelton, his secretary, and Charles D. Norton, Frank Vanderlip, A. Piatt Andrew, Assistant Secretary of the Treasury, and me."

Elsa interrupted him, "You must forgive me, Paul, but these are not the most altruistic of men. I am sure you would agree profits were their one and only goal. Senator Aldrich was a known Rockefeller kinsman, Davison was a Morgan Partner, second only to J.P. Morgan himself, Vanderlip was the President of the National City Bank of New York, a Rockefeller Bank, and Norton was President of the Morgan-owned First National Bank of New York. And though Andrew is a brilliant man, he has been associated with both the Morgans and the Rockefellers. You, yourself, are a partner of Kuhn, Loeb and Company, a for-profit company."

He smiled at her. "I understand how you feel, Elsa. Stability in the banking system is crucial to any bank's survival. Runs on banks, such as we saw in 1907, are unacceptable, especially when a sound system is within reach. You should know that most of these men are involved in very generous foundations, a fact rarely mentioned. I have anonymously donated hundreds of thousands of dollars, as they all have done."

Elsa snuggled closer. "Continue, Herr Warburg. Sorry," she said and kissed him.

"The first three days were spent on creating a sound system. For the next three, we separated into two teams, one to create financial projections and the other to review possible legal hurdles. Out of these emerged a best case and worst-case scenario. The final bill demanded the Central Bank be independent of the Treasury, that it managed all government loans, controlled rates of interest to be paid for such loans as well as all loans throughout the country, whether short or long terms and finally, it would control the printing of currency, thus managing its value and its gold equivalent. This, we knew, would create a stable banking system and a strong, controlled monetary infrastructure. The last three days were spent reviewing all the data and educating our Senator and his personal secretary. Senator Aldrich had spent years in politics where he became a master politician."

Paul reached out for the pack of cigarettes.

"We took the last day off and went duck hunting. Well … they did. I can't stand hunting of any kind. Once we believed our task complete, we boarded our train back up north. Remember, the Assistant Secretary of the Treasury was a full participant and valued member of our group because, in the end, all would need to be approved by the Treasury. This banking system had to be reviewed and modified under the strict rules of the Treasury of the United States. Any subsequent concerns were addressed during our journey back, or later in New York, in smaller groups."

Paul broke off and looked down to see her. She had fallen asleep on his chest. He moved her a little.

She turned, flipping her right arm toward the other side of the bed, uncovering her magnificent bare breast. He leaned forward and pulled the sheet over her. She was so bright, so beautiful, so sweet. He loved her as he had never loved anyone.

Paul leaned back on his pillow. Though he had been mostly truthful, he had not shared that the New York Banks were gravely concerned. It started in 1896 when William Jennings Bryan became the presidential nominee.

Bryan was a dominant force in the Democratic Party and strongly condemned the New York bankers and their insatiable appetite for power.

Paul remembered part of the speech the politician had delivered: *"When a crisis like the present arose and the National Bank of his day sought to control the politics of the nation. God raised up an Andrew Jackson, who had the courage to grapple with that great enemy, and by overthrowing, he made himself the idol…"*

With the "Cross of Gold" speech, a popular voice had risen—a warning of things to come. Had Bryan become President, more uncertainty in the financial system and a confrontation with the powerful New York Banks would have arisen.

Other cities such as St Louis and Chicago were growing faster than

New York, and their reserves were stronger, and the New York Banks were also losing their predominance.

He did not tell Elsa of the heavy financial backing provided to defeat Bryan. No matter the cost, McKinley would be promoted to the presidency.

Paul certainly did not share his anxiety at the greed his associates had demonstrated on Jekyll Island. If untamed, this greed, he believed, would either destroy their Federal Reserve System or the country. He heard footsteps and a knock. It came from the door to the suite.

"Felix?" He asked softly.

"Yes, Paul, it's me, Felix. I need to speak with you."

Paul responded he needed a minute. He dressed and left a note for Elsa, telling her he would be right back. He found Felix, who appeared nervous.

"I will be leaving for New York City tomorrow morning, Paul. As you know, Henry P. Davison was dispatched in August of 1914 to London and Paris to help the House of Morgan become the sole underwriter of war bonds for Great Britain and France. The Morgan firms have discreetly, though vastly, profited from this arrangement. Today, I learned that American soldiers have begun to arrive in France at a rate of 10,000 a day. The United States of America has entered the war."

Felix continued, "The Morgans were worried about your possible allegiance to Germany. This is the reason why you were not reappointed to the Board of the Federal Reserve."

Paul sat. "It does not matter, Felix."

"The next few months will be dangerous for Germany. The war will intensify. The M.M. Warburg Bank has lent heavily to the German Government. Could you review some numbers. Let's meet for breakfast at 7:00 tomorrow morning?" Said Felix.

"Of course, 7:00 it is. But Felix, do you really believe the Morgans would be afraid of a former German, now an American citizen, on the Board of the Federal Reserve? Personally, I doubt it. They are much too powerful. You know, I often worry their greed will never be satisfied." Paul responded. Sensing Felix was impatient and ready to leave, he stood and walked back to his room.

As he was leaving Felix said, "Paul, the papers I want you to review are in the office. Top right drawer. You know where the key is. I'll be out in twenty minutes at most. Thank you."

Paul entered his room to find Elsa fully dressed in a light gray dress, hair pulled tight in a bun. A pearl necklace softly framed her face.

She smiled at him.

"I am so happy to see you, Elsa," he said.

She walked over, and, resting her head on his shoulder, hugged him ever so tightly.

They stood there in silence for a minute—two lovers, knowing their impossible fate would soon be upon them. Paul was analyzing every possible outcome, for he loved Elsa dearly and could not bear to lose her.

She straightened and kissed him.

His hands rested on her hips, and he relaxed.

Elsa abruptly turned away and sat on the armchair nearby. She looked at him, and Paul could see tears in her eyes. She held her hand, reaching out for his.

Paul came closer and knelt before her.

"I dreamed of the day I would meet you, but never in my mind did I imagine the possibility of falling in love with you. Sadly, the percentage of success for this relationship is very small, Paul. The storm of life will pull us apart, my heart broken."

Paul reached out and held her hand tightly.

"I believe it may be time for us to part soon. I must return to my life, as do you," she said.

The two sat across from each other. Elsa and Paul decided to enjoy one last evening of freedom. Paul had selected to eat at a French restaurant a few blocks away, north of the White House. They left the Willard Hotel and walked arm in arm.

The restaurant was busy, and they were late, but the Maître D had kept a quiet table by the window for Paul. The opened windows let a gentle breeze blow in.

"Good evening Mr. Warburg."

Paul turned to the waiter, whom he vaguely recognized.

"My name is Jean. I have served you before, Mr. Warburg."

"Of course, Jean, I remember you," Paul smiled. "Jean, Miss Mueller, and I would like you to surprise us. Would you be kind enough to select a couple of your favorite appetizers and bring a bottle of Champagne? Merci." Paul said.

The waiter bowed slightly and left.

Elsa was looking at Paul with a tender smile. "The winds of time will take all away, Paul. But when dust I become, in the invisible entity we call the soul, I will forever remember these last few days. Thank you."

Paul reached out and held her hand. They shared pleasantries, avoiding discussing the cruel reality of separating. They chatted about Hamburg once more.

Paul learned that Elsa worked as an advisor to William A. Clark, the 'Copper King.' She explained that they had met in Paris. The kind man, upon learning she was an economist, asked her to solve a business problem; "The purchase price of a company, to be exact," she said. It took her fifteen minutes to come up with an estimated price. Stunned at her accuracy and speed, the "Copper King" hired her on the spot, and for the last six years, Elsa lived in the priciest mansion in New York City.

Elsa discovered that Paul had two children he loved but with whom he rarely connected. She learned that he loved his wife, "a friendly, platonic love, though," he admitted.

His family was currently in "Woodlands," Felix's extravagant country estates.

Elsa was, without a doubt, beautiful, elegant, charming, and so incredibly bright, he thought. *How are we going to ever separate?*

The meal had been exceptional. The Champagne, once gone, had been followed by some red wine, then more Champagne. In front of them were plates of desserts.

"So, Fraulein Mueller, what was the impression of the Herr Warburg you discovered in your research?" Paul asked.

She picked a small "Chocolate Religieuse" and took a bite.

He poured a little coffee and noticed the restaurant was quite empty.

"First, I do believe you deserve all the accolades you received. Without you, there would not be a Federal Reserve System in America. You worked tirelessly on this momentous task and succeeded. You did it because of your incredible knowledge of the intricacies of Central Banking, but mainly because you foresaw the changes needed to make it successful. You are a man of honor—respectful, kind, and socially conscious. Like most of the men who live to change the world, you stay focused on the task you are to accomplish and rarely stray from it. Unlike your accomplices, you lack their ravenous greed." Elsa paused to see his reaction, but none came.

Paul helped himself to the small "Paris Brest." The layered pastry looked delicious. He looked at her as if to say, "Continue."

So, she did. "As I am sure you know, Mr. Clarke is extremely wealthy, and when it came to knowledge, he cared little about the amount of money he would spend. He encouraged me to pursue all the leads related to the Federal Reserve System. During my studies at Columbia, I attended and read many of your speeches as well as speeches by the likes of Senator Aldrich and many others. Upon the passing of the Federal Reserve Act, Clarke and I met. He had just returned from a long trip to the West and, at 74 years of age, was more interested in growing his vast fortune than "seeing it crash as a result of some devil enterprise by a nefarious secret society."

"We knew from its inception the Federal Reserve System had been shrouded in mystery. Except for you, Paul. You were the public figure behind the need for a central bank, but the main conspirators were hidden. Though I am sorry to use the word 'conspirators' and mean no offense, the reality is I am convinced that what happened was, indeed, a conspiracy."

Paul sat back in his chair. Distant, he crossed his arms.

"By its definition, a conspiracy usually involves a group entering into a secret agreement to achieve some illicit or harmful objective. We cannot disagree with the "secret agreement" as part of the conspiracy. The Jekyll

Island meeting is an obvious example. So now, I had to define whether the creation of the Federal Reserve system was illicit or harmful?"

Elsa acknowledged the Act was certainly legal. The Federal Reserve Act had been approved and signed into law by Woodrow Wilson. It was undoubtedly created in secrecy by New York Bankers such as the Morgans, the Rockefellers, and Paul's employer. Kuhn & Loeb who had begun to see their dominance weaken. Between 1894 and 1903, growth in the banking industry declined for the New York Banks and appeared to trail the successful City Bank of Chicago and St. Louis by 30-40%.

Elsa grew nervous. Their eyes met, and Elsa searched for the tender Paul she had discovered a few days ago.

"Elsa, you are the most beautiful and intelligent woman I have ever had the pleasure to love," Paul said.

She decided to continue. "The Wall Street Bankers wanted a system they could control. In the Federal Reserve Bank of New York, they achieved their goal. It is the most powerful financial entity in this country and probably the world. Paul, let's be clear—a central bank, and due to the size of the country, a network of such banks, is a sound idea. One, no American should argue against. It could ensure a sound financial system. So, I say 'yes,' to a central bank, but one led by honest people dedicated to the success of our government."

Paul seemed to be growing impatient.

She retreated. "None of these matters, Paul. My life was like a leaf the wind had blown onto the surface of a river. You reached out and took me into your hands. This is what matters. All else is about numbers."

Paul reached out and held her hand and asked, "If these are all positive steps toward a stable and sound money, where is the problem?"

She leaned closer and smiled. "Let's go back to the hotel and make love, Paul."

He turned and waved at the waiter, who rushed over. Paul threw some bills on the table, and they left.

Washington, often hot and humid in the summer, was delightful. A light breeze sweetened the air. They walked, holding each other tight.

Paul suggested they'd make a stop at "La Rotonde," a French-style Brasserie, where they could sit outside.

She loved the idea, and they changed direction, turning toward Franklin Square. An open table outside awaited them. They ordered coffee.

Paul slowly brought the Federal Reserve System back into their conversation and finally asked what she thought was wrong with it.

They could hear a piano playing inside the Brasserie. The pianist played a delicate and gorgeous classical piece.

"This is Bach, I believe. One of the Goldberg Variations," Elsa said. "Legend has it Bach wrote the music to soothe the sleepless nights of one Count, who paid him with a cup full of gold coins." She leaned on his shoulder.

They left "La Rotonde," and he wrapped his arm around her.

"When are you returning to New York, Elsa?" Asked Paul.

Elsa remained silent. She did not want to think of leaving Paul and the life she had so enjoyed for the last few days. She turned and kissed him. "Certainly not tonight, Paul."

Finally, Elsa said, "What do I believe is wrong with the Federal Reserve?" She paused and took in a deep breath. "I do not believe a private entity should ever have been given such powers. I am sorry to say this, Paul, but I believe by such deceit, the powers bestowed upon the Federal Reserve and, therefore, its shareholders were taken rather than given— achieved through a multi-faceted campaign of misinformation, a manufactured financial crisis in 1907, and the enormous pressure and financial support given to politicians. In my view, the Government it is meant to serve, the Federal Reserve rules instead, because it is in possession of a complete and unequivocal independence. It is unlike any governmental agency and does not answer to anyone—not even the President. The Federal Reserve Act of 1913 created a monopoly over our financial system, and its power may never be subdued."

Elsa paused. She was nervous but felt strong and pulled him toward her.

This time he remained silent.

She kissed him on the cheek.

He smiled.

She continued, "Finally, Paul, my major concern is America's National Debt—the Debt that President Andrew Jackson vowed to get rid of and succeeded. Jackson, who said, *"...My vow shall be to pay the national debt, to prevent a monied aristocracy from growing up around our administration that must bend to its views, and ultimately destroy the liberty of our country."*

Paul, his arm around Elsa's shoulders, listened patiently, knowing every word she uttered was true.

"Debt has been the evil all along. Private bankers should not be running a nation's banking system," she continued.

They found themselves in front of the Willard Hotel and separated. Elsa walked straight for the elevator while Paul collected the key to the suite.

They rode the elevator quietly. The door opened to their floor. He followed her. The two could hear laughter in the suite but wanted no part of it and quietly entered Paul's private room.

Finally, they embraced, kissing each other lightly.

Elsa was gentle but strong.

Paul was madly in love.

They spent the night in each other's arms till finally, exhausted, they fell asleep.

Hours later, the phone woke them from their stupor. Elsa heard Paul answer the call.

"Yes, I know. I will see you in New York," he said in German.

She assumed he was speaking to Felix and closed her eyes.

"Fraulein Mueller, are you awake?" Paul asked.

She turned, smiled at him, and said, "Must we leave our paradise so soon?"

Paul would have done anything for this woman. He was crazy about her and felt like a teenager in love for the first time.

Elsa dressed in a navy-blue, pleated skirt, light-blue blouse, and a striped, knitted vest, her hair pulled back into a ponytail. She was about to walk out of the room when she turned around and put on her beret hat.

"I must run to the drugstore across the street. Could we meet in the Peacock Room for breakfast?" She asked. "Herr Warburg, what did you tell me the first night we met? Something about a rose... I loved it so much." She stood at attention, while he smiled.

"Out of a thunderous storm and the sailor's despair to survive another day, came the simple but striking beauty of a rose," he murmured.

She was delighted. "I must forever remember these words, Paul," Elsa said and approached him. They were so close, their lips almost touched. Their eyes met for a moment before she kissed him. Her hands remained on his cheek, holding his face tenderly.

"I love you, Herr Warburg," Elsa said. "I will see you downstairs in a few minutes."

What was he going to do? He could not imagine parting with Elsa. His mind raced in multiple directions when an odd feeling came over him. He felt light-headed and sat on the bed to let his body regain his equilibrium.

The feeling soon disappeared.

He picked up the phone and called Nina. The house was quite still, and she was afraid to wake the children. They agreed to talk later. He hung up, saying he would see her soon.

Paul dressed and walked down the flights of stairs. He spoke briefly to Monsieur Fernand and turned in the direction of the Peacock Alley. Realizing Elsa was not there, he decided to check the lobby. Oddly, the doorman was absent from his usual post, so Paul ventured outside.

It took him an instant to catch the commotion unfolding across the street. A dump truck, whose engine was still running, was stopped in the middle of the road, the driver's side door opened wide, and in front of the truck, a man stood, looking toward the sidewalk in disbelief.

The driver, Paul assumed, was in shock. Passersby covered their mouths to silence their cries of horror.

"She must not have seen the truck," someone next to him said. Paul turned. It was the doorman. Paul rushed across the street. His heart pounded in his chest as a palpable and cold fear overwhelmed him.

On the cobblestone sidewalk, Elsa laid in a pool of blood. Her arms were fractured in a few places. The delicate hand he had tenderly held was crushed, her right leg pushed backward, her chest bloodied.

His entire body trembled uncontrollably, and the warm blood filling his every vein turned into ice. Silence engulfed him as darkness fell upon his surroundings. All except Elsa faded into a desaturated and dark background. Paul kneeled and put his hand on her forehead. She seemed so at peace, her eyes staring at the blue sky above.

A hand tapped his shoulder.

Slowly, Paul ran the cusp of his hand over her eyes and shut them for eternity.

In the following moments, every second they had spent together replayed in fast forward. He could still feel the tender hands she had held on his face a few minutes ago.

Her voice echoed in his mind. "Must we leave our paradise so soon?"

A fireman threw a blanket over Elsa's crushed body as the silence which had surrounded him burst into a cacophony of concerned voices. There was another tap on his shoulder. Paul turned to see a fat Policeman.

"Sir. Do you know this young lady?" The officer asked in a heavy Irish accent.

Paul stared into the poor man's eyes but did not respond. Inside of him, his soul screamed loudly, "*No, Sir, I did not know this young lady. I loved her. She was the rose that, ever so briefly, illuminated my heart. She was the love I had waited for all my life. How can this be? I cannot lose this angel forever...*"

It took Paul a few days to deal with Elsa's tragic death. He felt broken, angry, and confused. He reached out to Elsa's family in Albany and spoke to her aunt, who burst into tears at the news. It was decided she would be buried next to her kin.

William A. Clark, the 'Copper King,' was horrified and offered to help. It was not necessary.

Three days after the accident, he watched the hearse carrying Elsa's mangled body drive away. He covered all the expenses and ordered the funeral home to inscribe "The striking beauty of a rose" on her tombstone.

Over the next few months, Paul relived every second he had spent with Elsa, hour by hour and moment by moment. He became withdrawn, and those close to him grew concerned.

Paul Warburg never returned to Kuhn, Loeb & Co., and when asked why he had not come back to work at the investment bank, he responded, *"My mind is not bent on making money—certainly not in these times."*

"Herr Warburg," as Elsa loved to call him, continued to sit on many boards of directors of some of the most prestigious and profitable banks, railways, and other corporations. He led the Council on Foreign Relations. But his world had turned grey. He missed Elsa. He missed the days they had spent together.

Paul wished he had been honest with the woman he loved so, for he never told her the truth about the Federal Reserve and the dark side of the events that changed America forever. He never shared the many back door deals, the many secret cash donations.

Elsa was right; the Federal Reserve System had been created for the profit of a few, though he believed, in due time, the central Bank would provide a stable and sound financial system. The large New York City Banks, with names such as the National City Bank, First National Bank, Chase National Bank, National Bank of Commerce of New York City, and others, owned most of the shares issued upon the Central Bank launch. In all these banks, the largest shareholders were the same; Rockefeller, J.P. Morgan, Kuhn, Loeb & Co., Rothschilds, and others, including himself, the private citizen, Paul M. Warburg. But secrecy was the rule these institutions demanded. Their names would remain hidden behind a dark, mysterious veil.

185

By 1928, Paul had grown disillusioned. The messenger for a Central Bank, the respected and revered man, was often ignored and, at times, ridiculed. The uncontrollable greed Elsa had predicted started to weaken the stable economic system he had tried to build. Paul publicly warned of over speculation and a possible dangerous bubble in the market. Most mocked him.

"Here comes old Gloomy Gus," someone shouted once as he entered the exclusive Century Club in Manhattan.

Shame on them, Paul thought. Later that same day, when he was booed at a director's meeting, he realized his voice was no longer welcomed.

A few months later, Paul Warburg, the gentleman, the "Father of the Federal Reserve," speaking of the climbing prices of the stock market, made the following statement: *"...if orgies of unrestrained speculation continue without control, the ultimate collapse is certain to not only affect the speculators themselves but also to bring about a general depression involving the entire country."*

The audience at the Annual Report of the International Acceptance Bank booed and hissed. Six months later, in September of 1929, following the London Stock Exchange crash, Wall Street collapsed. "Black Tuesday" sent America, and the entire world, into the Great Depression.

Three years later, as his prophecy of economic destruction raged on, Paul peacefully passed away. "Herr Warburg" had never returned to the Willard Hotel or shared Elsa's existence with anyone.

Felix never once mentioned either Elsa or Lara.

Paul forever missed the beautiful, gentle, and intelligent woman he had met and with whom he had spent some of the most wonderful days in his life. His family believed Paul Warburg, the mysterious, reserved, and self-conscious man from Hamburg died of a broken heart from being stripped of the helm of the Federal Reserve Bank. It had been the most shattering event in his life. It changed him so drastically, the family murmured at his funeral.

Weeks later, as the family gathered to celebrate Passover, James Paul Warburg entered his father's office. It had been left untouched. A great sadness overcame him, and he noticed the chair in which his father had sat for long stretches of time during his last few months.

The young Warburg turned toward the desk and noticed a small, folded piece of light blue paper under the desk. He reached out, picked it up, and unfolded it. In his father's meticulous handwriting, the following words were written: "Out of a thunderous storm and the sailor's despair to survive another day, came the simple but striking beauty of a rose."

CHAPTER 10

GREY EMINENCE

The real truth of the matter is, as you and I know, that a financial element in the larger centers has owned the Government ever since the days of Andrew Jackson.
— A letter written by FDR to Colonel House, November 21, 1933

MANHATTAN, NY, 1919

Though I aspire to protect the secrecy I have so cherished, a confession I intend to make. But not to you, my fellow Americans, strangers in this vast land. To you, I must remain unknown, and my deeds an inconvenient truth blamed on the president, I so misled. To the unborn men of tomorrow, to the future citizens of this beautiful country, I offer this confession born from the guilt that now troubles me. To you, I wish to reveal my deeds and the judge you may be.

My name is Edward Mandell House. Some may know me as "Colonel" House. I was an American diplomat, politician, and presidential advisor. A Colonel I was not. But I liked the appeal and ceremonious benefits it afforded me.

James Stephen "Big Jim" Hogg, whom I had helped become the 20th Governor of Texas, gave me the title long ago. I'll carry on forever with the deception. Why not?

I certainly was not the honest individual who became President Woodrow Wilson's most trusted and closest confidant.

My title was adviser to the 28th President of the United States of America. An informal title, for I refused any formal position. My father had provided me with enough wealth to never to have to work a day in my life. I neither needed the money nor the responsibility a formal position would have required.

However, my role demanded a particular nearness to the President. I was provided with my living quarters in the White House and operated of my own free will.

Woodrow Wilson and I were so alike, the President once described me in such a way; he *"...is my second personality. He is my independent self. His thoughts and mine are one."*

But guilt forces me to reveal the ugly truth. I repeatedly deceived and manipulated Woodrow Wilson. As a matter of fact, our entire relationship was based on lies—mostly mine, I must admit.

Wilson was a good man who tried to be a good president; a man I grew fond of, a man I dearly miss. But his failures were the fruits of the trust he granted in me.

In Texas, I was known as the "Kingmaker." The truth is, I was the King who crafted the policies which would define America for years to come. I was the true power behind the thrones, the grey eminence of American politics.

Yet, you don't know my name.

Men who change the world often commit their deeds in the shadows, unbeknownst to the public who happily disregard their influence and blame the leaders they counseled.

I acted on behalf of what Woodrow Wilson described in the New Freedom as *"a power somewhere so organized, so subtle, so watchful, so interlocked, so complete, so pervasive..."*

A shadow government of sorts ruling behind a curtain of secrecy; an entity the famed journalist and author Ferdinand Lundberg called the "de facto government," and claiming it was *"... actually the government of the United States, informal, invisible, shadowy..."*

One may wonder why Woodrow Wilson became so close to a man like me. He had, after all, expressed grave concerns for the newer form of economic domination he called *"informal imperialism."*

The author George Sylvester Viereck was working on a book called *The Strangest Friendship in History, Woodrow Wilson and Col. House.*

The author hoped to clarify a few points and reached out to me. During our conversation, Viereck asked me what had cemented our relationship.

"I handed him $35,000," was my answer.

"The nature of men is ambitious and suspicious.," Machiavelli once stated. Indeed, it is.

For the ruling class, the Morgans, the Rockefellers, the Warburgs, the Schiffs, and the Khans, I, by virtue of my friendship with, and influence over President Wilson, became the trusted and discreet soldier who delicately implemented their darkest schemes.

Unlike the kings of old, these men had skillfully retained the unlimited powers kings once possessed but transferred the country's governance to a puppet president; one they controlled. And he alone became the recipient of the dissatisfied citizens' anger.

Around 1910, I was approached and tasked with finding the next president. The prerequisites were an above-normal intellect, but gullible and honest enough to be easily compromised.

Governor Woodrow Wilson wanted the presidency, and I was searching for a man to be president. Wilson and I first met in a small room at the Gotham Hotel in New York City. It was a very unglamorous setting for what would become such a momentous relationship.

Ours was the perfect union.

A calculating man will always win over an insecure one; especially one with an inflated ego. Great men are often blind to their flaws.

Woodrow Wilson suffered from a grand sense of self-righteousness and superiority.

I possessed a special gift; I knew how to handle such a character.

"The trouble with getting a candidate for president is that the man that is best fitted for the place cannot be nominated and, if nominated, could probably not be elected. The people seldom take the man best fitted for the job; therefore, it is necessary to work for the best man who can be nominated and elected, just now Wilson seems to be that man," I said on August 30, 1911.

My friends, the elite, rejoiced.

My relationship with President Wilson was built on the sharing of common ideals and trust; two intellectual and inquiring minds basking in each other's grandness. I managed his campaign, reviewed his speeches, and introduced him to the men who financed it all from behind the scenes—the men who ultimately made him the 28th President of the United States.

But today, October 2, 1919, I received tragic news. The First Lady found President Woodrow Wilson unconscious on the bathroom floor, bleeding from a deep cut to the forehead.

According to his physician, Dr. Grayson, the President had suffered a massive stroke. It had left his entire left side paralyzed and his vision impaired.

I pray for my friend, knowing there is little hope for a full recovery.

In my mind, I replay the many hours we spent discussing politics, philosophy, and history. My heart grows dark.

But what despicable act must have I committed to offer such a confession, you wonder.

Well, many years ago, I joined the Cecil Rhodes Round Table group and soon grew fond of their four main projects: a graduated income tax, a central bank, the creation of a Central Intelligence Agency, and a League of Nations. Over the years, as my power grew, I implemented these goals.

First, I installed a puppet figure as the American president. Then, I manipulated Woodrow Wilson to embrace the policies we desired.

You see, I was the secret intermediary between the White House and the financiers who desired a central bank. I did everything in my power to realize their goal.

On December 23, 1913, Woodrow Wilson signed the Federal Reserve Act of 1913 into law.

Yet, you still wonder, what crime is there to confess, Colonel?

So, from you, the stranger of years to come, I request you inquire the amount of debt our country holds and to whom that debt is owed.

To you, I share these words written in 1863 by the Rothschild Brothers of London when describing their central banking system: *"The few who understand the system will either be so interested in its profits or be so dependent upon its favors that there will be no opposition from that class, while on the other hand, the great body of people, mentally incapable of comprehending the tremendous advantage that capital derives from the system, will bear its burdens without complaint, and perhaps without even suspecting that the system is inimical to their interests."*

President Jackson fought and destroyed the Second Bank of the United States, the Central Bank he believed would enslave our country.

In 1913, I revived its corpse into a new, more voracious monster into the system the Rothschild brothers described years ago.

Blameless and faceless, I was involved in drafting the Revenue Tax Act of 1913, a way to ensure the Federal Reserve would receive payments on the country's debt.

I traveled the world to negotiate peace and then negotiated America's involvement in World War I. I created the Inquiry, which probably means little to you, but for me and the elite, the members of the Inquiry were the experts our puppet presidents and our educated populace trusted.

The Inquiry was a group of 100 experts who advised the Government, often carrying the torch we requested them to. We paid for their programs, after all. The Inquiry became the Council on Foreign Relations, which grew to become the most influential non-governmental entity in the world.

On behalf of President Wilson, I joined the Council of Ten to negotiate the Treaty of Versailles at the end of World War I. But in my error, I disregarded too many of President Wilson's demands.

Wilson, upon realizing my deceit, grew furious. Then one day, the French Minister refused to negotiate with President Wilson and requested I present myself in his stead to complete the final drafts of the negotiations.

No longer was I the trusted adviser. I had become the usurper, the enemy.

Our relationship ended abruptly. The President and I returned from France separately. We never saw or spoke to each other again.

Though President Wilson did work on the League of Nations, most of its policies had been my doing. My role in these events was unquestionable, and their success unattainable without my guidance. Though no crimes had been committed in implementing these policies, it is essential to know they had been implemented under false pretense, behind a wall of lies, deceits, and manipulations. For the men I served, the power they possessed grew infinitely.

In closing and to justify this confession, I will, once again, quote President Wilson from "The New Freedom":

"Since I entered politics, I have chiefly had men's views confided to me privately. Some of the biggest men in the US, in the field of commerce and manufacturing, are afraid of somebody, are afraid of something. They know that there is a power somewhere so organized, so subtle, so watchful, so interlocked, so complete, so pervasive, that they had better not speak above their breath when they speak in condemnation of it."

To the men of tomorrow, may you kindly accept this confession, for I represented this invisible power. I was that power.

Colonel Edward Mandell House

CHAPTER 11

THE CRASH

Mr. Chairman, we have in this country one of the most corrupt institutions the world has ever known. I refer to the Federal Reserve Board and the Federal Reserve Banks ... and that this country was to supply financial power to an international superstate — a superstate controlled by international bankers and international industrialists acting together to enslave the world for their own pleasure.
— Congressman Louis T. McFadden, from a speech delivered to the House of Representatives on June 10, 1932

The depression was the calculated 'shearing' of the public by the World Money powers, triggered by the planned sudden shortage of supply of call money in the New York money market...
— Curtis Dall, Franklin Delano Roosevelt's son-in-law from his book, 'My Exploited Father-in-Law'

NEW YORK CITY, 2009

Over the Hudson River, in a burst of delicate shades of orange and pink, the sun was softly setting. The sky, scarred by plumes of smoke arising from the urban landscape, was a deep shade of blue. Through growing tears, Klaus Friedrich Hermann scanned the panorama before him. To the south, the Statue of Liberty stood glorious, arm raised in a show of strength and defiance. From his viewpoint, high above the streets, Hermann could see boats enter the harbor. There were small fishing boats and huge cargoes transporting thousands of people to the new world. He could picture the faces of the nervous immigrants, for only a year ago, he had entered the harbor, tense, but excited.

New York City, what have I done? Klaus thought in anguish.

An hour earlier, the German immigrant had entered the offices of the Bankers Trust Company Building at 14 Wall Street. Discreetly, Hermann had climbed up the stairs. Although, on what would become one of the worst financial crashes in American history, his efforts mattered little. No one cared for the presence of an intruder in their midst.

On the 18th floor, a toilet reeking of vomit became a hiding place. He waited a while. The floor was silent. He exited into the hallway and continued his climb.

Klaus, anxious and desperate, entered an empty office and locked the door. Bravely, he walked across the room and slid the large window wide open.

There he was, standing on the ledge of a window, 28 floors above street level, about to jump to his death. Strangely, his mind drifted, and he was amazed by how beautiful the city looked.

I lost everything. Every penny we had saved. All of it, gone, the young German thought. *Because of me, we are destitute.*

His heart was screaming in pain for his wife, Hannah, and Franz, their son, but it was too late. Courageously, Hermann ventured to look down at the street but only noticed the ragged shoes he had worn for the last few weeks. He smiled at the irony of what he had become in such a short time. Klaus rose his arms in a wide "V" over his head.

"Goodbye," he said, as he leaned forward and fell to his death.

Clara, startled by fear from the intense sensation of falling, sat up. Her dream had been so vivid, perspiration ran down her face. She was shaking like a leaf, in a stranger's bed and thousands of miles from her home. The clock showed 3:09 a.m. She picked up her cell and dialed. It would be 9:09 a.m. in Paris.

There was no answer.

Clara got up and found her way through the cupboard and found coffee, filters, and sugar. Once the coffee was brewed and a large cup filled, she turned to the stash of documents left for her to uncover.

Clara Peterman was a small, delicate woman whose charm and warm smile made her well-liked by most. Born and raised in Brooklyn, New York, she had, for the better part of the last ten years, resided in Paris, which she now called home. At 38, she had acquired the nonchalant elegance of a French woman. She wore just enough makeup to accentuate her well-defined face and only selected flattering clothes.

Years earlier, her college studies had led her to the Sorbonne in Paris. One evening, a few weeks after her arrival in the City of Lights, Clara felt a bit lonely and decided to reward herself. So, on a late Saturday afternoon, she ventured to the busy Rue Saint Jacques, where she sat at the terrace of a local Brasserie and ordered a beer. From her seat, she could admire the gorgeous light falling over the city. She was lost in a daydream when a tall, young, uninvited Frenchman sat at her table.

He announced she had to join him for a walk.

Clara, fluent in French, must have seemed surprised, for he immediately switched to perfect, though accented, English.

"My name is Henry. You must join me for a stroll. Please do not refuse, for you would forever break my heart," the young man declared theatrically.

Clara had smiled at the charming young man who resembled a decadent member of the Dadaist movement of the early 1900s. Long and thin, he had a messy head of hair, rumpled clothes, and a blue scarf informally tied around his neck. But she enjoyed his warm and inviting smile and agreed to join him for a short walk.

In very proper English, the young man spoke enthusiastically about poetry, politics, and the upcoming revolution, all the while chain-smoking Gauloises cigarettes.

They crossed through the Jardins du Luxembourg, meandered through the tiny streets of St. Germain des Prés and continued until they reached the Square du Vers Galant where he kissed her gently.

Clara and Henry had been together ever since. "L'amour fou," as they say in France.

Now, ten years later, Clara taught English at a private university located in the Bastille area. Henry, who had studied economy and philosophy, had written several books on the European Union. His work had been extremely well received, and he was regarded as one of the new Parisian thinkers. Of late, he had become a political consultant, working throughout Europe.

In early June, Clara received a call from a New York City attorney, a Mr. Jonathan Wilmore. He had left her a polite message requesting that she call him back. Though he had neglected to share the reason for his call, he had assured her not to be concerned.

She reached him the following morning.

Mr. Wilmore sounded just like a proper English gentleman. He informed Clara that her mother's cousin, Mrs. Hannah Wilkins, had recently passed away. "Mrs. Peterman, you are her only remaining family member," the lawyer said. Mrs. Wilkins' house in upstate New York was part of her inheritance. It also appeared that a house and some land in Germany, near Hamburg, were part of the estate. "Mrs. Peterman, would it possible for you to fly to New York City to settle this matter?"

Before she could answer, he informed her that Mrs. Wilkins' estate would certainly cover all her travel expenses.

Clara informed him it would not be necessary and promised to call and inform him when she would be able to travel.

The school year had just ended, and she knew that Henry had planned to be in Brussels for work over the next couple of weeks.

Clara flew to New York City on a Monday morning and arrived at JFK airport in mid-afternoon. A taxi drove her to the home of her old friend, Sara, who lived in the Brooklyn townhouse she had grown up in and inherited from her family a few years earlier. Even though it had long been her home, Clara always felt overwhelmed when returning to Brooklyn. There existed within her a certain disconnect.

The French use the word *"deraciné"* to describe the sensation. It means "uprooted." In a subtle way, she had lost her American identity but had never felt totally French.

Sara was at the house to welcome her. They spent a few hours catching up.

They soon walked to "Café Fada," a trendy French restaurant in Williamsburg, for dinner. Stephane Wrembel, a French guitar player, was featured. He was a master of the Gypsy guitar and delighted the audience with his gorgeous music and incredible playing.

Clara had a wonderful evening.

The next morning, in a fancy New York City law firm on the Upper East Side, Clara met Mr. Wilmore. Though he politely welcomed her, he immediately suggested they get a coffee.

Odd, she thought.

He led her back down the stairs she had just climbed. It felt unexpected and somewhat informal, but she was in New York City, she reminded herself.

Jonathan was a dashing and extremely polite man, though he certainly did not appear to be English.

"Don't you hate these Starbucks?" He asked with disdain.

"No need to apologize, Mr. Wilmore. We have those in Paris, too."

Clara sat at a large table while he ordered his coffee. The lawyer quickly returned, and they briefly chatted about her trip and her life in Paris.

"I must be honest with you. Hannah, your mother's cousin, was a dear friend of mine. It broke my heart to see her wilt away as she did. I am still heartbroken." He noticed Clara was looking at him inquisitively. "No, it was not what you think. We were more brother and sister than lovers, perhaps mother and son. She was a loving mother, of course," he said and then paused. "May I be perfectly truthful with you, Mrs. Peterman?"

She nodded, surprised by the turn of events.

"You see, I was 13 when I first met Hannah," he said. "Her son, Franz, was a neighborhood friend. One day, he invited me to come to his house. On this afternoon, there were a few of us playing. At one point, Franz asked me to get us some soda from the fridge. Excited to be given such responsibility, I sprinted into the house. In my blind rush, I ran full speed into Mrs. Wilkins. I can remember this moment as if it were yesterday. Hannah, who was tall, kneeled, held my face delicately and kissed my forehead. She asked if I needed to sit for a minute. Hannah was beautiful, gentle, and kind. As a child, I was always different. In those days, the feelings I experienced were left unspoken. For what appeared like an hour, we spoke on the sofa. Two souls, separated by the trials of life and time, finally met again."

"Over the years, we became the closest of friends. I was young. She was wise. She kindly listened to me and helped me accept who I was. One day, as I was about to leave for college, she asked me to sit with her for coffee. 'Jonathan, we have a saying in Germany, and it goes like this: *It's not beauty which determines whom we love, but love determines whom we find beautiful.*' She gently placed her hand on mine and continued.

"To be different is not a crime, Jonathan. We are just who we are meant to be. I hope you will find the strength to accept who you are and find yourself. I will always love you, my little friend, and already miss you."

The lawyer had tears in his eyes. "I am sorry, Mrs. Peterman."

As Hannah had done many years ago, Clara reached out and gently laid her hand on his.

"When Mr. Wilkins passed away a decade ago, Hannah contacted me to see if I could help her with legal matters. First, she needed her own will, but her overall concern was to straighten out all her affairs. A few years before her husband's death, Hannah inherited some property in Germany. As you may know, her son, Franz, had tragically died in a car accident when he was twenty-one years old. She was alone. It was my turn to reciprocate the kindness she had shown me long ago. I would have done anything for Hannah. This quiet woman had been the one and only person who never judged me, who never raised her voice to correct me. She was the rock I could return to when the storms of life reached my shores. Hannah was always there when life took me down."

Jonathan explained that he made the trip to Hudson, New York, with his partner, George. The two had recently purchased a place away from the city. It was a good excuse to visit Hannah and check on their place. The joy he had always found in her eyes had dissipated.

"Sensing my deep sadness, George was kind enough to keep himself busy while I spent the next couple of days with her ..." The lawyer paused.

"I am sorry. Enough about me. The inheritance. I would suggest you take a ride to see the house. You could stay there for a day or two to check if you find anything you would like to keep. I could arrange for movers to empty the house and prepare it to be put on the market. Everything else could easily be accomplished by phone, email, and bank transfer." He turned to Clara and asked, "Mrs. Peterman, how well did you know Hannah?"

Clara explained she may have spoken to her a few times. "Hannah always seemed reserved to me. When our family joined to celebrate the holidays. But she preferred to spend time with my mother, her cousin. The two would spend hours speaking German, laughing, reminiscing about their younger days in a faraway land."

Jonathan quickly returned to the legal matter and explained that the sale of the house would cover all fees, and no charge for his services would be forthcoming. She remained silent as he continued for a while. They agreed she would travel to Hudson in a few days. He would reserve a rental car for her and hire movers.

"Do you speak German?" Jonathan finally asked Clara.

She was a little surprised by the question but responded that she read German better than she spoke it.

"Hannah was a jewel," he said. "Her kindness toward me was the reason that our relationship existed. In her later years, she mostly lived alone and would spend days reading correspondence she had collected over a lifetime. There are three boxes full of letters, newspaper clippings, legal forms, and announcements. Most are in German. She kept these boxes in her living room and would open one of the boxes and read every single item it contained. Mrs. Peterman, I hope you will get a chance to discover the incredible person Hannah was."

His phone rang, then hers.

It was Henry.

So, after agreeing they would speak later, they parted.

Clara and Henry spent the next hour chatting about her meeting with Jonathan and the feeling she experienced being back in New York City.

Her husband was a calm man and always seemed to navigate life in his own peculiar but truthful manner. "Ma Cherie, tu es a New York, profites-en."

Once again, he was right. She was in New York City, a place she did love very much.

Don't feel like a stranger in your own home, she thought.

For the rest of the day, she let go of her feeling of being stranger, out of place. She walked along 5th Avenue and Central Park, stopped in front of the Metropolitan Museum of Art, climbed the stairs, and spent the afternoon discovering the incredible collection of 16th-, 17th-, and 18th-century paintings it hosted.

Over the next few days, Clara spent most of her time in the city; Union Square, Soho, Columbia University and St. John the Divine Cathedral. She fell in love with the Vessel, though most New Yorkers hated the thing. She found it one of the most fascinating sculptures built in recent memory. She meandered along the High-line and lunched at Chelsea Market.

Clara reconnected with old friends, explored certain neighborhoods at her own pace, rejoicing to be back home in some way.

On Tuesday morning, in Sara's typical Brooklyn brownstone backyard, Clara and her friend chatted for a long time.

Sara had barely changed over the years. She had remained the warm, energetic New Yorker with a thousand tasks and millions of questions.

Clara had little to say about Hannah, for she had barely known her. By 9 a.m., she left the house, picked up the rental car and started her journey to Hudson.

Jonathan had insisted she stayed at his place.

Clara arrived at his apartment in the early afternoon. It was a large loft on the second floor of what may have once been a factory. It was quite impressive with two bedrooms separated by a large kitchen and set in the back of the apartment. The front part hosted a large and opulent living room and dining room. She settled in the guest room. It had beautiful light streaming in through the tall windows which she opened to let the air in. It was a gorgeous day. She went for a stroll.

The town was quaint and friendly.

Clara settled in a cozy restaurant called the Governor's Tavern.

The next morning, Clara drove to Greendale Road, a few miles outside of town.

The house was perched on a small hill overlooking the Hudson River. Across the river was the town of Catskills, which she remembered having visited with Henry many years earlier.

The house was located two miles from Olana, the grand estate of Frederic Edwin Church, one of the major figures in the Hudson River School of landscape painting.

She fiddled with the keys a bit, and after a couple of tries, she opened the door.

Her phone rang.

It was Jonathan, wanting to be sure all had gone well.

She thanked him for letting her stay at his place and assured him all was well.

"By the way," he said, "there should be a note from Hannah, along with a few letters she left for you. I believe you will find them on a table in the living room."

They said goodbye and Clara entered Mrs. Hannah Wilkins' house.

The house was charming. Once again, she found herself opening windows to let the stale air out, and the beautiful light in.

Over the next couple of hours, she explored every inch of the place. The movers would arrive the next day and would need directions as to what to take and what to leave. She decided to explore the grounds. The house was a light grey with white trim.

Bland as could be, she thought.

The landscaping, however, was well designed and maintained. Behind the patio was a greenhouse hidden by a narrow edge of forsythia. The place was enchanting and certainly peaceful. She realized that only days earlier she had been in Paris—a noisy and polluted city—wrapping up her school year. She was quite taken by the turn of events of recent weeks.

Clara suddenly realized how famished she was and promptly returned to the house, grabbed the keys to the rental car, and headed to Hudson for lunch.

In a charming French bistro, she ordered her sandwich "to-go."

On her way back, Clara remembered Hannah's letters left for her. Upon entering the house, she quickly found them where Jonathan had said they may be. Clara found that there were two letters laying on the dining room sideboard.

Hungry, she carelessly picked them up and walked over to the patio, where she had left her lunch.

On each of the envelopes, her name was carefully written in a stylish script.

She sat, admired the beautiful handwriting for a moment, and opened the first envelope.

The letter was in German.

Clara, a bit rusty, slowly set about deciphering every word.

Hannah had written a polite letter, stating she was glad Clara would inherit the house.

"...however, while selling the house may, at first, appear to be the reasonable step to take, I would strongly suggest you reconsider and keep it."

The letter went on to explain she and her husband, after their son's death, had looked for a new place to live. It had been a lengthy search. "...We finally settled on this house because of the peaceful feeling we had both sensed during our initial visit. It was a peace I longed for and which remained with me to my last days," Hannah had written.

I cannot imagine myself living here, Clara thought, *but keeping the house was certainly an interesting idea.*

Clara laid the letter on the table. Slowly, she looked around at the beautiful landscape before her. In the distance, the sounds of the farm adjacent to the property could be heard.

The area was certainly beautiful.

Clara picked the second letter. Her name was written in the same beautiful cursive. She opened it. The first page was short and courteous. In meticulous handwriting, Hannah explained she hoped to share certain events.

"I must apologize for the burden I place on you. My story is the tale of the poor immigrant I was. But my story is your story in a way; and one, I feel, you should know."

Clara placed the first page on the table. She scanned the many pages in her hand. She stopped, took a bite, and leaned back in the chair. The sun was warm, the air pleasant. She began to read.

Dear Clara,

Of the three lives I have lived, the second was the one meant to be mine. The others were bookends to a period of love, friendship, motherhood, and discovery. My maiden name is Hannah Rose Von Furstenberg. To most of my contemporaries, my life was a fairy tale. By the age of 9, I had become a child prodigy. I could play the music of Bach, Mozart, and Chopin on the piano impeccably. My only limitations were I had not fully grown yet, and my hands were still small. Also, my lack of life experience restricted the various emotions I could instill into the piece of music. By 13, however, I had grown and toured Europe with my parents many times. Paris, London, and Amsterdam were the typical stops. I mainly played in smaller venues, salons, and private concerts. On a few occasions, I had the pleasure of traveling to Italy. When home, I delighted the wealthy upper class around Hamburg.

I grew to wonder about the possible reasons that my parents led me to live such a life. They were financially comfortable, so it was not for money. To this day it remains a mystery; one I no longer try to understand or justify.

Looking back at my youth, I feel my life was one in which all the joy and innocence of childhood had been removed. I did not particularly like or need the attention, and while I enjoyed playing the piano and loved music, I would have rather listened to music played by someone else. Instead, I practiced three to four hours daily, completed schoolwork with private tutors, and filled the rest of my days with piano classes or more schoolwork.

During my 16th year, a harsh winter fell upon Europe. The toll of years on the road finally hit me, and I fell ill. For the first time in my life, I remained at home for months. During this period, I drastically cut the amount of time I spent practicing. Instead, I worked to perfect the music I loved to play: Chopin, Bach, Mozart, and Liszt.

One day, an invitation came to the house. The note was from the local music school. The polite headmaster wondered if I would be kind enough to perform at their annual celebration. The school hoped to present a small recital with their star students and a few special guests to raise funds. My parents suggested I participate in the event, and I gladly agreed.

Sadly, during this cold winter, mother and father also became unwell. They seemed to have gotten much older, often lying in bed for most of the day.

On the evening of the recital, they remained behind. The house felt different. I found myself alone in front of the large mirror in my bedroom. I realized I had become a woman, no longer the child who had traveled Europe, delighting music fans with my prowess. I had learned my appearance was paramount to my success, so I took the opportunity to prepare. I selected a beautifully tailored red silk velvet dress and borrowed a little blush. I remembered the Italian tailor reluctantly adding the button-down sleeves to the design so as not to interfere with my playing. It looked wonderful and fit me perfectly. I put on my coat and walked the few blocks to the school.

The music school was filled with young musicians, and though I could hear most students struggling with basic pieces, their voices were full of joy and playfulness. It was something I had rarely experienced.

In the hall, a plump lady welcomed me.

I introduced myself and was led backstage, where I sat alone.

I was waiting for them to call me when a young man approached me and sat right across from me. The handsome, dark-haired, and tall young man introduced himself with the sweet innocence of a proper gentleman. "My name is Klaus Friedrich Hermann."

Dear Clara, the life which had, up to this point, been filled with music, suddenly grew into the deepest of silence; a silence in which my heart rejoiced while my soul lost itself in Klaus's eyes. Though frozen, my body trembled slightly.

"Hannah? What will you play tonight?" He asked me.

But, while I could see him, saw his lips move, and understood his question, I could not respond.

"Are you okay?" He asked as he laid his hand on mine. Upon his touch, the air in my lungs returned.

I smiled. It was the moment my first life came to an end. "I am sorry, Sir. I was going to perform a piece by Mozart but sensing such joy in the voices of the children, I will play Franz Liszt. 'Les Jeux d'Eaux à la Villa d'Este' I told him.

He smiled. To my great chagrin, Klaus disappeared, claiming he needed to return to some tasks.

On stage, a few minutes later, and to the delight of the crowd, I played the lively piece by Liszt. I poured my heart into the arpeggios and the amazing texture. The audience was spellbound to hear such a gorgeous composition. The generous applause warmed my heart.

On their feet, the crowd invited me to play another piece. I stood and walked to the edge of the stage.

"The previous piece was dedicated to all the young musicians whose joy touched me so deeply. However, I dedicate this piece to the young gentleman who kindly welcomed me."

I returned to the piano and performed one of my favorite pieces, Chopin, Nocturne, Op. 9 No.2 in E-Flat Major. I closed my eyes, breathed deeply, and played. I loved the tenderness of the melody.

Lost in the darkness of my mind, Klaus Friedrich Hermann's kind and smiling face appeared. I breathed in once more and looked down at the keys. Chopin's understated and haunting cadenza; the four simple notes repeating over and over created such a beautiful effect in closing the Nocturne.

Within a year, we were married. I left my parents forever. I often wondered if they had ever loved me or if it was the little monkey performing on the European stages, they so cherished.

Klaus was a wonderful, kind, and generous man who adored me. His family, who owned large plots of land on which farms produced a vast amount of food, warmly embraced me. The elder Hermann had recently built a small tool factory, and at the time, Klaus managed it.

At eighteen, I felt complete, one in mind and spirit. We spent four delightful years there. However, America, and the idea of a new life, were pulling us away from the places we had known all our lives.

My dear Clara, please remember the gifts we receive are often the ones we tend to ignore. Our life was wonderful in Germany, but nonetheless, we decided to leave it behind for a dream.

Klaus had done well with work. He had been able to save what we felt was a decent amount of money for our journey to America. His kind parents, though sad to see us leave (for they loved Klaus dearly), also helped us. Through the German Bank M. M. Warburg & Co, they transferred a large sum of money for us to settle in New York City.

In early October 1928, after Klaus' brother took over the factory, we left for New York on a transatlantic. Secretly, we were both a little nervous.

Within a couple of months of our arrival, our excitement for our new life in America had vanished. We spoke very little English and knew no one besides a quiet and unfriendly German family.

Our flat, while small compared to the one we had left, was on the lower West Side, on Duane Street, right across from a park.

Luckily, I started to teach piano lessons to a few children of German immigrants in the neighborhood. It was a little income while Klaus went to look for steady employment.

Joy returned momentarily when we realized I was pregnant. Our first winter away from home was a challenge, but Klaus and I managed well because we had each other. Truly, his mere presence filled me with joy.

As spring 1929 arrived, we welcomed Franz Max Hermann, an adorable little boy with the biggest and sweetest smile you have ever seen.

Over the next few months, however, the charming young man I had married became secretive and absent. I initially attributed the change to the difficulties he had finding and keeping work. I tried to ignore it and make our home a happy place.

It was a clear and beautiful evening on Tuesday, October 29, 1929. Franz and I had just returned from a walk when I heard a knock. I opened the door to see a young police officer who, upon looking at me, instantly burst into tears. I led the policeman, who was unable to speak, to the kitchen table, where he sat for a while, inconsolable. Perplexed, I served him a glass of sherry in hopes of calming him down.

"I am so sorry," the young officer kept repeating. Finally, between tears, he informed me that while on duty on Wall Street, he had found Mr. Hermann, my husband, dead on the pavement.

"Mr. Hermann had jumped to his death from the Bankers Trust Company Building at 14 Wall Street," he finally announced.

Searching for an identity, the policeman had discovered a letter addressed to me. The sight of my husband's body crushed on the pavement still horrified the poor man.

"I am so sorry, Mrs. Hermann. I had to come deliver this letter myself," the young policeman said as he stood to leave.

In a daze, I returned to Franz, the calm and quiet baby who strangely, was hysterical. Upon putting Franz to sleep, the unbearable reality finally hit me. The life I believed was forever mine had been taken away.

No words could convey the devastation his suicide had inflicted upon me. I was 23, and Franz Max was seven months old. I was far away from my home, alone, in the city we had joyfully embraced, but which sadly was now crumbling.

A few days later, I learned Klaus had begun to invest our money in the stock market. I heckled with the bank. Our savings were gone. I looked for the office of the Warburg Bank, where funds had supposedly been transferred for us. But, without any of the necessary documents, it was hopeless. He had lost it all.

Clara paused, tears swelling in her eyes. She had never known any of this. Reaching for her cell phone, she immediately realized Henry would be fast asleep. It was 2 a.m. in Paris.

The sun was setting over the Hudson River. A cool breeze gently rocked the trees.

Clara turned to look at the house.

"You were right, Hannah. This place is so peaceful," Clara murmured to herself. She continued to read the letter.

In the darkness of our flat, I reached for the letter the policeman had brought. Tears streaming down my face, my hands trembling. It informed me all was gone, My love, my companion, my friend, my husband, our money. All hope had suddenly vanished. Over the next few weeks, the collectors came to call. The landlord soon followed. Our debt was enormous, but so was everyone else's, and with no recourse, the lenders gave up. I had ransacked the apartment in search of money Klaus may have hidden or forgotten. Instead, I discovered his journal. It retraced my husband's slow descent into the abyss of despair and shame brought on by his unforgivable failure.

History offers lessons we all tend to ignore, so in the hope of restoring my husband's honor, I leave you these boxes of documents, all pertinent to my short and enchanted life with the man I so deeply loved.

My Dear Clara, we soon left the Lower West Side and moved in with your family in Brooklyn. Over the next few months, your mother and I became like sisters. Though she was much younger than I, she loved to help with Franz. By then, the misery inflicted on the country during that fateful October week had grown into a horrendous depression. But your family generously helped me.

Your grandfather called on me one day to sit with him in the living room. I followed him. We sat across from each other. He looked at me kindly and said, "We ought to discuss the future, Hannah."

As he spoke, a man entered the room. He introduced himself as Peter Francis Wilkins.

Your grandfather explained that Mr. Wilkins was a good man with a farm in upstate New York. But Mr. Wilkins was too busy with the farm and too shy to meet a woman with whom he could share his life. Mr. Wilkins was looking for a wife. He was a quiet German descendant whose mother had married an American. Wilkins was not a handsome man, but neither was he ugly.

Time stopped.

The piano music of Chopin suddenly filled me with an uncontrollable force. Suffocating inside, I closed my eyes.

I was transported on stage playing Chopin's Nocturne No.2 in E flat major, Opus 9, for the young man I had just met. The music I hadn't played in years was so beautiful, delicate, rich, and enchanting.

Goodbye, Klaus Friedrich Hermann. I will forever love you, but the life we cherished together, you took away."

The last notes of Chopin's beautiful nocturne played in my head, tearing me apart.

In an instant, the second chapter of my young life came to an end. I opened my eyes and said, "Bitte verzeih mir" (Please forgive me). Mr. Wilkins responded kindly.

The third life I lived was filled with emptiness.

Peter Wilkins was a kind man who had never felt passion. So, with little to live for, he passed through life a gentle soul whose only burden was to make it to another day. He was a good husband and kind father to Franz.

I, in exchange, was the good wife he desired.

At first, we grew to appreciate each other's qualities. The monotonous life we shared lasted longer than my two previous ones. The first two were full of the delicate beauty we humans are capable of.

After my son, Franz, passing at the young age of 21, these delicate feelings changed into the quiet acceptance of our tremendous differences.

My dear Clara, I hope you will forgive the burden I leave upon you with these old stories. It surely must come as an unwanted surprise, but I feel it necessary to share who I was with my only remaining family member.

I leave you now. I hope you will find it in your heart to forgive me for the request I place upon you. Please look through the documents I leave behind, for they are the testament of the lives I experienced. Were you to hold on to the house, may it be a haven you cherish as much as I did.

Sincerely yours,
Hannah

Clara decided to stay at the house. She found a room facing the river and made a bed in which she fell asleep instantly. She dreamt of Klaus Friedrich Hermann standing on the ledge of a window, 28 floors above street level. The dream had been so vivid that she woke, startled by fear and the sensation of falling. She had left her bed, made coffee, and opened one of the boxes full of documents in the living room.

The next day, the movers came and went. They carted off the furniture she disliked and emptied most of the garage. She used the car to drive to various donation centers to dispose of Hannah's clothes.

Clara extended her stay. The house was now almost empty except for the bed she used, the dining room table, and the many boxes of photos and mementos she had decided to keep before trashing them forever. A few days later, Clara returned to the city and called Jonathan. He picked up instantly.

"Hello Jonathan, how are you?" She said, before he could answer. "I am picking up Henry at the airport this afternoon. We are considering keeping the house, but I want him to see it before making a final decision."

The lawyer was happy to hear the news.

Within days, Clara and Henry had made up their minds.

The Frenchman loved the house. He enjoyed being in America. "C'est une excellente retraite," he announced.

She agreed. It was, indeed, a perfect retreat.

He returned to Paris while she stayed behind.

She wanted to go through the legal transfer of the property.

Hannah had left enough money to cover all the taxes related to the inheritance. The house would now be hers, plus the mysterious properties in Germany, which she would have to discover when back in Europe.

Jonathan refused to be paid for any of his services but insisted they meet for dinner later. "We can celebrate then," he gently said.

They met in Greenwich Village at a fancy but quiet restaurant.

Jonathan seemed excited.

The two of them had enjoyed getting to know each other. They discussed Hannah's letter at length. Jonathan had known very little of Hannah's life. Once again, he became emotional. To hear the trauma she had experienced touched him.

The dinner was wonderful, the wine delicious, and Jonathan was pleasant and fun to socialize with.

"We expect to see you in Paris soon," she reminded him.

In a formal manner, Jonathan ordered Champagne and announced he had to speak to her about a serious matter.

The Bottle of Dom Perignon arrived.

Jonathan waited for the glasses to be filled.

"Before her passing, Hannah had transferred special powers of attorney over a trust fund I had helped her create. Because she was concerned about the possibility that her cousin's daughter could be an unworthy beneficiary, she had requested I get to know you a little bit before transferring the trust over to you as a beneficiary. Hannah felt your mother's family had given her a home when she needed it and she never questioned the house should be yours. She was, however, unsure about the trust and requested I be the judge. Had you been an unworthy beneficiary, the funds would be transferred to a charity of my choosing." He paused.

Clara looked at him inquisitively, unsure what he was talking about. "I have decided you are a worthy beneficiary of the funds, Clara."

She smiled and reached out to hug him. Little did she know then that the trust was worth over two million dollars.

"You see," he continued, "the M.M. Warburg Bank had received the transfer from Germany for Hannah and Klaus, but due to some clerical error, it was not recorded until December 1929. By then, the great depression had overtaken America. A World War followed it. Hannah had disappeared. She was now Mrs. Wilkins. It was difficult for the bank to find her.

"In 1977, however, Hannah was contacted by the bank. A manager informed her that the funds had been available since the late 20s. The money had been placed into an account for Mr. and Mrs. Klaus Friedrich Hermann. After extensive research, the pleasant woman on the phone explained that the bank had found her. The banker informed her that the funds, which had grown substantially, were now available. A few months before Mr. Wilkins' death, Hannah traveled to New York City. At the bank, she presented all the necessary documents. She had kept her old passport as well as Klaus', their original marriage certificate, and his death certificate. Most of these documents were the ones you have seen. Hannah had never told Mr. Wilkins of the news. The poor man was on his death bed, suffering from advanced lung cancer. Somehow, from another life, Klaus had redeemed himself, but for Hannah, it was too late." Once again,

Clara had tears in her eyes.

My Dear Hannah... She thought, gratefully.

Closing her eyes, she saw the picture in Hannah's original passport; the beautiful young woman she had been. Chopin Nocturne, Op. 9 No.2 in E-Flat Major, played in her mind. She leaned on Jonathan and sobbed uncontrollably.

In late July, after five weeks in America, Clara returned to Paris. She traveled with two extra suitcases. Each contained the letters, journals, and newspaper clippings that Hannah had collected. She had spent an extensive amount of time reviewing each and every one of the papers and was so deeply touched that it had been impossible for her to part with them.

Clara arrived at Charles De Gaulle Airport on a grey morning. She was happy to see Henry, whom she had missed dearly. Their apartment in the Bastille district was full of flowers. Within a few days, her life in Paris returned to normal.

While away, she had received a call from the school, asking her to review some documents in need of her signature. On the day Clara went to school, she ran into Marc Blanc.

Marc was the history teacher. The two always had a friendly relationship. Over coffee, she recounted her adventures in America, minus the trust fund, and shared the story of Klaus Friedrich Hermann's demise.

"What a story," the Frenchman said. "You must write a book, Clara," Marc said in excitement. "This story would make a fascinating tale of the folly of society and the casino we call the stock market. Please call my friend, Adrien. America's banking history and the 1929 Crash are his specialties."

For Clara, the last few weeks had been such a roller coaster of emotions that she had begun to feel quite overwhelmed. She jotted down the telephone number of Marc's friend, Dr. Adrien Denuit.

Clara left her colleague and returned to the main office to sign the papers as requested. Clara had considered visiting the property she had inherited from Hannah in Germany before the start of school. She called Henry, who advised her to travel to Hamburg as soon as possible.

The next morning, Clara boarded a train from Gare du Nord. She pushed a few keys on her phone, and the music played—Chopin Nocturne,

Op. 9 No.2 in E-Flat Major.

Clara could not stop listening to the marvelous piano of Elisabeth Leonskaja. Her version touched her more than others. The music seemed to comfort her, to remind her of Hannah.

She was waiting for the train to depart for Hamburg when her phone rang.

"Allo, it's Adrien," a man's voice said.

Clara, a little confused, remained quiet long enough for the caller to continue.

"Je suis Dr. Denuit, Marc's friend." The voice on the other end announced.

She instantly remembered Marc had recommended she spoke to "Adrien," his friend.

Clara thanked Dr. Denuit for reaching out. She hated when people held long phone conversations in public spaces. But the train was almost empty, except for one other traveler who sat at the other end of the passenger coach.

Clara decided it would be fine to talk, satisfied that she would not be disturbing anyone.

At Adrien's request, Clara shared Hannah's incredible story. "I see," said the professor in a slow and considerate tone. "Le' Crash '…'" The polite professor said, "was caused by greedy New York bankers. Here in Europe, we associate the 'Wild West' with images of cowboys on horses riding into a colorful sunset, but New York City was the *real* Wild West. Thugs, disguised as honorable men, pillaged the country. The Crash was the end of an unsustainable dream—a dream created by the wealthy elite to benefit the wealthy elite. Three million Americans had invested in the stock market. Bell boys and shoe shiners played the stock on the pennies they earned."

Clara leaned back into her chair. She had never thought of bankers as thugs pillaging the country.

"Clara, you see, in the early '20s, the greedy bankers noticed that Americans had trusted the Market enough to place some of their savings into Liberty Bonds. These bonds had been issued to finance the first World

215

War. You have heard of the Liberty Bonds?"

"Yes, I have," she answered.

"A gentleman called Charles E. Mitchell of the National Citibank became one of the architects of this incredible scheme. He and a cohort of wealthy New York Bankers, through their control of the Newspapers, created a new idyllic image; investing in stocks was safe. Backed by huge financial entities, brokerage firms opened all over the country.

"Mitchell alone, through his various branches, sold millions of shares, totaling $650 million in value. The Crash of 1929 would completely wipe away the value of these shares."

"You mean to say the banks created this illusion of safety and marketed it to the masses?" Asked Clara.

"Exactly. The problems were, these sales used "call loans", which soon became how most investors purchased their stocks. A "call loan" allows you to put down only a small part of the total cost. However, the broker can call the loan anytime, hence the 'call' part. Upon the broker 'calling' the loan, the buyer must immediately pay back the entire loan. In 1925, the Dow Jones Industrial was at around 160. By 1929 it was a little below 400. Americans had bought into the dream and had begun purchasing stock.

"As it always does, the Market went up and down, but most stocks rose rapidly during this period. Brokers popped up everywhere. Clara, you could buy $1,000.00 worth of stock by putting down just 100 dollars— 10%. Of course, this number varied—usually between 10 and 30% —but 10% was common."

"Let me go through some quick but basic math. Let's assume you invest $1,000 in stock. Your purchase was made through a call loan, and you only offered $100 for the entire purchase. Now the value of the stock you purchased goes up just three percent in a week. Your profit would be $30. But since you have only put down $100 when, upon selling this stock, the broker would get his money back, plus a nominal fee. Your profit from this transaction would be close to 30% in a week. It is a very good return— an *excellent* return, in fact. In the 1920s, stocks' value rose drastically, and the stock market appeared to be a good bet. America was in a frenzy. Everyone played in the Market. I use the word 'play' to underline the reality of the time. It was a casino."

The train moved and soon the city faded away.

"In September 1929," Adrien continued, "the Market showed signs of strain and, at times, became extremely volatile. Thankfully, it stabilized, and everyone breathed a sigh of relief. Remember, an entire nation had poured what little it owned into the purchase of stocks and securities. Then a momentous event took place. On Wednesday, October 23, 1929, millions of shares were sold in the last hour of trading.

"The wealthiest people in the world, the 'elite,' and the New York City bankers could no longer withdraw their vast investments little by little. They wanted out, all at once. They couldn't care less about the results." Adrien paused.

Clara had been listening attentively. She imagined Klaus, the poor German immigrant, unable to find work, deceived into investing all their savings. It did seem to be a sure bet.

The Frenchman continued, "This tactical move of selling at the last hour, and in such an enormous quantity, could only come from the biggest investors. These wealthy investors owned the largest number of shares and controlled access to the exchange, allowing them to coordinate the enormous sales they placed. The goal was to dump their stocks in one sweep move.

"The next morning, the sense of panic and insecurity regarding the Market destroyed the hopes of millions. Most Americans, trying to save themselves, sold blindly. It was Thursday, October 24, 1929, when the Market crashed. Sadly, "Black Thursday," as it became known, was only the first phase of the Great Crash. Four hundred policemen were sent to Wall Street to provide safety. In the offices of J.P.Morgan, a group of bankers devised a plan to purchase large quantities of stock in the hope of calming the Market. These ostensible heroes committed $250 million to save the Market. It worked; at least initially. Over the next few days, the Market calmed itself a bit."

Adrien Denuit continued his brief history of the 1929 Crash and why it would ruin America and the world. On Monday, October 28, anxious brokers started to call in their loans. These brokers were not looking for the 10% or 30% the customers had offered to purchase their stock. They wanted the entire value of the loan to be paid back immediately.

When the brokers called in their loans, thousands and thousands of people started selling blindly. On Monday, October 28, 1929, the Market fell uncontrollably, losing 13% of its value in one day. The next morning, 'Black Tuesday,' all hell broke loose, and another huge sell-off occurred. The Market lost another 11%. The Stock Market had now lost 40% of its value since early September. It was now official. The Market had crashed.

Clara timidly asked, "But what would lead someone to throw themselves out of a 28th-floor window?" Clara could remember the vivid dream that woke her up in Hudson and a chill ran down her spine.

"Desperation, Clara. Desperation. Let's assume Hannah's husband had saved $3,000 and out of pure folly, had invested everything. A broker would welcome this kind of deposit and most likely grant Klaus permission to purchase up to $30,000.00 worth of stock. Now, if the stock goes up 3%, upon selling it, Mr. Hermann's earnings would be around $900.00, minus broker fees and possibly taxes. An excellent return. Clara, let me read you this part of a report I have before me: *"Based on (Tax) returns filed, the average net income reported for 1920 was $3,269.40..."* This information comes from the Department of Revenue and the US Internal Revenue Service. In the 1920s, $100 was the equivalent of approximately $1,700 based on inflation not on purchasing power which was far greater, so his profit would have equaled approximately $15,000.00 today."

Clara had pulled out a small notebook she kept with her and started to take notes.

Between the high on September 3, 1929, and Tuesday, October 29, the stock lost 40%. The $30,000.00 Mr. Hermann had borrowed had a value of around $18,000.00. When his broker calls the loan Hermann would have been short $12,000 plus fees. Clara, this sum is approximately $144,000.00 in today's value, and it was to be repaid immediately. Klaus Hermann woke up to the harsh reality that not only had he lost all his money, but worse yet, he was ruined."

A heavy silence set in. Clara looked at the empty car and the landscape passing by at high speed.

"So, what happened next?" Asked Clara.

"The cowboys with the biggest guns kept on riding, breaking into another bank and getting away with it," said Adrien.

"What do you mean?"

"Insider trading was normal practice. Think about this; Richard Whitney, the President of the New York Stock Exchange, was also the lead broker for JP Morgan & Co. How convenient? The Market was a big gambling casino for the richest Americans, mostly New Yorkers, but one they had rigged with professional bankers who controlled it, so it turned out that it became their piggy bank."

Clara, overwhelmed and feeling a little car sick, wondered if they could continue this conversation later. The kind Dr. Denuit agreed, and they ended the call.

Clara had read Klaus Friedrich Hermann's suicide letter.

"All is lost," he had stated. Clara now had a clear picture of events. She stood, walked away from her seat, and entered the restaurant car. The car was warm and comfortable.

She walked to the bar and ordered coffee, paid, and sat by the window. Clara called Henry. She loved their ability to chat for hours. He was a great listener, and they could debate any subject. She told him that Marc Blanc had suggested she write a book recounting Hannah's story.

Henry instantly loved the idea and proposed that the two stop everything, move to upstate New York, and give Hannah her fourth life.

She laughed at the idea. "Maybe?" She said. "Henry, maybe we should finish this school year, settle everything and do it."

Henry loved the idea because he had been thinking of writing a new book himself. "This would be the perfect opportunity. Frankly, I am sick of politics."

She arrived in Hamburg and grabbed a taxi to her hotel. It was six in the evening when her cell phone rang. It was Dr. Denuit. She had unsuccessfully tried to reach him.

"I am in Goury, on my balcony overlooking the Normandy coast with a glass of wine and a full bottle to refill my glass as needed. I would be happy to answer any question," the kind Frenchman announced.

Clara smiled. She could picture the magnificent coast of Normandy and the town she had once visited. "Well, I wonder what happened once the Market crashed. Hannah seemed so desperate that she chose to marry someone out of pure convenience."

"Life is controlled by the Yin and the Yang, the Light and the Dark, the balance between two opposites," he said philosophically. "Simply put, after a period of expansion comes a period of contraction. People who were owners and purchased on credit soon became debtors. Businesses that needed cash loans to run their day-to-day operation saw an end to credit, regardless of how good their credit may have been. The banks stopped lending. I am sure you know the movie *It's a Wonderful Life*. Well, this is what happened next. Every customer with any savings in a banking establishment, concerned about the possibility that the bank could fail, wisely withdrew their money *en masse*. When thousands of people do the same, it is called a 'run on a bank.' By 1931, over 2,000 banks had failed, and their customers' savings disappeared with these banks."

Hannah, the child prodigy, found herself far from home, penniless and at the mercy of well-meaning people who were themselves under the tremendous stress the Great Depression slowly inflicted on the economy and on the entire country.

Clara heard the glass being refilled. She could picture the kind Dr. Denuit in Goury, looking over the Normandy coast.

"Clara, the 1929 Crash happened in part because an illusion had been created—a dream of riches based on lies. The 'elite' or the people we call today, the '1%' created these lies. I call them the kings. The financial commitment these wealthy bankers had made into this horrible deception was enormous. Sadly, everyone was guilty—the elite for having created this scheme, the brokers for knowingly selling a false reality, and the Americans who foolishly trusted these devils."

She heard him shuffle papers.

"I have another call I must take. Let me call you back in a minute," said the Frenchman.

Clara, like most Americans, knew that the 1929 Crash brought on dark days. She was aware people had jumped to their deaths. Her phone beeped, announcing a new text. It was from Dr. Denuit who had forwarded a couple of images. They appeared to be from a book. It stated: *Credit from the banks to fuel the stock boom was supplemented by credit from the big corporations. Call loans to brokers in 1929 made by some leading corporations were as follows:*

Clara could not believe the amount of money involved: Bethlehem Steel Corporation, owned by Charles Schwab, had a little over $157 million in call loans. Morgan, of J.P. Morgan, through his various corporations, had approximately $200 million, Rockefeller had $100 Million, The Chrysler Corporation and Walter P. Chrysler over $60 million. In 1929, these were huge numbers, and in no way could have been investments approved by an underling. The commitments made to these "Call Loans" had to be approved at the highest levels.

She could remember Adrien saying that $100 equaled $1,700 in purchasing power. Clara's phone rang.

"It's Adrien," Dr. Denuit announced. "Did you get my text?"

Clara confirmed and expressed her surprise.

He explained that the pictures were from a book by Ferdinand Lundberg, who wrote a detailed account of the wealthiest families. Lundberg stated, *"The crisis of 1929-1933 America's sixty richest families were strengthened in relation to the hordes of citizens reduced to beggary."*

America was wounded, Denuit explained, but what followed became unsustainable. Businesses soon closed and unemployment spread to millions. Most Americans who had purchased on credit soon found themselves unable to repay their debts. This led to countless foreclosures, he explained.

"In my view, however, while the Crash of the Stock Market was the lightning rod, the Federal Reserve Bank failed to implement the necessary steps to battle the recession and stop it from growing into a prolonged event. On November 8, 2002, Ben Bernanke, who served two terms as Chairman of The Federal Reserve Bank stated the following: *"Regarding the Great Depression, ... we did it. We're very sorry ... We won't do it again."*

"The man admitted the Federal Reserve Bank, which was created to protect the infrastructure of the American financial system, had not only failed, but it was the very cause of the crisis."

"Hold on," interrupted Clara. "... the Great Depression was not the result of the '29 Crash? I am confused. What are you saying, Adrien?" Clara knew Adrien had a deep and sincere love for history, but being a Frenchman, his real passion was for the enjoyment of life; moments such as the one he was experiencing right now; A glass of wine on a patio overlooking a sunset on the Normandy Coast. There was no need to rush him.

The kind professor continued. "Clara, most Americans do not know it, but the Federal Reserve System is a private entity, wholly independent of the government."

Clara suddenly felt a little stupid. Though she considered herself educated, she did not know this.

"The current banking system, the Federal Reserve, is the fourth version of a system that the international financiers have incessantly fought to implement and inflict upon Americans. Their previous attempt, the Second Bank of the United States, was crushed by President Andrew Jackson, in a bitter battle he managed to win."

"Panics were good business, you see, especially when insider trading was lawful and common practice. Charles Lindbergh, a congressman in the early 1900s, stated the following: *'Under the Federal Reserve Act, panics are scientifically created; the present panic is the first scientifically created one, worked out as we figure a mathematical problem.'* Then, there is the question of the National Debt. The purpose of the Central Bank, as it is stated on their website, is as follows: *"It was created by the Congress to provide the nation with a safer, more flexible, and more stable monetary and financial system."*

Clara was writing furiously; Charles Lindbergh, Federal Reserve, financial panics...

"The Federal Reserve opened its door in November of 1914," said Adrien Denuit, "four months after the start of World War I. Listen to me carefully now. The War lasted four years, 1914-1918. Up until that time, annual federal expenses totaled about $750 Million. Four years later, yearly federal expenses were running at around $18.5 billion a year—an increase of enormous proportions. Approximately 70% of the cost of the War had been financed by debt which became the national debt and let me be very clear—much of this enormous debt the American taxpayers were responsible for was payable, with interest, to the Federal Reserve."

Adrien paused, and Clara could hear him chat with someone. He returned and announced it was time for dinner. "Could we speak later?" He politely asked.

"You have been most helpful, Adrien. Merci."

How could this be true? She opened her laptop and typed. Online, she found the work of Milton Friedman, an American economist who received the 1976 Nobel Memorial Prize in Economic Sciences. His report was bleak:

The recession was an ordinary business cycle. We had repeated recessions over hundreds of years, but what converted [this one] into a major depression was bad monetary policy. The Federal Reserve System had been established to prevent what happened. It was set up to avoid a situation in which you would have to close down banks, precipitating a banking crisis. And yet, under the Federal Reserve System, you had the worst banking crisis in the history of the United States."

Clara continued her search. The web was full of venomous criticism of the Federal Reserve:

"The Federal Reserve is neither Federal nor has Reserve...."

Clara knew information found on the web always needed to be filtered. She copied and pasted the information she found worthwhile so as to not forget its source.

Congressman Louis McFadden, who served from 1915 to 1935 as the Chairman of the House Banking and Currency Committee, commented:

"It [the depression] was not accidental. It was a carefully contrived occurrence... The international bankers sought to bring about a condition of despair here so that they might emerge as the rulers of us all."

Her shock at this incomprehensible truth grew at every search result. The Federal Reserve Bank a private, *for-profit* entity?

She discovered a site from the Mises Institute. The site appeared legitimate and hosted a series of articles titled: *"The Case Against the Fed."*

After clicking on the link, Clara found herself on what seemed a trustworthy site. It had an option to listen to the book they featured via their Audiobook option. She dug for her headphones, plugged them into her computer, and clicked 'play.'

Clara sat back, relaxed, and listened to the soft, feminine voice.

The content was clear and to the point. It discussed, point by point, the history of money and the birth of the Central Bank of the United States, as well as the monopoly it had on the entire banking system.

She looked at the landscape outside the hotel window. Clara discovered a PDF download of *America's 60 Families* by Ferdinand Lundberg, a book Adrien had mentioned. It was written around 1937. She downloaded it and read:

The United States is owned and dominated today by a hierarchy of its sixty richest families. These families are the living center of the modern industrial oligarchy which dominates the United States, functioning discreetly under a de Jure democratic form of government behind which a de facto government, absolutist and plutocratic in its lineaments, has gradually taken form since the Civil War. This is the de facto government of the United States - informal, invisible, shadowy. It is the government of money in a dollar democracy.

This is a powerful accusation, Clara thought. *Is this guy a nut?* She switched to her browser and Googled 'Ferdinand Lundberg.' Google, as always, delivered many pages. None seemed to imply Lundberg was a lunatic. She opened Wikipedia:

The Los Angeles Times described (Lundberg) as "witty, articulate, opinionated, marvelously well-read and not the least bit shy about telling us exactly what he thinks about America and the mess we've made of it." Lundberg was vocal in his contrarian viewpoints, describing the United States as an oligarchy, eviscerating prominent American families, including the Rockefellers and Hearsts, and denouncing the United States Constitution while calling for its replacement with a parliamentary system. Several of his dozen-or-so books on these topics were best-sellers.

This man did not sound like a nut, or, as they like to label vocal critics in America, a "conspiracy theorist."

Clara returned to the book, opened it to the period around 1929, on page 149. The chapter was called "The Politics of Finance Capital; 1920-1932." In the second paragraph, she found the following:

To such an extent was corruption interwoven with high government policies during the postwar years of Republican rapine (the violent seizure of someone's property)...The White House became, quite simply, a political dive.

Clara was stunned. Every word seemed a scathing critique of every president during that period. *'Amiable drunkard,' 'slob,'* and *'ignorant of common affairs'* were words Lundberg used to describe them.

The ruinous speculative boom that collapsed in 1929 was engineered, from first to last, by the wealthy families, and for their personal account. At every stage of the game, it was the richest, the most influential persons who were the prime movers in unloading inflated securities upon a deluded public. None of the truly rich came to grief, although some of their agents ... had to act as scapegoats.

Clara stopped, suddenly unable to continue. She remembered the New York City landscape in her nightmare. From the 28th Floor of the Bankers Trust Company Building, she, once again, could feel the still air and the sensation of falling. To think of the desperate German immigrant who had jumped to his death. She was disgusted.

A dark blue sky hung over Hamburg. She decided to go out for dinner. The information she had discovered was overwhelming and disturbing. Clara knew now she would tell Hannah's story, each part in its own context. The glorious beauty of the European music houses she had performed, her marriage to Klaus, the family she left behind, and the New York City she may have discovered at the time. But, above all, the injustice that led her husband to despair and had ruined her life, the crash. The misery of a loveless life that followed and the longing for the passion she had so often experienced.

The Hermann family had left Hannah a tremendous amount of land northwest of the city. Clara spent the next few days tending to all the legal paperwork needing her attention. Except for a quaint little house built by a brook, most of it was bare farmland. The house seemed to require work but had much potential. She met with a real estate agent, a jovial and slightly overweight man in his late thirties, who mentioned a developer he knew.

"He would most likely want to purchase your property," The young man proudly announced. He informed her the listing for her property would be posted immediately.

Clara called Henry and shared the details of the property. "I am still baffled by the events of the last few months and frankly, my head is spinning. There is a house on the land, which is very nice, but I do not see us attempting to restore it. I thought it would be nice to somehow give back."

Henry had remained quiet, but upon hearing this, said, "How about we give the house to a family of immigrants in need?"

She liked the idea and set things in motion.

Two weeks later, Clara and Henry returned to Hamburg to transfer the deed to the house to a Mr. & Mrs. Mustafa Benzema. The two entered a stuffy law office, where after some introduction, they sat around a table with the Benzemas.

Clara had met the family a few days before. Each had shared their story. Mustafa had been a doctor in Syria when the civil war broke out. Of their four children, two had been killed. The other two, ages six and eight, were running around the desk. Their tragedy led them to Germany, which welcomed them, but it had been extremely difficult.

Henry said in German; "Clara and I are delighted to be able to contribute to the welfare of your family. The house is yours to do as you please. Sell it, rent it. Whatever you feel may help you and your family settle comfortably." Henry paused and turned to look each in their eyes. He hoped to emphasize they were free. It was a gift without any strings attached. "We have opened a bank account with €10,000 to help you with the move."

Mustafa was fighting to hold back tears.

His wife, Fatima, had grabbed Clara's hand and held it tight, tears streaming down her face. The children, who had stopped running, leaned on the women. The social worker who had introduced Clara to Mustafa's family joined the group.

The lawyer handed Clara, the registered owner, one legal form after another. She separated from Fatima and started to sign each page, then passed it to Mustafa, who, after signing the page, returned it to the lawyer. The room was quiet until the final page was signed.

Mustafa held his wife, and they burst out in tears.

Clara turned to Henry and hugged him.

She returned to Hamburg a month later.

The land had sold, and though she could have completed the paperwork in Paris but decided to travel to sign the forms.

The Benzema family had settled nicely into the house. They had used some of the money to make upgrades on the house and purchase a car.

The children were now in a nice school, and Fatima had begun to make friends.

Mustafa welcomed her. He offered her some mint tea.

Clara sat at the kitchen table across from Mustafa, who was incredibly grateful. "I have to confess I am quite intrigued as to the reason why you have been so generous," he said.

"Hannah," she simply responded.

He wondered what kind of woman Hannah was and what had led Clara to donate so much.

"Hannah Rose Von Furstenberg," Clara said and shared Hannah's story. She spoke of her three lives.

"Her fourth life has given my family a *second* life. I'll pray for her soul. And yours, my dear Clara."

The children came running into the kitchen. They looked so happy.

Before leaving, she discretely left another check for €10,000 on the kitchen table. "From one immigrant to another."

CHAPTER 12

A MERCILESS WORLD

In the 1930s, in the Great Depression, the Federal Reserve, despite its mandate, was quite passive and, as a result, (the) financial crisis became very severe, lasted essentially from 1929 to 1933.
— Ben Bernanke - 14th Chair of the Federal Reserve.

I have ways of making money that you know nothing of.
— John D. Rockefeller.

ON THE ROAD TO SEATTLE, 1934

Wednesday 4 p.m., south of Seattle

Like ghosts in a merciless world, they approached the car uneasily, tentatively, their clothes in rags, their faces pale and dirty, their bodies gaunt. Three children stood next to the door of their car; fragile, absent; the palms of their tiny hands outstretched, hoping pity would win.

Marge turned off the engine. "Henry, I am going to feed these kids," she said.

He nodded. They were accustomed to the misery the Great Recession had brought on.

Marge was a photographer working for the Farm Security Administration.

Henry was an economist specializing in the farming industry.

Both had witnessed the enormous economic devastation and its human toll.

With a blanket and food in hand, Marge turned to the children. "This way."

Obediently, they followed her to the edge of the filling station. They sat in a semi-circle around the blanket. Each was handed an apple and a morsel of bread. Soon, a can of beans was opened and passed around.

The children, ravenous, devoured their food in silence. When the food was gone and another car pulled into the station, the kids, in a synchronized motion, stood and rushed toward the vehicle, hoping for another display of generosity.

Marge collected the remnants of the meal. Once behind the wheel of their car, her tears ran free. She turned to Henry and said, "What do you pray for when all is lost?"

Henry knew his wife needed to vent and remained quiet.

"You pray for a miracle, perhaps, knowing, deep in your heart, miracles are absent imposters in a reality far too harsh for fairy tales." Marge's hands tightened around the steering wheel. Her foot pushed on the accelerator.

Wednesday 4 p.m., north of Seattle

Pierre Finkler entered the Royal Bank Tower. He was accustomed to the ignorant who found his diminutive stature and odd appearance amusing. So, oblivious to the stares his entrance generated, Pierre marched on. They were "Ne'er-do-wells" in his mind, people who could not make anything of themselves and found relief laughing at others.

The bank manager, who had been expecting Pierre's arrival, stood outside his office, and waved upon seeing him. "Good afternoon, Mr. Finkler. It is a pleasure to see you."

"Greetings. This is my associate, Mr. Wasserman. He'll accompany me to the safe," Pierre said nonchalantly, pointing at the tall man who stood by his side and carried a heavy briefcase.

Sensing a slight degree of impatience in his customer's voice, the manager invited them to follow him at once. "This way, gentlemen."

The trio marched to an elevator where an armed guard stood by. Pierre, five feet and one inch, looked minuscule between Wasserman's six-foot and one-inch frame and the slightly shorter bank manager.

Within minutes, Pierre, whose birth name was Peter Levi Finkleman, stood alone inside the vault room, two floors below the Royal Bank of Canada lobby. Before him, his brown leather briefcase rested on the mahogany table.

Pierre straightened. This would be his last trip across the border to smuggle his treasure. He released the locks, lifted the cover, and gazed at its content.

The gold coins, stored in thick, burgundy fabric, were closest to him and to the left. The rare jewelry, in rigid shell boxes, was next. The gold bars filled the remaining space. Eight were stacked sideways and four laid across the top.

The chair rattled as Pierre stood. He unlocked the door to one of his four rented lockers and pulled the heavy door open. The locker was quite full already. The fourth locker was empty and would host the gold bars and jewelry. A few minutes later, he shut the door to the lockers.

This is it, thought Pierre, his task completed. *My gold is out of America and away from Roosevelt.*

By transporting his gold out of America and into Canada, Pierre Finkler had defied FDR's Presidential Order 6102, demanding all gold coins, gold bullion, and gold certificates be presented to the Federal Reserve Bank in exchange for their equivalent in currency.

"Screw the bastards," muttered the diminutive Pierre. "This is my gold, and no one will take it from me, especially not this idiot of a president." After checking to see he had all the keys to the lockers with him, he left the bank.

Wednesday 8 p.m., south of Seattle

Their car hummed along on the road north toward Seattle. They had left San Francisco a couple of days earlier on an assignment for the Farm Security Administration. She was to document the eight "Hoovervilles" around Seattle.

As the sun was setting on the magnificent landscape before them, Marge, a photographer by trade, wondered how much more misery she could handle to document.

Beside her, Henry, an economist, and a faculty member at the University of California, was staring into the distance. Though the FSA had hired him to work alongside his wife before, this time, he was just along for the ride.

"The kids were famished, and the little one had a cut, needing attention. How awful," she said.

"Black Tuesday happened five years ago, and America has yet to recover. Farmers have been hit especially hard. The parents of the kids we met were most likely penniless," Henry said.

The landscape before them was glorious. The Pacific Ocean, extending as far as the eye could see, was slowly turning gold as the sun came down in a cloudless sky.

Henry reached out and rested his hand on her shoulder. His wife was heartbroken to see such misery. The fact that it affected the children broke her heart.

"How can it be? FDR took office a few years ago, and nothing has changed," she said. "What a failure."

"Well, his 'New Deal' has merits, Marge, and in time it will help America, but the crisis was catastrophic, and changes will take time."

"Yet here we are, hired to document not one but eight Hoovervilles. How many shantytowns can there be? How many malnourished children, desperate mothers, and helpless fathers will we see? How many times will I have to hold back tears?"

Henry reached out a little further, his hand now resting at the base of her neck, which he gently massaged.

"Sometimes, I wonder if it is my duty to photograph these scenes. I had a wonderful life taking portraits in my cozy studio. My heart aches so much, Henry. I receive money to document people's misery," Marge said. "Do you remember the mother I photographed in Arkansas? The one staring at the road, with her two kids looking away?

"I do."

"Well, everyone wants to use this picture. It has been printed all over the world. I have gotten more checks for this photograph than any other. In the meantime, the poor woman, most likely, still lives in misery."

Henry turned toward her and said, "Your work is critical, Marge. Your photographs will exist for eternity. One day, someone will wonder what a Hooverville was. Your images are a testament to our times."

Wednesday 8 p.m., north of Seattle

Upon securing his treasure, Pierre drove to the Georgia Hotel. In one of its plush suites, he would kill the next few hours before returning to Seattle early the next day.

Wasserman stood by the door, useless until someone knocked. "Miss," he said politely, and opened the door wide.

"Come on in," Pierre said and waved for her to join him.

The young lady was petite, with pale green eyes and long flowing red hair.

"Wasserman, there is an envelope for you on the mantel. As always, thank you for your patience and professionalism."

Wasserman picked up the envelope, opened it, and smiled. Three 100-Dollar bills stared at him. "Thank you, Mr. Finkler. Do not hesitate to reach out anytime."

But Pierre, distracted by the young beauty before him, did not respond. The door closed softly.

"Sarah," the young woman said. She walked further into the room and began to undress. "My name is Sarah."

Hours later, Pierre, a light sleeper, paced around the room as the exhausted Sarah slept heavily. He had made six trips to transport his gold out of the country, traveling in the middle of the night and under protection. But this had been his last trip, and he was happy. Gold would undoubtedly rise in value, and the profit would be his.

The moonlight fell upon the beautiful and naked Sarah. Pierre approached the bed and slowly ran his hand along her entire body.

She shivered and opened her eyes. The little man wanted more. They always wanted more. She pulled him toward her.

Thursday 5 a.m., south of Seattle

Marge entered the motel room they had rented for the night with two cups of coffee and a couple of muffins.

Henry was exhausted. After breathing the stench from a cheap and dirty pillow for hours. He had finally thrown the stinky pillow on the floor and had soon fallen into a deep slumber.

Marge was ready to start her day. "Well, precious, I'll start loading the car. The light is beautiful this morning."

Henry forced himself to sit. Fifteen minutes later, he took the wheel while Marge read the map and directed him.

They soon arrived at the abandoned Skinner & Eddy Shipyard. Once thriving, the location currently served as one of the largest Hoovervilles around Seattle. A little more than a thousand people populated the location, each poorer than the next.

Marge sprang into action and quickly opened the legs of her wooden tripod. Next, she mounted the heavy Graflex 4×5 camera on it, and finally, she strapped the large leather bag holding the film holders, light meter, and black cloth over her shoulders and swiftly proceeded to capture the wide views of the quiet shantytown. The light was soft, the area quiet.

Henry stayed in the car, where he kept an eye on his wife from a distance. He knew all too well the pattern she would follow. First, the wide shots while the population of the makeshift town was asleep. She would then come closer, sit with the desperate mothers, and talk a while before capturing the dramatic photos that had made her famous.

At one point, he would join Marge to protect her against the aggressive and deranged men who sometimes inhabited these shantytowns.

There was a little wind, and the stench was nauseating. The two used their bandanas to cover their faces. While the scenes were tragic and hopeless, most of its inhabitants were kind and appreciative.

Everyone agreed that former President Hoover deserved to have his name attached to these shantytowns. Hoover had presided over a crisis during which a 607% rise in the unemployment rate, a 46% drop in industrial production, and a 60% fall in the prices of crops brought America to its knees. Ultimately, none of President Hoover's attempts at solving the economic crisis amounted to anything, and the Great Depression inflicted enormous misery. Soon, hundreds of shantytowns sprouted all over the country and were appropriately named Hoovervilles.

Thursday 5 a.m., north of Seattle

A thick layer of fog had fallen over the city, and Vancouver looked dreamy as Sarah and Pierre walked out of the Georgia Hotel.

She turned to the man beside her inquisitively.

Pierre looked into her pale green eyes, clueless as to what to say. "Bye, Sarah," he finally muttered.

Sarah paused. She knew Henry was a man with little compassion or willingness to inquire about the people around him. But Sarah had been generous with her body, and so had he with his money. She clenched her purse tightly, and they parted ways. Her two young children came to mind as the night replayed vividly. She narrowed her focus and looked away.

There would be food on the table tonight, she thought and hurried back home.

Pierre was distracted. From New York, three hours ahead, his broker had called to inform him that the market had risen sharply. Now, he pondered his next move; steel or oil? Which would provide the most return on his investment?

The grave and worrisome issue of the Levine family had also resurfaced. They had been the most prominent loan shark family in Brooklyn, and two of their oldest sons had been murdered in a back alley, supposedly by Italians. A turf war would ensue. He knew it and longed to be back in New York City.

Right before leaving, he had called Washington seeking news on the progress made to dispose of President Roosevelt. He had spoken softly and away from unfamiliar ears. The plot was slowly taking form, he was told, and hung up, cheerful.

Thursday 7 a.m., south Seattle

Thirty feet away, Marge spoke to a well-mannered Irishman. Makeshift suspenders held the pants that had once fit him.

The poor man must have lost at least thirty pounds, thought Henry.

Haggard and beaten, the man spoke in a low voice.

The man's wife, scrawny but dignified, held the youngest of their four children on her lap. Her movements were measured and deliberate as if she were attempting to save her energy.

From a distance, Henry could see the inside of their makeshift home.

Their shack was built of discarded planks and various odd pieces of old tarp. It lacked flooring, and in its furthest corner stood a pile of rags, which probably were their blankets. In the middle, the trunk which may have once carried their possessions, served as a table. On it stood a crucifix, a cruel remnant of a life long gone.

Henry came a little closer.

"This is where I worked. Right there," said the Irishman, pointing toward the docks. "I would direct a group of twenty hard-working men. Now we have nothing but misery. My children are little starving things, and my wife refuses to eat until their bellies are full." The powerless father lowered his grimy face as his right hand rested on his forehead. Fighting the tears real men refuse to accept, he walked away.

Marge reached into her pocket. "Sir," she said, and walked toward him.

The Irish man stopped in his track and turned.

"Please take this." Marge had emptied her pocket of the coins and small bank notes. Her heart trembled.

"Thank you, Ma'am."

Thursday 7 a.m., north of Seattle

Twenty miles away from Seattle and his mansion in the Fort Hill neighborhood, Pierre pulled over. The small town hosted a diner he liked. He ordered a coffee and used the telephone.

"Good morning, Jocelyn. I am thirty minutes away."

"I must leave soon, but I'll wait for you. Hurry up," his wife said.

"Baby, I assume you took all the jewelry out of the safe. I checked it last night, and it was empty."

"Sorry, Darling, I forgot to tell you. I got everything out of the country, and our gold is now safe."

"Ok," she said and quickly ended the call.

Pierre loved his gorgeous wife but was sick of Seattle. A New Yorker at heart, he had followed her to a new job as the editor of a local newspaper. Neither needed to work—they were very wealthy—but it made her feel good about herself. She was intelligent and beautiful, kind and generous. But he had grown to detest the white, suburban mentality and hated the local wasps with their five o'clock martini parties.

Thursday 9 a.m., Seattle

A woman's voice interrupted Henry from his reveries. He turned to see a tall, attractive woman with long flowing blonde hair, rushing down the path toward Marge.

"Jocelyn, over here."

The woman passed by Henry and reached Marge, who gave her a big hug.

Henry was introduced to Jocelyn and immediately charmed by the beautiful woman. After a bit of persuading, Jocelyn was able to recruit Henry to help her distribute food. Over the next hour, Jocelyn gave out an enormous amount of canned food and bread. She hugged every mother, and each one held her hand tightly as they parted.

"Bless you, Miss. Bless you," the women said with teary eyes.

Jocelyn ignored the display of appreciation, asking how else she could help. "Your children, are they okay?" During each interaction, if there was any issues, Jocelyn wrote it in her notebook.

Henry followed, astonished. Here was this woman who could have had the world in the palm of her hand; such was her beauty, kindness, and intelligence.

Yet, all she wanted to do was to help these desperate families.

"I am going to bring a doctor along next time. These poor children are in such poor health. Should I bring blankets and shoes? What do you think, Henry?"

"You are wonderful, Jocelyn. Anything you do will be much appreciated, though I agree a doctor would be especially beneficial."

Soon, her car was empty. They searched for Marge, who had disappeared further into the Hooverville.

"I'll see you tonight," Jocelyn said upon finding her. They hugged, and she left.

"We are staying with her tonight, Henry," Marge said.

Thursday 9 a.m., Seattle

The offices of Wilson & Markowitz were modest but efficient. The law firm had strong connections with the mayor's office and could, for the right amount of money of course, work out any deal its clients desired.

Pierre was curious about making a real estate investment. He believed Seattle had many prospects to offer.

"Mr. Finkler," said a gravelly voice.

Pierre turned to the man calling him and away from the gorgeous brunette managing the office.

"Markowitz, how are you?" Pierre said, extending a hand.

The two walked into a large conference room. Architectural drawings and maps covered the long, wooden table in its center.

"Well, Mr. Finkler."

"Pierre. Call me Pierre. No need for formalities."

Markowitz said, "The Skinner & Eddy Shipyard would be an excellent choice and a perfect location for your development. Sixty three-story buildings would host 180 families. Here are some financials for you to review." Markowitz slid over the fifteen-page document. "Would you excuse me? I must take a call."

"Of course."

The short, bold, and overweight Markowitz did not intend to take a call. Instead, he rushed to the bathroom—the sixth time so far that morning.

Too many trips to the bordello, Markowitz thought. *I'll have to see a doctor.*

Alone, Pierre reviewed the numbers. With 20% down to cover the land purchase and then pay all the cost of construction, he would be paid back within a year and own the property within three; it was a great deal, especially now, when every desperate worker would work for half the normal pay.

"So, what do you propose we do?" Pierre asked when Markowitz returned.

"Assuming you are ready to move forward, we will set things in motion. First, we must evict the thousand or so tenants of the Hooverville. It should be easy."

"Where will they go?" Asked Pierre.

Markowitz, curious, paused, sat back in his chair, and said, "Pierre, you are my client. You want the land. I get you the land. Nothing else matters. Correct?"

Pierre thought of Jocelyn, who had been so concerned with the people at the Skinner & Eddy. Were they to be evicted, it would break her heart. She would certainly show him contempt if she knew he was responsible.

"Great. Let's move quickly. But we may have to create an anonymous company to disguise my ownership." Pierre stood. "Thanks, Markowitz. Keep me posted."

Thursday 8 p.m., Seattle

Once the Skinner & Eddy Hooverville was fully documented, Marge and Henry drove east a few miles to visit the area's four other shantytowns: Airport Way, Washington Ironworks, Massachusetts St., and the Louisville Hooverville.

The day weighed on them, and a somber mood had taken over. Of the four Hoovervilles, Washington Ironworks had been the most dreadful. A mysterious illness afflicted many children. Henry attributed it to high metal levels in the water but was unsure. A test would be necessary.

Henry shut the trunk of the Ford. Their long day was over. The next three Hoovervilles, further north, would be documented the following day. Interbay, the furthest north, then Lighthouse Broom Co., and finally the Waterfront Park Hoovervilles.

Twenty minutes later, they reached Jocelyn's house in the plush Fort Hill neighborhood. Jocelyn burst out of the front door to greet them as they pulled into the immaculate driveway.

A short little man followed. Round in the middle, and balding, the man appeared to limp slightly.

"This is Pierre," Jocelyn said, reaching out for her diminutive husband.

Marge and Henry waved inquisitively. "Really?" Murmured Henry in disbelief.

"Come in, come in," said Jocelyn excitedly.

They entered the grand hallway in shock at the immensity of the place. From the outside, the house looked of decent size. The minute you walked in, its impressive marble entrance, grand stairway, and the long hallway behind it informed the visitors the house was massive. After spending the day in ghettoes, Marge and Henry looked at their surroundings in disbelief.

They were led to a quaint living room for aperitifs.

Staring at the two humans before him, Henry tried to comprehend the union. Sitting in the large chair before him, Pierre seemed like a child lost within the enormous piece of furniture. But the real shock happened upon seeing Jocelyn. The human being God had created as a model of perfection, within and without, in flesh and spirit. She had changed into a blue tunic and loose-fitted beige linen pants. She looked stunning.

Henry was so distracted by the scene before him that he did not hear the little man speak.

A sharp elbow nudged him, as Marge attempted to snap him out of his daze.

"Sorry," he said.

"I was asking, what do you do for work, Henry?" Repeated Pierre, oblivious at his distracted guest.

"I am an economist," Henry said and described his work, both as an academic and a researcher.

A discussion ensued about the possible forecast in real estate.

Jocelyn stood and invited Marge to follow her to the kitchen. "Darling, will you join us on the porch? Dinner should be ready in twenty." She leaned forward from her six-foot perch and kissed Pierre.

"What a failure this president has been. In four years, FDR will manage to destroy this country," Pierre proudly avowed.

"Not a big fan?"

"I detest the impotent. His New Deal is a fool's errand and will amount to nothing."

"If our government was created by the people and for the people," Henry said, "shouldn't it serve all the people? The wealthy as well as the poor?"

"I am a financier," Pierre said, "and all I see is a bunch of lazy people blaming others for their misery. You see, I made a fortune before the crash, during the crash, and will do so after the crash. I never complained about being a victim."

"I am sorry, Pierre. I can't imagine anyone suggesting that."

Pierre moved forward in his chair and let his feet touch the ground. "First, FDR demands we transfer our gold at a devalued price. Then he will void all gold contracts. How crazy! Henry, I want to be honest with you; I do not know anyone who turned in their gold. Why would they? Because FDR said, you had to? My gold ended up in Canadian coffers," Pierre said, expecting a response, but Henry, as uncomfortable as he appeared to be, said nothing.

"I just returned from Vancouver this morning to hide the last of the gold bars I had here," Pierre continued. "By the way, I heard you visited the Hooverville in the shipyard. I was told it's been emptying, and people are returning to work."

Henry explained that during his time at the Hooverville, there were few signs of a decline in its population. "Every shack was occupied, every space filled, every man waiting to be called back to work."

The martinis were strong, and Henry started to feel the effect on his temper. "Let's go rejoin the ladies," he said.

Pierre and Jocelyn's house was magnificent. Each one of the rooms they passed was richly decorated. There was a billiard room painted a ruby red, a library with floor-to-ceiling wood shelves full of books, and an overall baby blue theme. Finally, they stepped out onto a stone patio full of giant plants.

"Italian Travertine," Pierre said, assuming Henry knew he was referring to the stone the floor was made of.

"There you are," said Jocelyn.

The meal was perfect, the wine delightful, and Pierre was soon a little drunk.

Henry, who had tried to limit his alcohol intake, was about to lose it.

"May I tempt you in a game of billiards, Henry?" Pierre said.

The two men departed the patio for the billiard room, where upon arriving, Pierre filled two glasses with expensive Cognac.

"Don't tell Jocelyn, but I am going to acquire the land where the Skinner & Eddy Hooverville is located. We will have to relocate the last few families staying there, but it should not be a big problem."

Henry cut him off. "I am an economist, Pierre, and a good one. I know the unsustainable machinations of the New York City bankers created the 1929 Crash. Morgan, Rockefeller, and their cohort had millions invested in call loans made to shoe shiners and the like. I also know none of the culprits paid the price for their crimes. The Hooverville we visited this morning is full of unemployed workers. Evicting them will not be a problem for you, of course. For them, the misery will deepen, and the suffering will increase. The president you detest is at least trying to help the majority. At the same time, his New Deal may appear to be a transfer of wealth from one group to another. But, in time, I believe it will create a strong middle class."

Pierre surveyed his guest. After a quiet moment, he smiled and said, "I wondered when you would finally respond to my taunts. You see, I do not believe the New Deal, with all its merits, will end the Great Depression. Why? Because the depression is far too deep."

"What would you suggest then, Pierre?"

"A lot more money spent on targeted projects to get people back to work, Henry."

"Isn't it exactly what FDR is attempting to do?"

"An attempt it is. However, a more forceful response is required, and taking away our gold does not seem to be helping."

At each corner of the room were plush armchairs.

Henry took a seat, a little defeated. Within reach was his Cognac. He took a sip. "A group of scholars at my university developed a study to examine the possible effects of a much larger governmental investment. The results were stunning. The unemployment rate would shrink within a year. This was based on a doubling or tripling of the cash injection into the economy. The study projected that within two years, the economy would recover, or at least stabilize. So, you may have a point."

Pierre laid his cue on the pool table and pulled an armchair up to Henry. "There is such a gap between the 'have' and the 'have-not' today, and each side blames the other for their misery. In the end, most see FDR as the savior. I see him as a narrow-minded aristocrat whose policies on gold are ludicrous and dangerous."

"In the meantime, FDR's efforts help the millions of Americans who go to bed shoeless, starving, and desperate," Henry said.

"But sadly, the daily misery you witness will go on for a while, Henry. Our economy is years away from a full recovery."

Henry stood and walked to the pool table. He knew the depression would fade with time, but how long would it take? Was Pierre correct in his forecast? He leaned on the edge of the table. Holding his cue firmly, he aimed for the white ball. Bad shot. He returned to the armchair. "Years, you say?"

"Punishing the wealthiest in times of crisis forces them to hide their

243

treasures for safety," said Pierre. "Until the financial elite feels it is safe to invest in the economy, our country will struggle. So, yes, it will take years. The American people need to get back to work, and factories must produce, and none of this will happen without the financial elite paying for it." Pierre paused.

"However, a war could help get Americans back to work."

CHAPTER 13

THE BANK PLOT

There exists a shadowy government with its own Air Force, its own Navy,
its own fundraising mechanism, and the ability to pursue its own ideas of
national interest, free from all checks and balances, and free from the law
itself.
— Daniel K. Inouye, US Senator from Hawaii

WASHINGTON, DC. 1939

Thomas McGovern reached out for the typewriter and laid his fingers on the keys. "What is fiction and what is truth but one and the same? Two sides of a coin, each destined to be forgotten. We, as men of virtue, must fight to see that truth is never forgotten." He paused. "Sounds too serious. Let's try again."

Tucked away in the corner of the temporary offices of the Temple University News, he was glad his study kept him busy. He had begun to work on a paper due the following week, whose subject was "Ethics in journalism."

Tom, as most knew him, had always aspired to become a journalist. A senior at Temple University, he was a few months away from graduation. One day, he hoped to be working at a newspaper back home in Jefferson City, Missouri.

Today, however, Tom felt guilty for being at school while his mother and sister remained home trying to hold on to the remnants of their family. His father's passing six weeks earlier had been like a slow but never-ending earthquake, shattering windows one after the other. Unsure of the benefit his studies may provide, Tom's moods swung from sadness to gratitude, from worry to the comfort of friendships. Invariably, loneliness became his refuge, the shelter he sought was the one in which he reflected on his father's life and the devastated landscape his departure had produced.

Upon receiving the unfortunate news of Arthur McGovern's sudden death, the University's main office had sent Miss Faulk, the President's Secretary, to fetch Tom from his English class. She was usually reserved, but as he walked out of the classroom, she welcomed him with a sweet smile on her face.

"How are you, Thomas? I am sorry to bother you, but I need you to come with me to the office. But no worries, you are not in trouble."

Miss Faulk put her hand on his arm and moved out of the way to let him through the door and out into the yard.

The morning was grey. They walked a little way silently as he wondered why he had been taken out of class.

But the Secretary was pretty, and her fragrance, smile, and easiness made him feel comfortable. "I wonder, which class did I interrupt?"

"The class was 'Social order in medieval times,' Miss Faulk. It may sound boring, but Professor Anhauer always finds a way to lighten our discussions."

They walked through the courtyard and entered the office. The president shook his hand—a firm handshake, one implying seriousness and purpose.

Tom received the news as someone would after unexpectedly getting punched in the stomach; breathless, stunned, his hands slightly shaking. Miss Faulk put her hands on his shoulders. He instantly slouched. The thoughts of his mother, of his father. A blur, a breath, then silence. A heavy and unbearable silence.

The days passed. On the surface, the wound healed. Tom still doubted the purpose of his being in school, away from his family, who he knew too well, was in distress. Unable to change their fate, he searched for quiet places to hide. "Fiction seen through a set of colored glasses is truth, just as truth, viewed in the same manner, may become fiction. We, as men of virtue, must fight to see truth remains truth, the unmovable and powerful pillar on which our society exists." *This felt better.* He thought.

Behind him, the office door slowly opened.

"Tommy, my father's car is ready for us," said George P. Easton, Jr., who had just arrived to fetch him. "Where is Paul?"

George, also a senior at Temple, always entered a room with a storm of smiles, a breath of kindness and confidence.

George reminded Tom of the time he and his late father had walked downtown on a lazy, sunny day, years ago. It was a Sunday afternoon in Jefferson. They were on their way to get an ice cream at Albert's Drugstore on Main Street. It was a beautiful afternoon, and the town was busy, with parents strolling around, chasing their young children, keeping them out of trouble. Attracted by the sound of music coming from the other end of the street, they walked toward it. As they came closer to the park, Tom and his father heard a rambling voice calling on the passersby to gather.

"Tien Li, The Marvel of China," roared a large man standing in front of a colorful carriage parked by the fountain. The large man stretched out his index finger to the sky. For a moment, the man froze as in a trance, then slowly, he turned around, staring into the face of the motionless crowd.

Sitting on a wooden box behind him was a small man whose skin was dark as night. He was tapping on a drum.

"Tiennnnnnnnn... Liiiiiiiii." The large man roared as the drum grew louder.

Suddenly the man stepped back. Silence fell over the crowd. The children's eyes grew wider. Time and life suspended. Their breath held frozen by the suspense. They stared at the scene in disbelief.

The Marvel of China seemed to float in the air as he appeared from behind the carriage. Tien Li raised his chin high, smiled, and saluted the crowd.

He elevated on one foot, and a pirouette followed. When he smiled, the breath in the lungs of every man, woman, and child returned. In an instant, with a twist and a smile, he had won their hearts.

For a moment, they had forgotten all the daily sorrows' life had presented. For a moment, they were happy.

When George entered a room, he was Tien Li. The world brightened. Hearts warmed as all became insouciant to the worries of the world.

George rummaged through the long narrow office and finally entered the little room in the back. With a smile on his face, he said, "Come on, old chum, no time to be working. We must get on the road."

Tom immediately noticed the beautiful black suit his friend was wearing. He could not help but say: "You are looking very distinguished today, George. Paul is probably in the cafeteria."

"Well, let's meet him there. I need some coffee," George responded.

As they walked down the stairs to Johnson Hall, Tom McGovern looked at George P. Easton, Jr. with slight envy for the rich and elegant life he led, but today he mostly envied the suit his friend wore.

Since his father's passing, Tom's money had been extremely tight. Without the generosity of the school board, who completely waived his tuition, he would have had to go back home, seven months away from graduation. But still, while the cost of his studies was no longer an expense to his family, purchasing new clothes was out of the question.

Tom was a lanky, 6'2" young man.

George, a little shorter, was your typical football player, with broad shoulders, large arms, and a big, square jaw. To most women, these were the most appealing features in men, but what they found most attractive in George were his light blue eyes, wavy blond hair, his warm smile, and the caring twinkle in his eyes.

Paul Ashton, in contrast, while healthy, was more of a bookworm interested in the sciences. He had spent so much time in dark rooms that his fair skin tone had vanished and had been permanently transformed into a light grey, mixed with subtle shades of green.

As expected, they found him at the cafeteria. In front of him were a large cup of coffee and an even larger book. Paul looked over his shoulders as he heard footsteps coming toward him. "Gentlemen, good to see you.

Sorry, I got lost in 'A treatise on Electricity and Magnetism' by James Clerk Maxwell. Fascinating." He took a last sip of coffee.

"My friends, I am so excited about the journey we are about to undertake. General Smedley Darlington Butler, 'Old Gimlet Eye,' 'The Fighting Quaker.' Fantastic. George, how were you able to arrange for us to interview such an illustrious character?" Paul waited for an answer but impatiently continued, "I find the question almost as thrilling as the quest. Well, on we go." Paul stood and marched away toward the door, leaving his friends staring at each other. Paul seemed to have woken up on a good foot and full of energy.

Tom took it as a good sign. They would need his sharp mind.

He put his hand on George's shoulder and followed him to the car.

It was a clear, crisp day in February of 1940. A couple of months earlier, George had arranged for him and his two fellow students to meet retired General Butler. The general had agreed to an interview for an article in the University's newspaper. The article would present the general's long and distinguished career.

George's father, a local businessman in Newton Square, had met and befriended the general, who had recently settled into a new house outside of town. The two had met at a fundraising event for the veterans, and George P. Easton, Sr. admired General Butler. During the social dinner, many fascinating conversations ensued, and a friendship was born.

Their ride from Philadelphia would take a little over an hour. In the back seat of the 1930 Ford Model A, Tom and Paul felt like kings. The two-toned brown car with black trim was beautiful and very comfortable.

George sat next to the driver but faced his friends.

On their way to Newton Square, they discussed the interview. It was decided they would start with a safe question. Long notes from Paul's research were pulled from their bags. A new list was quickly created. After a short while, the discussion switched to the upcoming school dance. Their main concerns were which girls each would invite.

The three students arrived at the door of the classic suburban house in

Newton Square.

General Smedley Darlington Butler welcomed them with a warm smile and a strong handshake.

Following brief introductions, he led them into the library, where they sat admiring the photographs and framed letters from foreign ministers, presidents, and other various dignitaries. The retired general asked about their schooling and their interests.

The French doors opened, and Mrs. Butler, a tall, strong woman with delicate features, entered the room and introduced herself. She welcomed them and offered tea and pastries, which the General highly recommended.

The three gladly accepted the offer and quickly relaxed.

The General was a likable man, as was his wife. They all felt at home, with family, a dedicated uncle, or a grandfather maybe. Someone who offered you his full attention, so when you spoke, you felt like the only person who mattered.

A fearless man of conviction, a politician, and a dedicated man. Thought George.

The General had noticed his suit was made of expensive material, the shirt he wore had been bleached and ironed, and his shoes were made of excellent leather. But most recognizable to the General was George's demeanor. It showed the carelessness of the young men who knew nothing would prevent them from reaching their destiny. Rich at birth, these young men were destined to grow a little richer. They'll have rich children whose only worries will be to not lose their wealth. Like Smedley Darlington Butler, George was from Westchester, and both had quaker roots.

The pastries arrived and as promised, were delicious, the tea was warm and strong.

Paul devoured a few of the delicacies in seconds.

George was inquiring about the picture of the General with a group of Oriental men lined up in front of a Pagoda.

Tom sipped tea, feeling suddenly melancholic.

The General reached out and laid his hand on George's shoulder and said: "Well, gentlemen shall we proceed with your interview?"

The three immediately shuffled through their bags to fetch their most recent list.

"Sure, General, we have a list here," Tom McGovern said. The 6'2" tall young man from Missouri was ready to deliver their first question. He had been the one to lead the group in seeking out General Butler. "Sir, on our behalf, the University, and the newspaper's readers, who will certainly be most fascinated by this interview, we want to thank you for giving us your time. General Butler, our first question is, in your long, illustrious military career, what would you say is your proudest moment?"

The "Fighting Quaker" looked down for a second, his eyes momentarily lost in a distant past. He leaned forward to rest his elbows on his knees and looked at Tom.

"When I saw in the trenches of distant lands, the tears of dying men turn into gold for the profit of capitalists hiding behind a corrupt government, I walked the fields of death no more."

Tom tried to repeat the answer to himself, unsure how to respond.

The air was still. Paul, who had agreed to take notes, kept on writing. George's face had turned to stone. *To most men,* thought Tom, *the General looked at peace, his kind eyes looking straight at you, without judgment or prejudice, but they were cold as steel.*

A body shifted into its seat, Paul, probably, breathing.

"My proudest moments, gentlemen, was when I walked the fields of death no more," said the General. "This is my proudest moment."

He settled back into his armchair, crossed his legs, and continued. "I successfully fought many wars for which I received praises, promotions, respect, envy, and money. But soon, I began to question why I had enlisted in the Marine Corps a month short of my seventeenth birthday; why had the foundation on which I had built my beliefs started to crack? Why had doubts arisen? The value of my actions became cloudy. No longer did we serve and protect. We pillaged, and the vermin came in for the scraps. Whatever the scraps may have been, natural resources, land, people, it did not matter. The loot we had unknowingly been sent to fetch was now theirs. It was their treasures, and blood had run in the trenches to acquire them. Who are 'they,' you may ask? — the invisible power hidden behind what we call our government." The General suddenly looked straight at Tom, staring right through him as if to ask; *Are you listening, young man?*

Butler soon continued. "I feared for my soldiers and saw their anguish. Dark tomorrows were approaching, and they knew it, they sensed it deep inside their souls, and they were right. Back home, I met the men who benefited from our wars. They lived in the most distinguished homes of the most distinguished neighborhoods of Washington, Manhattan, and other fancy state capitals. They debated the progress made in the regions we had ruined, so they could acquire control over the stolen treasures: oil, mining, jewels, coffee, and finances. They pillaged and controlled, and they did so with our unlimited power." He briefly paused to offer a little rest.

"Sorry, Tom, for being so abrupt, but the truth is bloody, raw, and hard to look at. Often the truth is better left hidden. Yes, I could have told you of the friendships I made, the medals, the accolades, and the battles I won, but they all have left me with a bitter taste. Gentlemen, I have looked into the eyes of corpses left on the battlefields. They stared back at me and asked why. Most times, I had no answers, but to this day, their faces still haunt me."

George was about to say something when he realized the General seemed to cherish the silence. He waited.

General Butler reached out for a book on the shelves beside him.

War is a Racket, typed printed across its cover in large bold type. He read.

"I spent 33 years...being a high-class muscle man for Big Business, for Wall Street and the bankers. In short, I was a racketeer for capitalism... I helped purify Nicaragua for the international banking house of Brown Brothers in 1909-1912. I helped make Mexico, and especially Tampico, safe for American oil interests in 1916. I brought light to the Dominican Republic for American sugar interests in 1916. I helped make Haiti and Cuba a decent place for the National City [Bank] boys to collect revenue in. I helped in the rape of half a dozen Central American republics for the benefit of Wall Street...In China in 1927 I helped see to it that Standard Oil went its way unmolested...I

had...a swell racket. I was rewarded with honors, medals, promotions...I might have given Al Capone a few hints. The best he could do was to operate a racket in three cities. The Marines operated on three continents..."

Once again, a short pause.

"It is why I said, when I saw, in the trenches of distant lands, the tears of dying men turn into gold for the profit of capitalists hiding behind a corrupt government, I walked the fields of death no more."

"Sir, your powerful words will stay with me forever," George said as he walked across the room to shake the General's hand.

Paul was scribbling a few notes.

"Let me see your list of questions," General Butler said. "It may save us time."

Paul, quite cool and collected, offered the handwritten list of questions to General Butler, who started reading it.

George, who had returned to the couch, turned toward Tom, who looked a little frazzled by the turn of events and the mostly unanticipated response.

Butler scanned the list, looked up, and turned to George. "Gentlemen, have you heard of the McCormack-Dickstein Committee?"

The three students looked at each other inquisitively.

"How about the House Committee on Un-American Activities?"

"Yes, I think I heard of it," said Tom.

The other two were clueless.

"Tell your driver to come in for some coffee and a meal. After we have lunch, I will tell you about the "Business Plot." I believe you will find it an interesting story. Follow me, Gentlemen."

George went to fetch the driver and left him in the kitchen with a beautiful plate of food and a cup of coffee.

Mr. and Mrs. Butler were generous hosts.

The three young men were delighted by the food and the pleasant company.

The General had vast knowledge of the world, and Paul seemed to have an unlimited number of questions. They returned to the living room, where the three students were offered cigars.

George excitedly welcomed the opportunity, but the other two declined, fearing they may get sick.

General Butler sat in a large armchair. "Gentlemen, what I am about to tell you is the story of a plot to take over the American Government; a plot in which, unfortunately, I became an unwilling participant. The events I am about to share were followed by the press, though my testimony was kept secret."

The General seemed to savor the opportunity to tell his story. The young men sat quietly, fascinated.

"A few years ago, in ember of 1934," the General began, "I testified in front of the McCormack-Dickstein Committee, as it was called initially. Later, it became the Special Committee on Un-American Activities. The Committee's task was to investigate Nazi propaganda activities in the United States. John W. McCormack, the chairman of this Special Committee, requested I share the events I was involved in."

The General paused, reached for notes he had collected, adjusted his reading glasses, and said: *"May I preface my remarks by saying sir, that I have one interest in all of this, and that is to try to do my best to see that a democracy is maintained in this country."*

A long pause followed.

General Smedley Butler knew fear, he explained. He could recognize its smell, its color, and its sound. Far too often, he had witnessed the moment when a man realized his last chance to spare himself was before him. First, panic arose, then slowly but uncontrollably, fear moved in. He had seen the strongest of men become speechless, suddenly trembling or losing control of their bladders.

"On that day, fear ran through the room," the General explained. "The men before me knew how important their roles in our democracy were to me. But it was their power I doubted, and for me as a soldier, a man without power is no man at all. Sadly, the mighty powers these politicians trusted were only an illusion. It was like the rabbit which disappeared

254

under the hat upon a magician's order."

"I shared my tale when I was interrupted. This time it was J. Will Taylor of Tennessee, pointing his finger in the air, *'You expect me to believe that a fascist group was trying to overthrow our government? What foolishness do you pretend us to believe?'* I looked at him with fire in my eyes," General Butler said. "With all due respect, sir, I care little for what you trust is the truth or isn't. I am here to state the facts as I know them to be. I swore to tell the truth and nothing but the truth. So yes, sir, a fascist plot to take over the Government. A plot financed by Wall Street interests, designed not to overthrow President Roosevelt but to remove from him all authority to govern."

The three students shuffled uncomfortably in their seats.

Paul was writing.

George looked at the general in awe, hoping he could, one day, possess such power.

Tom, who had folded the paper on which their list of questions had been written, listened intently.

"My voice rose a bit," said the General. "I do not lie, sir. I was approached by Gerald MacGuire, who presented certain ideologies; ideologies from which a message soon emerged, loud and clear. They needed me to lead a rebel army of 500,000 ex-soldiers toward Washington. First, an ultimatum would be presented to Roosevelt, suggesting that he formally announce he is too sick and incapacitated from his polio to run the affairs of the country. The President, after much deliberation, would inform the country that he had found an acceptable answer and a new position of 'Secretary of General Affairs' would be created who would run the government in President Roosevelt's stead.

"I don't think we can write about this," Paul said, interrupting the general.

Everyone turned to Paul, who apologized.

General Butler also agreed the subject might be too controversial for the university's newspaper but offered to provide a lengthy article. "It will provide you with everything you'll need to know about my career and accomplishments."

"Thank you," Paul responded, "and I am sorry for the interruption."

255

"So, what happened?" Asked George.

"Roosevelt would be told, if he were to refuse, that I would force him out with an army of 500,000 war veterans from the American Legion. Of course, the new Secretary of General affairs would be carrying out the orders of the Wall Street Financiers, the puppet masters behind this shadowy fascist dictatorship. I asked McGuire whether the American people would believe Roosevelt was too sick to govern. His response shocked me: *'You know, the American people will swallow that. We have got the newspapers. We will start a campaign that the President's health is failing. Everybody can tell that by looking at him, and the dumb American people will fall for it in a second.'* I was stunned."

General Butler continued to explain that his understanding was money was no object. He had been told that Mr. Robert Clark, one of Wall Street's richest bankers and stockbrokers, confirmed he was ready to spend up to $60 Million of his own fortune.

But the General believed others, more discreet partners, were involved.

Grayson M-P. Murphy, he had been informed, was also behind the plot. Murphy was the director of several companies controlled by the J.P. Morgan interests, including the Guaranty Trust Company.

The afternoon sun had moved lower in the sky. The room seemed darker, heavier.

"These men hoped I would spread their message, slowly recruiting an illicit army using the American Liberty League, which once again was headed by Morgan and the Duponts, to finance the plot. It soon became clear that U.S. Steel, General Motors, Standard Oil, Chase National Bank, and the Goodyear Tire and Rubber Company were all involved. In short, Morgan, Dupont, Murphy, and Rockefeller." The General paused briefly to sip a bit of water.

Tom, hands folded, elbows resting on his knees, registered the General's every word and the emotions they carried.

George, standing erect as if ready to pounce in order to defend his newfound hero, looked like an offensive lineman during a most crucial play.

Paul had sunk into his chair, his analytical mind racing furiously. *What is the purpose of telling us this incredible story? What are we to do with the information? If this is true, and I believe it is, a 'coup' to take over the government had really been planned.* He thought.

The General continued; "Fearing the scheme to be so nefarious, I reached out to Paul Comley French, a trusted confidant. I needed someone to be a witness to this crazy plot; one in which I had unwittingly become a part of. During Comley French's testimony, he confirmed each one of the facts I had presented. He also shared his visit to New York on September 13, 1934, where he met with Gerald P. MacGuire in the offices of Grayson M.-P. Murphy & Co. He arrived on the twelfth floor of 52 Broadway, shortly after 1 o'clock in the afternoon."

The three young men were stunned by the General's story.

Retired Major General Smedley Butler continued. "As I said, in late 1934, I went public and exposed the conspiracy. I revealed the details of the coup attempt in sworn testimony before the 'McCormack-Dickstein Committee,' and the plot collapsed."

The General reached out for his coffee and took a sip. He informed them that this was the story he wanted to share.

A question came from Paul. "Why, sir? Why tell us this incredible story, and what are we to do with it?"

Butler turned toward the young man and smiled. "Truth is the weapon tyrants conceal, but it is also the weapon men of honor brandish. As a result of my testimony, the committee soon held hearings in six cities, questioned hundreds of witnesses, and when it was all said and done, they had collected 4,300 pages of information."

George said, "Why would they attempt such a takeover of the government?"

"Gentlemen, you probably were too young to pay attention to world events in 1934," Butler said. "During the first 100 days of his presidency, Roosevelt transformed the financial world in powerful ways. Executive Order 6102 made it illegal to hoard or export gold. Everyone had to present their gold to one of the Federal Reserve Banks and sell it for a set price. The President had forced everyone, including the wealthiest, to abide by this act. But no one appreciated being ordered to sell their gold for paper money. The President soon devalued the dollar by almost 40%, another major blow to the American financiers whose wealth had just diminished by such a percentage. Then Roosevelt voided the 'Gold Clause' in which lenders were to be repaid in gold. This affected all and any contracts, past, present, and future. Once again, it dealt a blow to the large financial powers. Finally, FDR's new deal raised taxes on the wealthiest to benefit the less fortunate."

Paul was now writing speedily and barely breathing.

"It is not my belief that wealthy American financiers were fascists," the General continued. "In my humble opinion, they saw Roosevelt as a dictator and believed they could rule the country without the responsibility of governance. Financiers had little interest in governing a country. They just wanted to uphold the racket they were perpetrating upon the citizens of this country. All that these men desired was to control the policies which advanced and grew their influence. Remember, the plotters would not depose the President but render him useless while their puppet, the 'Secretary of General Affairs,' would do their bidding," said Butler.

"What was the outcome of your testimony, General?" George asked.

"What do you think happened, Mr. Easton?" Butler responded. "When my testimony was completed, I stood on the steps of the Capitol and paused for a moment. The air was crisp, and the sun was setting behind the Mall. It was then I realized the futility of my testimony. I laughed at myself. *What a fool*, I thought. To suppose my words would destroy such an invisible power. To suppose I could win. To believe the truth would be my weapon, the weapon which would free us from the tyranny of the shadow powers who rule us." General Butler paused and looked at the three students.

"Nobody cares about truth," he continued. "In politics, truth is like a long-lost pocketknife of which only its memory remains. I fought an invisible power, you see. This power controlled all and lived hidden behind a wall of wealth and privilege."

The room was silent. The three students, breathless, waited.

"But to answer your question, Mr. Easton, this is what happened. Mr. MacGuire, who vehemently denied trying to recruit me, passed away from pneumonia a few weeks after his testimony. Most of my critical testimony was suppressed out of the reports in back door deals, and the names I spelled out were edited."

General Butler handed Tom a newspaper clipping and asked him to read it aloud.

"There was no doubt that General Butler was telling the truth... We believed his testimony 100%. He was a great, patriotic American in every respect," Representative John W. McCormack said in an interview.

The Committee believed the facts the General had shared. Though gravely concerned, they did not have the power to prosecute. Plus, once the Committee realized how close its investigation was getting to some of the most powerful men in America, they backed off.

"The final report was useless," Butler said, looking tired. It had been a long day.

The three students were in shock and remained silent.

How could one doubt Smedley Darlington Butler, a man of such integrity?

The General paused to apologize.

The young men demurred at the apologies, saying it had been such an honor to be in his presence and learn of these events.

Butler smiled and said, "You thought I was about to tell you all about what a great general I had been; what an honor it had been to serve ... not the shame I felt protecting the Rockefeller Oil interest in China. But I will share with you an article written about my glorious achievements. Use it for the article in your school paper." The General called his wife and asked her to fetch a copy of the article he had mentioned.

She disappeared.

"Gentlemen," he said. "In the end, this is all about money—who controls it, and how much of it do they control? In my speeches and the book that came out of it; 'War is a Racket,' I described the following:

"The World War, or rather our brief participation in it, has cost the

United States some $52,000,000,000. That figure means $400 debt to every American man, woman, and child. And we haven't paid the debt yet. We are paying it, our children will pay it, and our children's children will probably still be paying the cost of that war.

"The normal profits of a business concern in the United States are six, eight, ten, and sometimes twelve percent. But war-time profits... ah! That's another matter; twenty, sixty, one hundred, three hundred, and even eighteen hundred per cent, the sky is the limit. Uncle Sam has the money. Let's get it..."

The General was angry, his speech quicker, his eyes sharper.

"Or, *let's take a look at United States Steel,"* he went on. *"The normal earnings during the five-year period prior to the war were $105 million a year. Not bad! Then along came the war and up went the profits. The average yearly profit for the period 1914-1918 was $240 Million.'* Does War pay? It paid *them....* The coal companies made between 100% and 7,856% on their capital stock during the war. The Chicago packers doubled and tripled their earnings. I do not need to continue. War is a racket, gentlemen. War creates fortunes for those who benefit from it, and misery for everyone else."

The young men were speechless.

Mrs. Butler returned at the most opportune of times, for General Butler seemed agitated.

She held a copy of the article her husband had requested and noticed his appearance. She turned to the three young men and politely thanked them for their visit. It was time for them to leave.

"Well, if you'll indulge me, I leave you with this;"

Mrs. Butler stood by her husband as he rose to his feet. His bright blue eyes were damp, and his hands shook ever so slightly. He said, "When I saw, in the trenches of distant lands, the tears of dying men turn into gold for the profit of capitalists hiding behind a corrupt government, I walked the fields of death no more."

The three thanked the General and his wife profusely for the generosity they had demonstrated.

They woke the driver, who, after a delicious lunch, had retired to the comfort of the car. Their trip back to Temple University was quiet. Once there, each quickly retired for the day.

Before separating, Paul informed his friends that he had stopped taking copious notes midway through the interview. Overwhelmed, he could no longer concentrate on writing and had to just listen.

"I believe we were quite unprepared to hear General Butler announce that a fascist attempt to take over the government may have taken place," said George.

The three decided it would be best for them to meet and discuss their recollection of the events over the next few days. They never did.

Paul used the article General Butler had given them to create an informative account of his brilliant accomplishments and ignored the "Business Plot."

On June 21, 1940, General Smedley Darlington Butler passed away in the Naval Hospital in Philadelphia.

By then, the three students who had visited the general four months before had completed their school year.

Tom McGovern had finished his school year most honorably, and while he was offered a position at a reputable Philadelphia Newspaper, he decided to return home to Jefferson, Missouri. The young man followed his dream and became one of the most successful journalists of his time, winning many awards for his dedication to helping uncover the hidden crimes of the upper class.

Over the years, he documented politics, the various presidents, and the many wars, including the Vietnam War. He also reported on the assassination of President John Fitzgerald Kennedy as well as Kennedy's brother, Robert. On his bookshelf, to the right of his desk and always within reach, was a copy of *War is a Racket* by General Smedley Darlington Butler.

George P. Easton Jr. returned to school to study law, which he practiced until he became a politician. He rose to become a congressman and then a senator. His career was punctuated by a demonstration of brilliance, honesty, and concern for the common man whose voice was often ignored.

Paul Ashton received a master's in economics and worked at the Treasury for many years. He held a few patents, grew his wealth using a keen knowledge of the stock market, and retired at the age of 47. These days, Paul was mostly traveling and writing books on various subjects.

Though the three had stayed in touch by mail, they only met once more later in life.

In Washington, DC, to receive another journalistic award, Tom decided to reach out to his old friends and invite them. They accepted the invitation, and on a rainy evening in Washington, they met at the office of Senator George P. Easton Jr. at the Capitol.

George excitedly gave them a brief tour.

The three were so happy to be together once again, and though they had changed so much physically, their connection seemed unbroken.

At the end of a long dinner, Paul talked about their meeting with General Butler. "Have you ever shared the story Butler told us with anyone?" He asked his friends. "Frankly, there is not a day when I do not think of General Butler and of being in his presence and of his words about 'walking the fields of death no more'."

Tom, the journalist, said he had contemplated writing a book on the event but had been too busy to do so. He shared that he kept a copy of Butler's book *War is a Racket* by his side.

George, sitting behind his oversized desk, looked imperious. "I started my career as a lawyer for the privileged, or, as I grew to know them, the thugs, for they often are one and the same. Butler touched me deeply. I was disillusioned with my practice of the law and decided to change in the hope of making a difference."

A long pause followed.

Finally, Tom said: "As a journalist, I spent my life documenting many events that reminded me of Butler. Whether the subject I covered was focused on war, politics, business, or something else, it always seemed to come back to money and who controlled it, and the shadowy elite secretly controlling it all. On a gloomy evening on January 17, 1961, I was assigned to attend President Eisenhower's farewell speech. Though it would be a TV address, a select group of journalists was invited to witness the event live. We arrived and were directed to a quiet room. A few chairs were scattered around the room, a TV running in the background."

"Upon arriving, we were handed a copy of Eisenhower's speech and directed toward the side table covered with delicacies, wine, and coffee. Uninterested in the festivities, I read the speech. I sat, shocked at the words I was reading.

"Tom recited parts of President Eisenhower's speech word for word:

'...We annually spend on military security alone more than the net income of all United States corporations ... Now this conjunction of an immense military establishment and a large arms industry is new in the American experience. The total influence—economic, political, even spiritual—is felt in every city, every Statehouse, every office of the Federal Government. We recognize the imperative need for this development. Yet, we must not fail to comprehend its grave implications. Our toil, resources, and livelihood are all involved. So is the very structure of our society.'

Tom turned to his friends; "In my mind, as I read the speech, Butler's words, 'War is a Racket,' resounded. Eisenhower, the only general to ever be elected president in the 20th century, clearly expressed General Butler's dire warning. Further, into his speech, he reiterates his warning saying":

In the councils of Government, we must guard against the acquisition of unwarranted influence, whether sought or unsought, by the military-industrial complex. The potential for the disastrous rise of misplaced power exists and will persist. We must never let the weight of this combination endanger our liberties or democratic processes. We should take nothing for granted..."

Tom sat back in his armchair. He looked at his friends and said, "We, as men of virtue, must fight to see that truth remains unmovable, unchangeable, and undeniable."

CHAPTER 14

PRESIDENTIAL ORDER 11110

History records that the money changers have used every form of abuse,
intrigue, deceit, and violent means possible to maintain their control over
governments by controlling money and its issuance.
— President James Madison

The high office of the President has been used to foment a plot
to destroy the American's freedom, and before I leave office,
I must inform the citizen of this plight.
— President John Fitzgerald Kennedy, Ten days before his assassination

KNOTTS ISLAND, NC, 2004

The calls came during the last week of May, and messages were left on Peter Ford's personal cell phone—the phone he placed inside the glove compartment of his government-owned sedan. The last call came as Peter stared at blurry screen images of a terrorist suspect.

The man was on his way to meet with someone to plan a terrorist attack.

Though his team had followed him for the last two days, a heightened alert level had been given and a team was assigned to track his every move.

Peter wanted to know who backed this group of domestic terrorists and what their plans were.

The man was currently traveling through the bowels of Manhattan's train system.

Peter sat in the back of the large room in New York City's Homeland

Security Office.

A team of four controlled thousands of cameras below and above ground. Two technicians managed the civilian photography satellite three hundred miles above the city, which had been re-directed to follow their commands.

The suspect emerged from the subway at the Canal Street Station.

"Oh no. We are going to lose him," said Peter.

The team responded nervously, shifting uncomfortably.

A camera followed the suspect as he continued toward Chinatown, then suddenly he turned on Baxter Street.

The screen refreshed to a different view from a new camera angle.

The man's face could be seen. He lowered his cap, turned right, and went into one of the many novelty shops.

Peter stood. "He's not coming out of there. We should have had men on the ground. Damn, we lost him."

There was a flurry of activity. New angles appeared. Each screen offered a different camera angle from a block away and then two. Some screens zoomed in. But it would be useless.

Peter knew that for $50 in cash, the man would be guided through a maze of underground tunnels, never to be seen again.

"Call me if you track him down," he said as he left the dark surveillance room.

A lead investigator in the New York City office of Homeland Security, Peter had been working hard on a growing list of domestic terrorist threats. Though the practice of tracking suspects remained the same, the new reality of domestic terrorism still unnerved him.

Peter was looking forward to relaxing with his girlfriend, Lucia. In a few hours, he would be off for the long Memorial Day weekend; a well-deserved break.

Peter was interrupted by Paul Madeiros.

The station chief entered his office. He needed something. "Peter, could you go to 36 Thomas around lunchtime?" He asked. "I was supposed to attend a meeting there, but something came up."

Something always comes up, especially since Paul started an affair with the new secretary. Thought Peter, who smiled innocently. "Of course," said Peter. "36 Thomas," the abbreviation used for the NYC State Police Office downtown. Maybe he could kill the afternoon in a useless meeting after all.

"Great. Come by my office before noon. I'll fill you in."

Forty-five minutes later, Peter was on the elevator to the lobby of 633 Third Avenue. The building, located in midtown Manhattan, was quite luxurious for a government office. He picked up a coffee and walked down two floors to the basement parking.

Peter did not notice the blinking screen on his iPhone on the passenger seat when he entered his car. But when it buzzed, Peter quickly found the phone and answered it.

"Hello," he said.

"Hello, Mister Ford. This is Maria, the nurse at the Ocean Breeze Retirement Home. I called earlier. Did you get my message?"

"No, I am sorry, Maria. What is going on?"

"Your father is not very well, Mister Ford, and I think you should come see him."

"Ok. Anything happened?"

"Well, Mr. Ford almost fell today, and I was very worried."

He sensed a slight nervousness in her voice.

Maria was the dedicated nurse who had befriended the elder Ford. "He is not well," she said. "He asked me to call you."

"Thank you very much, Maria. I am going to call him." Peter was a little surprised but grateful for the call.

"Ok, Mr. Ford. Bye." She hung up.

Over the next thirty minutes, Peter repeatedly called his father. There was no response. He tried the front desk at the retirement home. They informed him that his father was fine, but they could check on him if necessary.

Peter declined.

At 2:30 pm, he called the Ocean Breeze Retirement Home and asked if they could check on him.

They offered to call him back.

Upon his arrival at the NYC State Police Office, Peter checked in at the front desk and was directed to a large conference room. He recognized a few faces but sat in the back. He exited the room a few times to try calling his father. He then spoke to the front desk of the retirement home. "Please text me his status, as I am in a conference," he said.

A text came in very quickly; "All is well. Your father, Clive A. Ford, is taking a nap."

Peter was a little frustrated, not knowing what was happening and unable to reach his dad. He could feel his phone vibrate and decided to exit the room to answer.

"Hello, my love. So excited to see you. My flight from Miami has been delayed, though, and I won't be in the city till midnight," Lucia said.

"Hey, Babe. It's okay. I'll pick you up anyway."

"You are so sweet. I'll text you my flight info. Thank you. Are you okay?" Lucia sensed some nervousness in Peter's voice.

"My father is not well, I guess. I can't get any information, and I am unable to reach him."

"Maybe you should go see him. Why don't you take the weekend and drive down?"

"This weekend? I was looking forward to spending it with you," Peter said.

"I am in the city for a week. Go see your dad. He will be happy to see you."

The two continued for a little while and he agreed he would go see his father and they would meet Monday night at his place.

Peter was only a few blocks from the Holland Tunnel. He called his station Chief. "Paul, listen, I am at your meeting. It is the most boring conference, and I just got a call from my father's retirement home. They said he is not doing well."

"Peter. Get the information from the conference supervisor. Bring them to the office Tuesday and get the hell out of there," Paul Madeiros said. They hung up.

The drive out of Manhattan was slow early on. There was some congestion at the Holland Tunnel, but he did not mind. Thirty minutes out of Philadelphia, he left 95 for Route 1 toward the coast.

Peter would miss his father, who, at 82, was tucked in bed by 8 p.m.

He decided to take a detour to Ocean City. The family had spent many summers there. The ride would be a little longer, but much more enjoyable. After a delightful dinner by the sea and in no rush, Peter walked along the beach.

Clive A. Ford sat up, startled as shots rang out in his dream. His past troubled him. The clock showed 4:28 a.m. He decided to get up. At 82, the elder Ford started his day by stretching and practicing yoga. He had been an FBI agent for 36 years. His personal fitness had always been of the utmost importance. The news would start at 5:30 a.m. By then, he had dressed, washed, and now sat at his dining room table, waiting for the morning nurse to deliver his breakfast.

After his wife's passing, it had been difficult for the elder Ford to be alone. A year and a half earlier, he had moved into the Ocean Breeze Retirement Home and appeared happy.

Only a few miles away, Peter sat in his hotel's restaurant, staring at his laptop's screen. He loved to be quiet in the morning, sipping hot coffee leisurely, answering a few personal emails, and browsing through various websites to get his news. He returned to his room and left to see his father.

The nurse on staff recognized Peter and welcomed him warmly. She directed him to room 421, where the father and son embraced and chatted for a few minutes. Each knew he loved the other but never showed any overflow of emotions.

"Peter, could we take a day trip?" Clive A. Ford asked.

"Of course, Dad. Wonderful. Where do you want to go?" Peter sensed the excitement in his father's voice.

"I wonder if we could drive south toward Knotts Island," suggested his father.

Peter thought it was an excellent idea, and they agreed it would be their destination.

The nurses were informed he would be taking his father out of the center for the day. The office staff was pleased to hear that Mr. Ford would enjoy a day with his son.

Peter's last visit had been a few months earlier, and his father seemed to have aged. He certainly seemed slower and a little bent forward. "Dad, would you like a coffee for the road?" Peter offered.

But his father did not respond and exited the building in a hurry.

The two got into Peter's car and headed south.

"Peter, I would love a cup of coffee, but let's get it on the road."

"Dad, Maria informed me you were not well. That's why I came to see you."

His father turned toward him and rested his left hand on Peter's forearm. Clive A. Ford said he did not have long to live, and Peter laughed.

"No one knows when his time is coming." He responded.

"Peter, I know, though mathematically the chances are that I will pass before you do. But don't worry, I am fine. And please don't be mad at Maria. I asked her to leave you these messages." Clive A. Ford said. "She is a good person, a single mother with three young children, trying to survive in this crazy world. Truly, she has been the only small ray of sunshine during these long, slow, and boring days."

Peter smiled. He had been tricked but did not harbor any anger. He was a single man, his lovely girlfriend traveled most of the time, and for her, family came first. She would understand he missed the long weekend with her to see his father, whether he had been tricked or not.

Peter briefly turned to look at his dad, who looked straight at the road before them.

His father, whose skin had minor reddish and dry blemishes, had droopy eyes, and seemed older. "So, what's going on, Dad?" Said Peter.

"As you get older, the pace slows, and nothing much happens. Your days are filled with a void, a waiting room of sorts, where the most important events in your life seem to replay over and over in slow motion. Your mind repeatedly asks you, 'Look at the choices you made. Would you make the same choices now?' Your own purgatory, perhaps," his father said. "I lived through certain events, and they overwhelm me during the day and keep me up at night. Every morning, their questions still unanswered, these events return—a repeat performance I wished I did not have to attend. Now, I am helplessly searching for a sign I did the right thing, but I am unsure whether I did or not."

Peter was surprised by the feelings his father showed and stayed quiet. Never had Clive A. Ford appeared weak or doubtful. On the contrary, he had forever been the strong, polite soldier and the resolved father and husband.

"I am sure you are wondering if I have lost my mind. Do not worry. My mind is stable and healthy, but I am becoming a little forgetful every day." His father broke off and pointed toward a distant shape. "Let's pull over at the Black Horse Farm. They have delicious coffee and fresh pastries. We can grab a table on their deck. It has magnificent views."

Peter complied.

Within minutes, the two were ordering lattes and a couple of enormous muffins.

"You have been here before, Dad?" Asked Peter.

"Maria and I used to spend the afternoon here once in a while and talk," he said. But noticing an inquisitive look from Peter, he quickly continued. "Don't worry. We are just friends."

They walked over to the deck. The view was, indeed, spectacular.

Peter's father seemed to enjoy being outside.

"I have had a wonderful and very rich life, Peter. Your mother was an angel, and I miss her dearly. The story that has been tearing me apart is the assassination of President John Fitzgerald Kennedy."

Peter was aware that his father had somehow been involved with the Warren Commission and the investigation related to this horrific moment in American history. But they had never discussed it. Both were in the intelligence business and knew privacy was a much-appreciated quality.

His father was sipping his coffee and munching on the last pieces of his coffee cake muffin. "I am so happy you are here, Peter. It is so hard to be lonely, feeling like a bother to everyone. Maria seems to be the only person glad to see me." He paused, took a sip of coffee, and said, "Peter, I do not mean to make you feel guilty. You have been a wonderful son. I am so proud of you."

For the second time today, the elder Ford had reached out and placed his hand on his son's forearm lovingly.

"Peter, as you know, in every investigation, means, motive, and opportunity are the keys you must examine. They usually lead you to the guilty party. My entire career was built on this motto; and I usually found the criminal."

Clive A. Ford explained the Warren Commission was formed seven days after the President's assassination. This was, after all, the killing of an American President; a momentous effort would be made to find the culprits.

Clive A. Ford was assigned to the case for almost a year. He often acted as a liaison between the FBI and the Warren Commission. "As the months went by, our team shrunk. Oddly enough, I remained on the investigative team until its conclusion in September 1964," he said.

Peter, who could not remember his father speaking for so long about anything, remained silent.

"Initially, a team of around 100 agents was created. Our first task was to define the means: Who had the ability to commit such a crime? Three teams were created; one focused solely on the theory of the lone gunman, the other two teams split to study a possible national plot, the other an international one," his father continued.

Peter had read a couple of books on Kennedy's assassination, but that was long ago. "Dad, forgive me, but from what I read, this had been a very odd investigation."

His father, whose eyes were fixed on a distant point, turned to his son. "...so strange it still haunts me."

Behind them was some sort of commotion. A dissatisfied customer was yelling at the server behind the counter.

Peter stood and walked over to see what was going on. "Sir," Peter said as the man turned around and looked at him. "I am not sure what is going on here, but would you mind lowering your voice and showing some respect to this young woman?"

Peter Ford was tall with broad shoulders, eyes of steel, and ready to punch the poor man, who was a short, overweight coward. His raging anger disappeared, soon replaced by fear.

"Well, I already paid for my coffee."

Peter made half a step forward and cut him off. "Your server will be grateful for the tip."

The diminutive man left in a rush.

The young, nervous waitress apologized.

He smiled at her, threw a few dollars in the tip jar, and returned to his dad.

The Fords finished their snack and decided to continue their journey south. An hour remained on their drive to Knotts Island.

The grateful waitress offered them a free refill.

They both accepted.

Back in the car, Clive A. Ford continued where he had left off. "Whoever had killed the President, whether it was a national or international plot, had to have serious planning, a sharpshooter, and a plan of escape. In the case of the lone nut, the culprit had to possess the skill to shoot with such deadly accuracy at such a distance," his father said. "In this case, the lone shooter was located at the perfect location because, to take the turn, the extremely heavy limousine had to slow almost to a stop. The gunman, with his target moving so slowly, would have been provided with a rare and perfect opportunity. The luckiest man on earth could not have planned this better." Clive A Ford said.

"I agree," said Peter. "I vaguely remembered the police chief had ordered his men to face the limousine instead of facing the crowd. As a result, none of them noticed the barrel sticking out of the window of the School Book Depository Building. A few witnesses did, but most ignored it, thinking it was part of the security apparatus."

"When our teams reconvened in Washington a few weeks later, the mood was somber, his father said. "Sadly, each group had tried to assess the motives for why one would want to kill the President of the United States. JFK had made so many enemies that it was not a surprise he had been shot. On the international front, you had the Russians and Fidel Castro. On the National Front, the Mafia were the featured miscreants, but there were others. With a touch of fear, we discussed the possibility that this had been an inside job. Lee Harvey Oswald had ties to the Russians and the FBI. Remember, the only words he pronounced after being arrested were, 'I am just a patsy.' It may have been the truth. He was shot dead two days later. Case closed."

These events haunted the older Ford, Peter realized. He kept his eyes on the road but listened attentively.

His father explained the truth was much different. Good leads were not followed. A large group of witnesses were dismissed, or their testimonies were distorted.

The Warren Commission's requests for information from the CIA were often ignored or returned incomplete. The Commission was often provided with misleading information.

"Our team quietly agreed that an autopsy should have been performed immediately, not hours later, in a remote military hospital under cover of secrecy. When the Warren commission requested to see the photos taken at the time of the autopsy, their request was denied," his father said. "The President's limousine was, by 3:30 pm, only a few hours after the assassination, loaded onto a plane back to Washington and hidden from view in a hangar at an army base. These odd events went on and on. We were tasked to find the truth. When we did, the information was filed away forever. Weeks after the start of the investigation, most of us knew that the truth would never be discovered. Lee Harvey Oswald, all by himself, had successfully planned and killed President Kennedy. This was the theory we had to prove true. This was our one and only task."

"We should arrive in five minutes," Peter said after noticing his father was getting upset.

Clive A Ford perked up a little, excited to see the town where, as a family, they had spent so many of their summer vacations.

They took a walk along the beach. The landscape before them was beautiful.

"Have you read any books on JFK's assassination?" Asked Peter.

His father had but preferred to talk about the many summers they had spent here.

So, Peter talked about the family holidays and the annual fishing expeditions they took with his cousin, Paul. They remembered the lazy evenings spent playing cards on the decks of their rented houses.

The "Sugar Shack Fish Market," an old favorite, was mentioned, and after a quick search on Yelp and Google, Peter found out "The Shack," as it was nicknamed, was still in business and they decided to visit the place.

They drove the three miles silently and found that the "Shack" had retained its "run-down" feel.

Both ordered fish and chips and a Coke.

"Of all the books I read on the Kennedy Assassination, one stood out," said Clive A. Ford. "Had I read it in 1963-64, I would have thrown it out the window as pure garbage. By 65, I would have certainly considered its content seriously." He turned to Peter. "How often is the term 'Conspiracy Theory' used in defense of indefensible acts? During the years following Kennedy's death, many citizens took it upon themselves to investigate the assassination and the ensuing events. While their findings were often ridiculed, these people continued to investigate."

Peter listened to his father attentively.

"My colleagues and I labeled them crackpots and conspiracy theorists, nuts you kindly ignored because they seemed to be so simple-minded, and their premises just too far removed from reality. Sadly, anyone curious enough to dig a little would have realized the stated conspiracies may have been the only stories resembling the truth," Clive A. Ford said.

It was a gorgeous day.

Peter was happy to be with his father, but he knew his dad was not at peace. A wound had never healed.

They continued to eat quietly for a few minutes and decided to get a coffee on the road.

Back in the car, the elder Ford mentioned the possibility that the President's enemies may have joined forces to enable the assassination.

"Look," Clive A. Ford said. "In Chicago, a warning of an assassination plot had been not only ignored but was never shared with the Secret Service in Dallas. I don't believe the Mafia alone could kill the President of the United States, Peter. Not without help. Their involvement with the CIA was well known and documented, and JFK had threatened the CIA multiple times, saying,

'I will splinter the CIA into a thousand pieces and scatter it to the

275

winds. The President's most powerful enemy may have been the CIA itself." The elder Ford shook his head in disbelief.

"Maybe growing up so wealthy, the President mistook his name for a shield—a white knight wearing impenetrable armor. Camelot. A fool, I now say," he concluded.

They arrived in Kitty Hawk and decided to get a coffee there. Peter stepped out and walked around the car to help his dad. They sauntered to a local café a short distance away. Peter could see his father was getting tired.

The town was calm and the sun warm. The coffee shop was quiet. It was a brief and well-deserved break in Peter's hectic life.

During his investigation, the elder Ford spent a week in Washington. He had been assigned to interview the people Kennedy had closely worked with—the men and women who had known or had been around the President before his assassination.

"On the morning of December 12, 1963, I arrived at the Treasury Department to meet one James J. Saxon. After a brief wait, I was led to his office. Saxon, the Comptroller of Currency, shared that he had much respect and admired the President. 'Mr. Ford, please forgive me but I need to speak to my secretary. I may have a scheduling conflict. Would you mind coming with me?' Saxon said as he stood. I followed him outside his office. His secretary's office was one floor below. We used these windowless stairs, which were a less glamorous option, but a faster one, I assumed. As we went down the quiet stairwell, Saxon appeared nervous. He looked up and down to see if the stairs were being used. Saxon quickly turned around as we exited the stairwell and placed a note in my suit pocket. Before I could respond, we were out of the stairwell, in a large and busy hallway."

"Pretty strange," said Peter.

"We joined his secretary, who looked at us, surprised. Saxon informed her he had another appointment. 'Polly, please answer any question FBI Agent Ford may have. I am sorry I cannot be of more help. Thank you, Mr. Ford,' Saxon said and left. Half an hour later, I left the Treasury and read the note. It listed an address and a time."

Clive A. Ford realized he had barely touched his coffee or cookie and paused.

It was a beautiful time of the year.

Peter ventured to ask if he had gone to the address on the note.

"I did, Peter," his father said. "It was odd for an official of the Kennedy administration to suggest a discreet meeting with an FBI agent. The address led me to an old Irish bar in a Washington suburb. I sat in the back at a quiet table. Saxon soon arrived and joined me. 'Mr. Ford,' he said, 'I am sorry for the inconvenience, but I feel discretion is required. I must trust this meeting will remain private. The facts I am about to share, while public, have remained discreetly concealed, out of the limelight, and for good reasons, Mr. Ford.' Saxon was a handsome man with grayish hair, and the mild temper of a Midwesterner, though the poor man certainly looked nervous. The two of us sat there in the dark and dingy bar while he wondered whether truth could be offered. Saxon walked to the bar, ordered a beer, and returned to the table."

The bar was a suburban hangout and pretty quiet.

"Saxon returned and asked me what I knew of Kennedy's recent action. I responded I knew nothing. 'Are you aware of Executive Order 11110?' I was not. Saxon shared that for months he and Kennedy had been at odds with the Federal Reserve Board on various matters. One evening, the President and I discussed monetary policies. He offered me a drink. I accepted, and our conversation took on a more informal air. The President and I seemed to agree on many aspects of America's financial state. Our mutual respect grew, and over the following months, our trusting friendship blossomed."

"Months later, the President asked Saxon to join him at Margot, a French Restaurant near the White House. The President wanted to discuss the long history of the Treasury. He was quite knowledgeable about the First and Second Bank of the United States. Kennedy knew of the herculean effort Andrew Jackson had gone through to destroy the Second Bank of the United States, which was, at the time, the equivalent of our

Federal Reserve. The President admired Jackson, who had prevailed and destroyed the central bank. 'But JFK had grave concerns about the power of a central bank system in the private hands of an elite group of shareholders,' Saxon said. "JFK believed this system kept our country in a perpetual and ever-growing cycle of debt. But Kennedy was no fool and had no desire to battle the Federal Reserve Bank."

Peter's father looked at the landscape before them, happy to be out of the senior home. He soon continued. "Quietly, Kennedy devised a plan: Executive Order 11110, which he signed in June of 1963. The Executive Order called for the issuance of over four trillion dollars in United States Notes, which were to be backed by Silver. 'Do you follow me, Mr. Ford?' Saxon asked. I did not but nodded I did, and he continued."

Clive A. Ford explained JFK felt only Congress should coin and regulate money, not a private, for-profit institution like the Federal Reserve Bank.

Saxon agreed with him.

"The Federal Reserve prints one million dollars' worth of banknotes at the cost of the paper and the ink, and the American people, owe the Federal Reserve the one million plus interest on it. How crazy was this? They hand us paper money, and our debt grows endlessly," President Kennedy had told Saxon.

Clive A. Ford turned to his son, wondering if he was still listening.

Peter sensed the stare from his father and looked at him. "Dad, this is fascinating. Every word of it." It was getting late in the afternoon, and Peter knew he had to reach out to the retirement home. "I think we should start our ride back north. I propose we stop on the way, have dinner by the water and enjoy the sunset. I'll call the home and tell them you will be back later," Peter said.

Their drive out of town was slow. The traffic was heavy. Peter called the home and informed them that his father would arrive later.

"Dad, I am sorry to have interrupted you earlier. I vaguely knew you had somehow been assigned to the investigation in the Kennedy assassination but had no idea of how involved you had been."

"I hope you'll forgive me," his father finally said, somewhat embarrassed to bore him with this long story.

"This is no burden. On the contrary, Dad." Peter was thrilled to hear his father's story and summarized the events Saxon had shared with his father 60 years earlier.

The two agreed what Mr. Saxon had implied was John Fitzgerald Kennedy disagreed with the Federal Reserve Act of 1913, which had given the Federal Reserve Bank the right to coin and regulate money.

Kennedy believed it to be unconstitutional; that it was a power only Congress should have been granted.

As a result, the Federal Reserve kept America in a cycle of debt.

Kennedy's answer was to quietly create US Bank Notes, which, unlike the Federal Reserve Notes, would be backed by Silver.

"Its intended goal was to render the Federal Reserve notes obsolete and wrest away the printing of currency from the private Federal Reserve, freeing the country from its ever-growing national debt," Peter said.

Clive A. Ford seemed satisfied that his son had clearly understood the story he had shared. "Exactly, Peter. We were in a dark bar on the outskirts of Washington, and Saxon looked at me with a touch of sympathy and patience in his eyes. I could sense fear in him—a deep, dark, and insurmountable fear. I remained silent, and once again, Saxon asked me, 'Do you understand what I just told you, Mr. Ford?' I must have looked at him with a blank stare because he soon continued.

"Congressman Lindbergh, upon the signing of the Federal Reserve Act, stated: *'This Act establishes the most gigantic trust on earth. When the President signs this bill, the invisible government by the Monetary Power will be legalized. The people may not know it immediately, but the day of reckoning is only a few years removed.'*

"In his autobiography, Theodore Roosevelt, the 26th President of the United States, wrote, *'Behind the ostensible government sits enthroned an invisible government owing no allegiance and acknowledging no responsibility to the people. To destroy this invisible government, to befoul the unholy alliance between corrupt business and corrupt politics is the first task of the statesmanship of the day.'* Please, you are an investigator, do your research," Saxon said. "Remember, the power we give cannot easily be taken back."

After a pause, Saxon rose to his feet. "In 1920, the President of the Bank of England, Sir Josiah Stamp, discussing the central banks power of printing money, stated the following: *'But if you wish to remain the slaves of bankers and pay the cost of your own slavery, let them continue to create money and to control credit.'* With all due respect, Mr. Ford, the Mafia could not kill the President, nor could anyone else, without help. This is much bigger than you think. It was good to meet you, sir. Please be careful." Saxon was about to leave but said, "Do you follow the stock market, Mr. Ford? Do you know what short selling is?" I looked at him, but Saxon abruptly turned and left."

Peter checked his speedometer. He was driving ten miles below the speed limit, fascinated, but in disbelief at the words he was hearing.

Clive A. Ford continued, "I had come to see Saxon hoping for answers but found myself left with many more questions. No, I did not really follow the stock market, and of course, I had no idea what 'Short-Selling' meant and felt like an idiot. I spent a few more days in Washington but never returned to the Treasury." The elder Ford seemed exhausted.

Peter did not want to push him. A few miles ahead, he pulled over to a diner.

The sun was setting, and though the place was informal, it had an outdoor eating area in the rear. It was ideal.

"So, Dad, what is bothering you? You did what you could."

The elder Ford agreed. "At one point in the ensuing weeks, I traveled to New York City for an unrelated assignment. By then, I had investigated the stock market and discovered on Friday, November 22, upon the news of the Kennedy assassination, the market had dropped dramatically. This drop was described as the greatest stock market panic since 1929. The afternoon after the assassination, roughly $15 billion in paper value had been wiped away. During my stay in New York City, I visited Bill

O'Donnell, an old friend who had left the FBI a year earlier for a job as a New York Stock exchange trader.

"I caught him right before his lunch break. We were happy to see each other. During lunch, he calmly and patiently explained what short selling was. It is basically a bet against a stock. Let's say the stock in General Motors is currently worth $80 per share. You believe the stock is going to lose some of its value and fall to $72 per share in a week, so you place a 'short sell' order and sell 100 shares of a stock you do not own, never purchased, or intend to pay for at the time the order is placed. Then a week later, if the stock is at $72, you make, in this case, the difference; $8 per share, times a hundred, for a total of $800. It's pure speculation," he said. "November 22 was a dark day around here, but a few days later, on the 26th, we made a killing, and those who foresaw this huge drop made a fortune."

The restaurant they were in was busy and loud.

"It is estimated the profits made just from this one day drop on November 22, and its turnaround was around $500 Million," Bill said.

"Upon rejoining the team, I presented my discoveries. First, I shared the existence of Executive Order 11110, which could have triggered a battle between the White House and the powerful Federal Reserve. Then I informed my team of the enormous benefit someone had made from trades on November 22, 1963. Two days later, I received a call from one of my superiors."

"What happened, Dad?" Peter said.

"I was told, in no uncertain terms, Lee Harvey Oswald had acted alone. My task was to find supporting evidence for this theory, not go on some random investigation. My superior sounded extremely stressed and insisted I stay away from this. I was furious."

The dark blue sky over them was full of stars. On the horizon, a band of rich orange and pink hues glowed. The sun was about to disappear.

Clive A. Ford was enjoying the last of his French fries. Mostly, he seemed to cherish the time with his son. "I felt the murder of a president required every possible motive to be investigated. Foolishly, I decided I would present my case to the Warren Commission. For a week, I prepared, away from prying eyes. But then, a rumor about an agent called Abraham Bolden spread like wildfire around the agency. Everyone knew Bolden because Kennedy, concerned with the lack of minorities on his security detail, had personally selected him to join his security team."

"Never heard of this," Peter said.

"So, Abraham Bolden joined the Secret Service detail. Sadly, the first black man to serve in the secret service was most unwelcome. But he was an exemplary agent who soon found a surprising laxity in the White House detail. Bewildered, he mentioned it to his superior. Bolden was immediately transferred to Chicago. Three weeks after the assassination, Bolden discovered certain information about a plot to kill Kennedy in Chicago had not been shared with the Warren Commission."

The elder Ford straightened up and reached for his drink.

"Of his own volition, Bolden decided to make a trip to Washington to share his knowledge with the Commission. Upon his arrival at the airport, he was arrested, returned to Chicago where he was accused of discussing and attempting to get a bribe with a criminal, and quickly received a lengthy prison sentence," Clive A. Ford said. He stirred in his chair, troubled at the cruelty the agent had been subjected to.

"At the FBI, men talked," The elder Ford said. "Everyone agreed Abraham Bolden was a good, honest man who stepped on the wrong toes. Cowardly, I reconsidered my decision to present the information I discovered to the Warren Commission. This is what has bothered me ever since. It haunts me. At the time, I feared losing you. One day, I spoke to your mother. She immediately stopped me. In September 1964, the President's Commission on the Assassination of President Kennedy delivered its reports. McCloy, a powerful banker, appeared to have brokered the consensus. The lone gunman theory was the outcome of their investigation. Case closed."

It had been an emotional marathon for Clive A. Ford, and somehow his body seemed to have deflated. For over fifty years, he silently kept this story to himself. He looked thinner somehow, paler for sure. He stared at the sky silently.

This time it was Peter's turn to reach out and lay a warm hand on his dad's forearm.

His father turned toward him. "Thank you for listening, Son," he said.

Once they were back in the car, Clive A. Ford soon fell asleep.

Peter arrived at his hotel a few hours later. He was happy to have spent the day with his aging father. For the two of them, the day had been a roller coaster of emotions. Never had he seen his father so talkative, especially about such matters.

Peter grabbed his computer and searched the internet: "Executive Order 11110." The facts were as he had been told. Kennedy had begun to print United States Notes.

Peter reflected on his father's story and investigated the stock market on the fateful date. He searched the internet for a while and found a book about the assassination. It was accompanied by many reviews stating it was written by a conspiracy theorist and useless.

This is the one I want to read, he thought.

Peter continued his search. John Jay McCloy of the Warren Commission had dealt with the most powerful men of his time. He had been the second president of the World Bank, Chairman of the Chase Manhattan Bank, the US High Commissioner for Germany, supervising its reconstruction after World War II. McCloy had been involved with intelligence, advised presidents, and worked in close association with the Rockefellers. Of course, McCloy had been chairman of the Council on Foreign Affairs. He was one of the powerful "Wise Men" who helped craft such institutions as NATO, the World Bank, and the Marshall Plan.

Further research led Peter to look at the roles of the various agencies, Secret Service, CIA, and FBI.

The results were terrible. A 2014 public report released by CIA Chief Historian David Robarge stated CIA director McCone was "complicit" in a Central Intelligence Agency *"benign coverup"* by withholding information from the Warren Commission. It reported that the agency had instructed its officers to give only *"passive, reactive and selective"* assistance to the Commission. The agency's goal was focused on what it believed was the *"best truth; that Lee Harvey Oswald, for as yet undetermined motives, had acted alone in killing John Kennedy."* The CIA was also covering up evidence confirming it may have been in communication with Oswald before 1963."

Peter wondered what the typical American in 1964 thought of JFK's death. He was astounded to find after a quick search, a survey by Gallup found 81% of Americans believed other people were involved in a conspiracy to assassinate President Kennedy, while only 13% supported the theory that Oswald had acted alone.

It was getting late, but a link intrigued him. It was a video called: "JFK - The Speech that Killed Him." Peter could not sit through the entire video. Instead, he scanned the internet to get a transcript of the speech. It was President Kennedy's speech to the American Newspaper Publishers Association on April 27, 1961. Peter found a transcript and read John Fitzgerald Kennedy's forewarning speech:

"For we are opposed around the world by a monolithic and ruthless conspiracy that relies primarily on covert means for expanding its sphere of influence--on infiltration instead of invasion, on subversion instead of elections, on intimidation instead of free choice, on guerrillas by night instead of armies by day. It is a system which has conscripted vast human and material resources into the building of a tightly knit, highly efficient machine that combines military, diplomatic, intelligence, economic, scientific, and political operations. Its preparations are concealed, not published. Its mistakes are buried, not headlined. Its dissenters are silenced, not praised. No expenditure is questioned, no rumor is printed, no secret is revealed..."

CHAPTER 15

THE MERCHANTS OF DEBT

*Over their 4000-year history, the Merchants of Debt have rarely, if ever,
contributed anything to a society's patriotic improvement or moral uplift
other than to assist in their destruction now and then.*
— Professor Caroll Quigley Tragedy and Hope

*Wall Street owns the country. It is no longer a government of the people,
by the people, and for the people, but a government of Wall Street, by Wall
Street and for Wall Street... Our laws are the output of a system which
clothes rascals in robes and honesty in rags...*
— Mary Elizabeth Lease, Lecturer, writer, and political activist. 1890

NEW YORK, AUGUST 1971

Francis Turner took his seat at the head of the kitchen table. Maureen, his
wife, was rushing between the counter and the fridge. Somehow, the
mayonnaise jar had been misplaced. She paced around the kitchen,
frantically opening cabinet doors. Unable to find it, she grew annoyed.

"Patrick, come down. Breakfast is ready," she called to her son, a floor
above.

Francis noticed Maureen's temper flaring, her body tense, her lips
pursed. He decided to fetch the newspaper. When he returned, a steaming
cup of coffee and buttered toast waited for him. He was delighted.

Maureen sat across from the red Formica table they had just purchased.
She loved their new table and though she wished the chairs matched, she
no longer cared they did not. Perhaps they would purchase the ones
matching the table in a month or two. She could wait.

Francis had refused to use credit to buy the chairs and had proudly quoted part of Proverbs 22:7, "... and the borrower is slave to the lender..." to the confused salesperson, who insisted no one would become a slave over so small a credit.

But Francis insisted and continued with a line from Ralph Waldo Emerson; "A man in debt is so far a slave."

The salesperson gave up, satisfied with the sale of the table and glad to see them go.

Maureen had resigned herself to her husband's peculiar thinking. But on this ordinary morning, she looked at Francis and wondered, *Could I walk out on him?*

Patrick finally came down the stairs and interrupted her thoughts. His steps were heavy and slow.

Maureen stood and poured her son a glass of orange juice and placed it on the table.

"Oh my God," screamed Francis as he slammed down the newspaper. "I can't believe this!"

Maureen turned toward her husband. "What is it, Dear?" She said. But suddenly, her mind escaped the room and traveled to Macy's, her place of employment, where John, a flirtatious and handsome young security guard, had made advances. Now, she was torn between the lust John had engendered and her duty as a wife.

Maureen turned her gaze to Patrick, their eight-year-old son, then to Francis, buried deep behind the newspaper. She was thirty-eight, attractive, and passionate.

Unlike the security guard, who looked like James Garner, Francis was overweight, balding, and eight years older. Worse yet, her husband lacked any drive, especially in the bedroom.

"Nixon ended the Gold Standard," Francis announced as he turned the front page of the *New York Times* toward her. It read, "NIXON... SEVERS LINK BETWEEN DOLLAR AND GOLD"

"What's it supposed to mean?"

"It means that the Federal Reserve can print your dollar bills without having gold in reserve to back it. In the past, to print one million dollars in new bills, the Federal Reserve needed a percentage of its value in gold."

"Well, you work at the Federal Reserve. Maybe you'll get a raise so you can pay for the matching dining room chairs," Maureen said.

"I am just a lowly accountant, Maureen. The one to profit from this will be the Federal Reserve Bank's shareholders."

What a surprise, she was about to say as she looked at him. But she kept the comment to herself. The security guard looked better with every moment she spent in this damned kitchen. *Lunch with the security guard would not be a crime, after all, would it?* She told herself *...unless, of course, we end up visiting the storage room two floors underground, where no one would hear us.* Sexual longing warmed her body.

"Maureen, you look very pretty this morning," Francis said.

She had applied a little extra lipstick, a blue eye shadow, and extra perfume and was delighted by the comment. *So, he's not completely dead after all*, she told herself. "So, what is the big deal with this Gold Standard?" Maureen asked.

"Debt," answered Francis. "Nixon has removed the last and only guardrail to sanity, the only protection against the merchants of debt, and soon they will peddle their paper money backed only by the 'full faith and credit of the U.S. Government.' When Patrick turns thirty, or maybe fifty, you watch; our country's debt will crush us."

"Nice, Honey." Maureen answered and turned to her son. "Patrick, don't forget your sandwiches, and wash your hands before you leave."

Francis returned to the newspaper, eager to read more about the event, soon known as the "Nixon Shock." When Nixon proclaimed that the American dollar was a *"hostage in the hands of international speculators."* Francis knew this was a pretext. From that moment on, U.S. dollars changed from "lawful money" into "legal tender", whatever that meant.

Francis sat back in his chair, his son by his side, and wondered what changes would burst forth on the international market.

"Dad, what is debt?" Patrick asked.

Francis explained the meaning of debt as simply as he could, and after a few more questions, his son appeared to understand the concept.

"But, why is it bad?"

"Debt, in itself, is not bad if controlled and properly managed, but the danger is we have a new president every four years. Every four years comes new promises, new budgets, and soon, the debt balloons. One day, it becomes too big. This is why it's bad." Francis smiled at his son, as if his eight-year-old son had understood any of his answers.

Maureen returned from the bathroom. She did look radiant this morning. Her bright blue eyes were striking against her pale skin and dark hair.

"See you tonight, Dear," said Francis as he folded the newspaper, grabbed Patrick's hand, and started down the stairs when the phone rang.

"Good Morning. Turner residence," said Maureen. "Hello, yes…one moment."

Maureen pulled the receiver to her chest. "Francis, it's a Robert Ferguson for you. I'll take Patrick to school. See you tonight." She left for work holding Patrick's hand but wondering if she would see John, fall madly in love with the handsome and sexy guard, and live happily ever after.

"Good morning, Robert," said Francis.

"Francis, did you read the news?"

"Yes, Tricky Dick did it again."

"Listen, there is going to be a lot of money to be made."

Maureen returned home after work to find the house empty. She felt lonely and uneasy, for she had hoped being home would help silence her carnal thoughts.

The entry door opened and closed. Francis quickly climbed the stairs and rushed toward her. He gently pulled her into his arms and kissed her passionately.

That's more like it. she thought.

Francis announced he had left Patrick with his mother. They were going out for dinner to celebrate. "Ferguson offered me a job at J.P. Morgan this morning. I accepted it."

The discontent Maureen had felt slowly dissipated. With his new job, Francis' salary grew immensely, and soon she quit her job and forgot about

John, the security guard. Francis was more joyous, tender, and attentive. As their life changed for the better, her fantasies vanished, pushed away by destiny.

Strangely, out of that insignificant morning, she never forgot their conversation about the National Debt. Over the years, it piqued Maureen's curiosity. Every so often, she checked its never-ending rise.

Her husband had been correct.

In 1971, when Patrick was 8, she noted the National Debt amounted to $398 billion. When her son turned twenty, it had grown to $1.377 trillion, then to $4.441 trillion when he turned thirty.

Ten years later, in 2003, on Patrick's fortieth, Maureen checked once more. It was $6.783 trillion.

Patrick eventually became a professor of advanced science at Columbia University. Now married with two young boys of his own, he visited them often. Every once in a while, Patrick teased Maureen about her interest in the National Debt. But to their amazement, it never stopped growing.

In 2018, a few months before Maureen passed away, the world was much different. A nationalist movement had risen in America. It divided the country. America's National Debt was then $21.2 trillion. Three years later, in 2021 at the end of a presidential term led by a self-centered and hateful president with an inferiority complex and little interest in governing, the debt had grown, in three years, by $7 trillion to approximately $28 trillion.

"Do you remember the red Formica table and how we could have purchased the chairs on credit?" Maureen asked Francis one day.

"Of course. It was a few weeks before I left the Federal Reserve Bank of New York. What about it, Dear?"

"I can still picture you quoting Emerson to the flabbergasted salesman," she said, laughing. "...'debt' ...something. The poor man looked at you as if you were an alien."

"A man in debt is so far a slave," Francis said. "I remember you asked me what was the problem with a little debt."

Francis paused, reached out for her hand, and held it. "I also recall telling our clueless eight-year-old son that debt was fine if controlled and properly managed," he said as they laughed.

"In 2008, the interest on the debt alone was $253 billion," Francis said, "and this fortune is mostly owed to the few shareholders of the privately owned Federal Reserve Bank. Still, no one cares. Now, talk about the Yankees or football, and everyone has an opinion."

Francis tightened his grip on her hands. She was frail now, but her fiery, crystal-blue eyes were still strong.

"But the machinations of our corrupt ruling class are too complicated. The foolishness of men, my dear Maureen, is to trust a system operated by well-dressed thieves," Francis said, "men read the Bible but ignore its content, for if they paid attention, they would acknowledge Proverbs 22:7, which states:

"The rich rule over the poor, and the borrower is a slave to the lender."

CHAPTER 16

THE SCHEME

Based on various industry reports and FBI analysis,
mortgage fraud is pervasive and growing.
— FBI 2005 Financial Crimes Report to the Public

From what I saw, the types of things I saw...it [fraud] was systematic. It
wasn't just one individual, or two or three individuals. It was branches of
individuals, it was regions of individuals...
— Mary Foster, Executive Vice President of Fraud Risk Management at
Countrywide.

Rampant fraud in the mortgage industry has increased so sharply that the
FBI warned Friday of an 'epidemic' of financial crimes which, if not
curtailed, could become 'the next S&L crisis'...
— CNN reporting on the FBI repeated warnings, 2004

LAS VEGAS NEVADA, 2004

Mohammed wondered if this was his version of the American Dream.
Stuck in a Crown Victoria outside a Las Vegas Walmart with a perfect
moron and eating a two-dollar burger whose meat had been so flavored no
one would ever figure out what part of the animal it came from—leftover
body parts most likely. He stared at the cheeseburger before him, annoyed.
The ketchup had slowly begun to collect into a lump about to run along the
side of the bun. The pickle stuck out. But the French fries flooded the car
with a glorious aroma. He tightened his grip on the burger.

His mind floated away as the gruesome images that occasionally populated his mind returned; Tabriz, the city of his youth, where Iraqi bombs fell all around him. The "War of the Cities" it had been called. But his home was not a city, just a three-story building far from the violence of an unnecessary war.

Mohammed pushed the thoughts away forcefully, but he felt defeated and lowered his meal.

"So, you ran like a scaredy-cat," John said from the passenger side front seat.

The burger came back into focus.

Mohammed turned his gaze toward his colleague. "Shut up, you ignorant redneck."

Mimicking the voice of a crying child, John continued. "Mummy, I am scared... Mummy, I am scared."

"You're a cretin with a brain the size of a pea, Johnny Boy."

"Hey, no one calls me a whatever you called me." John said. Furious, he tried to reach back and punch Mohammed. But a hand of steel locked itself around his forearm.

"John, you wanna fight someone, you fight with me," said Denver, the 6'2" retired army ranger who ran their team of mortgage originators. "We got a big day," he said. "Let's close the deal on these damned mortgages."

Mohammed took a bite of the burger. The truth was, he had run. But the truth bears many shades and is never as simple as it appears.

The Iran-Iraq War had been in its fifth year when Tabriz was bombed. Though the city was far from the Iraqi border, it had become a target. Unable to reach his family from his college dormitory, where he studied engineering, Mohammed decided to rush back home.

Horror filled the streets, burned victims cried in desperation, and the stench of death filled the city. A neighborhood kid, who had witnessed the events, told him that a bomb had fallen straight onto his house. Mohammed asked the kid if he had seen any survivors.

The kid explained he was across the square, a distance away from his house. "I am so sorry, Brother," the kid said, apologetically, "but the explosion was so powerful that the three-story building vanished in an instant."

And so, yes, Mohammed ran; first, through Europe, where he learned to speak Spanish, and finally to the United States. Today, he no longer missed Tabriz Grand Bazar, its beautiful Blue Mosque, or the sweet evening breeze. Iran was a long-gone memory.

Outside the car, the temperature was over 102 degrees.

The red Crown Victoria LX hummed along nicely as the three men enjoyed the superior air conditioning.

"Momo," continued Denver, using the nickname he had given Mohammed, "you take care of the Spanish-speaking customers. We have four this afternoon and two this evening. I'll drop you at La Paloma. I'll go check on the other team and pick you up later. All you'll need are pens and the applications. They're in the trunk. There are four Nina Loans and two Ninja loans. They don't need nothing. Just a license." Denver pulled a cigarette from a brand-new pack of Marlboro. He offered one to John, who took it. "Now, each mortgage on these spec houses is around $350,000. 2.1 mil altogether. Twenty grand in fees, boys."

John interrupted, "So Mohammed deals with the customers. I handle the paperwork, and we get the hell out of there ASAP."

"You got it, man."

"Good, I don't like hangin' at La Paloma. Too many Mexicans."

"Will you shut up, John," said Denver. "I told you my girlfriend is Mexican. These are good people, and you're certainly no better than them."

"Denver, your girlfriend is OK. She's pretty, for sure, but the others, they take our jobs, our money."

Denver reached out and grabbed John by the collar. "Now, listen to me," he tightened his grip. "I don't care for your insults or your ignorant comments. You are judging people you don't even know. Now, we have a job to do, a very simple job. Can you handle doing it without the verbiage?"

"No need for big words 'D.' We cool." John said.

"Thanks, John. Momo, you good?"

"Yes, Boss." But he was not. *I should have been an Arabian prince— the one who saved Tabriz from the bombings.* he thought.

In the back of the car, Mohammed's shoulders slumped, his mother's face flashed in his mind. *I should have been the prince who saved his parents, his five-year-old sister, and his eight-year-old brother.*

"John, get us some coffee, will you," Denver said as he handed him a ten-dollar bill. "Come up front, Momo."

Mohammed got out of the car. He was just a little taller than the top of the Crown Victoria and noticed John walking away. His right hand was raised, his middle finger erect. *Screw you, redneck,* he thought.

Denver was a nice guy. In his mid-sixties, he had traveled the world many times during his career. "By the way, nice job calling him a cretin."

"You know me, Boss, I knew it would infuriate John not to know its meaning, making the insult sting even worse."

"Well, sorry about John," Denver said, gently tapping Mohammed's shoulder. "Tried to get rid of him a few times, but we're short-staffed, you know."

"Thanks, Boss."

"What's the trouble, Momo? You look like you seen a ghost."

"I probably have," but other, more present matters, troubled him. "Boss, you know I own three condos with 'interest only' mortgages? I am having a little trouble finding good tenants, so I pay the mortgages. I am a little worried. How long is this euphoria going to last?"

"Sell these stupid things as soon as you can and sit tight. This house of cards is about to crash, and it's going to be a doozy."

"Sell?" Mohammed repeated, scratching his beard.

"Momo, we are in the sub-sub-subprime business. We're many floors below the basement. We've dug a cave so deep below the basement, it may take the entire building down. We grant $350,000 mortgages without checking for income, assets, or jobs. You know what NINA and NINJA loans mean, don't you?" Denver turned to look at Mohammed, waited a moment, and getting no response, continued. "Three-quarters of our mortgages are tampered with," Denver said. "Momo, have you ever filled out the blank parts on mortgage applications?"

"Yes, Boss. The applications needed to be filled out."

"Momo," Denver paused for emphasis. "This is fraud. The blank spaces need to be filled by the customers, not for us to make up crap."

Mohammed remembered his training and how little details had been covered.

Ameriquest, who had employed him for three years now, had been a godsend. He made good money for very little work, and they had certainly helped him with his own mortgages.

"Boss, what do you mean 'fraud'?"

"Momo, did you get trained to do this?"

"Yes, you know…"

"Momo, on your first day of training, they gave you a package. The second page describes the SEC (The U.S. Securities and Exchange Commission) Rule 10b-5. Does it ring a bell?"

"Boss, they gave us a package but told us to ignore it. We spent our time going through various scenarios of mortgage applications; what to fill out if an applicant is unable to do it, you know, this kind of stuff."

"I spent three years as a trainer," Denver said. "SEC Rule 10b-5 pertains to,

'Employment of Manipulative and Deceptive Practices,' and it starts like this: *'It shall be unlawful for any person…'*"

But Mohammed could not remember opening the introductory package even once during his training. They played games, checked his Spanish fluency, and ate a lot of pizza. Not much else had happened.

Denver continued reciting the rule.

"B; To make any untrue statement of a material fact or to omit to state a material fact necessary in order to make the statements made, in the light of the circumstances under which they were made, not misleading…"

Mohammed looked confused.

"The keywords are *'untrue statements and misleading,"* Denver said.

John returned with the coffees and slammed the car door; furious he had been relegated to the back seat.

"John, how many mortgage applications have you filled out where some information was missing?" Asked Denver.

"D, every application need tweaking. It's our job to fill in the missing parts. What the hell?"

"How about SEC Rule 10b-5? The second page of the package you received during your training?"

"All I know is, if any information is missing, make some stuff up. This is what I was told. No income entered. Write a hundred grand. Boom, done, mortgage approved," John said.

Denver's massive hands clamped the steering wheel. Though he was upset, he knew better. The scam had been going on for years now. Another year or two of work, and he and his girlfriend, Alejandra, would pack it in and be done.

The three sipped their coffee silently.

"Johnny Boy, do you have any mortgages?" Asked Mohammed, curious.

"Moron, do you think I am stupid? I cashed out. Just waitin' for the storm to blow, so I can buy them back dirt cheap."

"As I said, sell," Denver concluded.

Silence returned.

Mohammed felt like an idiot. Even John knew better than to hold on to mortgages in these times. He looked through the window at the Walmart parking lot.

People were streaming in and out of the store, unaware of the crisis he felt within him.

"Why is Ameriquest approving these mortgages if they know the people who apply can't afford to pay them?" He asked.

"Momo," Denver said. "We are mortgage originators. We create and sell them. Our company does not hold the mortgages. Therefore, the company does not hold the risk. We charge a fee to the customer, hallelujah. Then our employer sells these mortgages in bundles and at a huge profit to a big bank called a 'securitizer,' more large fees, hallelujah. From then on, I, and especially our employer, don't give a damn what happens to these mortgages. You and I get our fees. The company get its fees, and everyone lives happily ever after."

"That's right, D," said John. "This is the American Dream."

"Well, if it's fraud, couldn't we go to jail?" Mohammed asked timidly.

Denver and John burst out laughing.

"Sorry," Denver said. "Look, in America, money rules. Our Secretary of the Treasury, Hank Paulson, is worth around $400 Million. He was head of Goldman Sachs, one of the well-meaning banks which currently buy our worthless, fraudulent mortgages. Do you think he is going to call his old colleagues to inform them of the harsh punishment he is planning for them?" Denver shook his head. "How many teams run the streets of America, peddling these worthless mortgages? Hundreds? Thousands? We are tiny little ants in a big, big world. This scam is bigger than the three of us."

Mohammed felt a sense of relief. He had spent his entire life being a tiny little ant no one noticed. It had been his survival mode.

"Momo," Denver continued. "Selling rubbish isn't a crime, if approved by the Government which regulates the sale. No one will go to jail, Momo. No one. These people are too powerful."

CHAPTER 17

THE COLLAPSE

The truth is that many people saw the crisis coming and tried to stop it to curtail the excessive risk-taking that was fueling the housing bubble and transforming our financial markets into gambling parlors...
— Sheila Bair, Chair of the U.S. Federal Deposit Insurance Corporation (FDIC) from 2006-2011

There's a tsunami coming our way, Hank, and you're on the beach hesitating over what color of bathing suit we should wear!
— Christine LaGarde, Head of the IMF and formerly the French Finance Minister reported warning to U.S. Secretary of the Treasury Hank Paulson in the summer of 2007.

MANHATTAN, 2006

On a moonless night, the remnants of a tropical storm landed upon New York City in a fury of torrential rain and powerful gusts of wind. Central Park was engulfed in darkness. The irregular shapes of tree branches defined against the random streetlights arose from the blackness. New Yorkers had retreated to coffee shops, department stores, and train stations. The Friday evening traffic had turned the city into a parking lot.

"What kind of trouble are we in?" Parker Jones demanded.

"Hard to say. You know these analysts always tend to confuse you with loads of incomprehensible data," the caller responded. "Listen, all I know is this guy has been our lead analyst for over ten years and has been with the company for twenty. Everyone I spoke to believes he's the best."

"But why are you calling me if you can't even say if we are in trouble

298

or not?"

"Parker. When your best analyst starts a conversation with 'a complete collapse of the financial system,' you listen. All I am asking you to do is call the guy and have a talk. You are much better with these intricate details."

Parker Jones thought about the words, "Complete collapse." It sounded severe indeed. "Pat, of the three people this analyst presented his findings to, you are the third to call. Maxwell was hysterical, warning of an imminent real estate crash and calling his team to review our exposure. James called me an hour later with grave concern about our CDOs, and while he sounded calm, I could sense the gravity in his voice. I'll get Maggie to set up a time to meet him Monday. What's his name?"

"Parker, if we must push the panic button, we're better off pushing too early than too late. Do me a favor and call him now. His name is Sam Wescott."

"Will do." Parker Jones leaned back.

They were at the corner of 83rd Street and Fifth Ave. The car, in the worst traffic he had ever seen, was barely moving. The sidewalks were emptied of people. Central Park had become absent from reality, a mysterious silhouette.

Jones picked up his cell phone, "Maggie, can you reach out to a Sam Wescott? He is an analyst at the firm. Please see if we could meet sometime tonight."

"Sure, Mr. Jones. I will get right back to you."

Jones reached out for the remote, and with a few strokes, Miles Davis' "Nuit Sur Les Champs-Elysées Take 3" started to play. Tenderly, and in delicate brush strokes of pure genius, Miles transported him away from the crisis. He had become so accustomed to dealing with these unfortunate turns of events, that they no longer affected him.

Parker Jones turned toward the dreary scene outside. His phone lit up. "Yes."

"Good evening, Sir," said Maggie. "I have spoken to Mr. Wescott, who politely declined your invitation to meet, but, if this were an emergency, offered to welcome you into his home."

"His home? I'll call him."

"I can patch you through, Mr. Jones."

"Great. Thanks, Maggie."

The phone was quickly picked up.

"Hello."

"Hello, Mr. Wescott. This is Parker Jones. You apparently freaked the hell out of my directors today, and they urged me to speak to you."

"I certainly did not intend to freak anybody out."

"But you did."

"So, it seems."

"Should I be concerned, Mr. Wescott?" Jones leaned forward, resting his elbows on his knees, one hand under his chin, waiting for an end to the silence.

"Haven't any of your directors briefed you, Mr. Jones?" Sam answered timidly.

Jones realized that he would get nowhere and should just meet Wescott. "My secretary shared your address, Mr. Wescott. I should be there shortly." Jones hung up. "Sameer," he called out to his driver. "Change of plans. We're going to the corner of 113th Street and Morningside Drive.

"No problem, Sir." Sameer looked into his rear-view mirror. As always, his boss was on the phone. Sameer was an Iraqi ex-patriate who had struggled to find work when, one morning in 2004, he and Jones had struck up a conversation. They were at a local diner on the Upper West Side, Sameer in dirty sneakers, jeans, and a cheap overcoat purchased at Target long ago, Jones in thousand dollars shoes, a custom-tailored suit, and a $500 tie. The two could not have been more different. But Parker Jones loved the Arab world and thought its people were the warmest and kindest he had ever met. Over the next hour, the two shared memories of their travels. Each had loved Egypt and Lebanon.

"It's been tough, you know; us Arabs are not the most welcome guests in America right now."

"You seem like a good man, Sameer," replied Jones. "I need a new driver. Call my secretary. If things work out, I'd love to offer you the position." Jones handed him his business card, stood, and left the diner.

Sameer had been driving Parker Jones ever since. He gently pulled the car to the curb. Armed with a large umbrella, he rushed to open Jones' door.

Parker Jones entered Sam Wescott's apartment when Miles Davis' trumpet exploded into a frantic melody.

"Diner au Motel," said Parker Jones, who instantly recognized another song from "L'ascenseur pour L'Echafaud."

"I was just listening to another tune on this album. Are you a Miles Davis fan?"

"For sure," answered Sam Wescott; "this album especially. It was a touch of genius by French director, Louis Malle, to let Miles improvise as he watched the movie. Absolutely brilliant."

"I've watched the movie so many times. The scene where Jeanne Moreau wanders the streets of Paris is amazing," Jones said. "Jeanne Moreau seems to respond to Miles's brilliant melody—her expressions, gestures, and Paris in the '50s, the B&W. Pure genius."

Parker Jones, glad to have something in common with his employee, relaxed and took in his surroundings. He noticed a strange display across the room. It was made of three large panels. Pinned articles, graphs, newspaper clips, photographs, and handwritten notes covered its entire surface. It reminded him of the movie Conspiracy Theory with Mel Gibson and Julia Roberts.

"What the hell is this?" Jones asked anxiously, wondering if his employee had lost his mind.

Hesitantly, Sam Wescott said, "A year and a half ago, while at a conference, an old colleague of mine made the strangest comment. Staring at the group I was with, he said, 'Are you ready for this house of cards to crash?' The guy was known as a jovial and playful person but was often inebriated."

Parker Jones squinted a bit. His sharp eyes focused on Sam.

"Somehow, ignorant people find it easier to assume the fault in others than to recognize their unwillingness to accept the truth." Sam continued, "I had known the person in question to be an incisive trader, who was

extremely precise in his research and very forward-thinking. Later on, that day, I wondered if he had discovered an anomaly none of us were aware of."

"Mr. Wescott, are we in trouble?"

Sam leaned back. "The outcome of my research is extremely concerning, Mr. Jones. In fact, I believe the financial system as we know it is about to implode. So, yes, as a small to mid-size Hedge Fund, we could be in serious trouble."

The front door opened, and Brigitte walked in.

Parker Jones straightened a bit, his face ashen by Sam's alarming news.

"This is my wife, Brigitte Dumont. Brigitte, this is Mr. Jones."

Brigitte extended her hand politely but seemed confused as to who the man was.

"Mr. Jones is my current employer at Jones & Albright Financial, the Hedge Fund I work for."

"The boards are out," Brigitte asked. "What's going on?"

"I met with three of the company's directors and expressed my..." Sam paused and corrected himself. "I expressed our concerns to three of the directors at the office. Mr. Jones heard from them and wanted to meet with me immediately."

Parker Jones turned to Sam. "Is there any way we could discuss this matter in private?"

"I am sorry, Sir, but it is Friday evening; we are in our home, and Brigitte is quite knowledgeable on this matter. You could say she helped me create this display. But, if privacy is critical, I would be more than happy to meet with you at the office on Monday."

Parker Jones leaned back in his armchair and faced Sam. He clasped his hands together, gently rubbing them against his chin.

Sam knew Jones to be a nice man, polite, straightforward but stoic, firm and unapologetic, and certainly unaccustomed to having his requests denied. Tonight, he had to give in.

"Coffee?" Offered Brigitte.

"Anything stronger?" Asked Jones.

"Of course. Follow me." Brigitte led Jones to an antique Art Deco Liquor Cabinet. "Help yourself."

Jones poured a copious glass of Johnnie Walker Blue Label Whiskey and returned to the couch. "You freaked the hell out of our directors today, Mr. Wescott. You are one of our most trusted analysts, so please proceed with an explanation of this insane display."

"My presentation was brief. In a few words, I informed them of my personal research and the conclusion I was led to...."

"Yes, the entire financial system could collapse," interrupted Parker Jones.

"Correct," Sam responded, annoyed. "However insane this may sound to you, Mr. Jones, these boards helped Brigitte and I uncover the many problems about to lead our country straight into a major crash." Sam paused.

"Sam, I am going to get some dinner," Brigitte said.

"Hold on," said Jones. "What kind of food do you like?"

Sam and Brigitte looked at each other.

"How about I let my driver, Sameer, surprise us?"

Before they could answer, he had picked up his phone and walked across the room.

"How do you feel?" Asked Brigitte.

"A little freaky to have Parker Jones in our living room, but all right, I guess."

"You really freaked them out."

Parker Jones turned to them and offered a smile. He made another call and, once done, joined them around the coffee table. He seemed eager to hear about the display.

"The left board represents the 80s," Sam said. "...the center the 90s, and on the right, the 2000s." He walked closer to the left board and placed his index finger on the red tape.

"Let's start here. During the 80s, large commercial banking institutions on Wall Street grew restless. They saw the 'Shadow Banking System, us, the hedge funds, investments banks, private brokers and other entities amass huge profits from riskier businesses."

Sam explained that for years the large, regulated commercial banks had not been allowed to deal in riskier areas of the business. At the time, the subprime-mortgage market had exploded, and the incredibly profitable securitization of asset-backed commercial paper was out of commercial banks' reach.

"Let's imagine you represent the traditional, 'safe' banking system: Bank of America, Citibank, Chase, etc. I represent the hedge funds. You, the boring and traditional banks, must follow a set of regulations; drive at the speed limit, stop at a red light, pay to park, tip your waiter, be polite, on time and always dress properly. But because these regulations do not apply to me, the unregulated banking system, the shadow banking system, I drive as fast as I want, view red lights and other regulations as options I select whether or not to follow."

Sam pointed at a newspaper clip. "In the 80s, the commercial banks grew frustrated by the number of regulations controlling them and now wanted access to these profitable markets. As a response, Donald Regan, Merrill Lynch CEO until 1980, was made Secretary of the Treasury in 1981. He was the perfect insider who would now do the commercial and safe banks' bidding."

Sam traced his finger over the blue tape. "1984. The Secondary Mortgage Market Enhancement Act is made into law."

"I vaguely remember this. Can you clarify?" Said Jones. "What enhancement are they talking about?"

"There *was* no 'enhancement.' In our industry, these fictitious titles often mean nothing and are well designed to be obscure. The Federal Reserve is the perfect example; it is neither Federal nor has any Reserve, yet because of its title, everyone thinks otherwise."

Sam described the 1984 Secondary Mortgage Market Enhancement Act as extremely important because it allowed large, "regulated," commercial banks to purchase any mortgages, prime or sub-prime, and pool them together to create mortgage-backed securities. The commercial banks could group hundreds, perhaps thousands of mortgages into a 'security' to be sold to investors.

"The first flaw I discovered was that fraud ran rampant in the subprime mortgage industry. The second flaw was that Wall Street, and these large and extremely powerful commercial banks forced the credit agencies to rate these mortgage-backed securities, or MBS, at the highest rating available, no matter what the actual quality of the mortgages were, high quality or pure crap," Sam explained.

"Ok, so commercial banks, supposedly safe, were now allowed to take risks. But instead, they cheated their clients by selling low-quality securities under the pretense they were of the highest quality and therefore free of risks," Parker Jones said.

"Correct. Soon, Wall Street realized these securities would sell better if they had a tax benefit. In 1986, REMIC, the Real Estate Mortgage Investment Conduit, was enacted."

"I remember using it a lot," Jones said.

"REMIC created tax advantages for the purchaser of these Mortgage-backed securities. The MBS (mortgage-backed securities) instantly grew extremely popular. It was a tax loophole for the huge banks that were not big fans of paying taxes, except when it's for the 'little people;' my wife and I."

Sam slid his finger down the board. "It is important to note the total volume of MBS—the mortgage-back securities which made a lot of money for these banks—grew drastically; In 1984, it amounted to $11 billion; in 1994, $200 billion; and by 2006, almost $3 trillion."

"It is a lot of money," said Brigitte.

Parker Jones did not take the bait and waited patiently.

"The same year," Sam continued, "the Federal Reserve, which, as you know, is a private, 'for-profit entity, allowed commercial banks to create, own, and manage affiliate companies to handle certain securities—the ones that were illegal for them to deal with before."

Sam paused for a moment. With Brigitte by his side, he felt a little calmer.

"What is the Riegle...something?" Asked Jones. "There, on your right."

"The Riegle-Neal Interstate Banking and Branching Efficiency Act granted the right to commercial banks to merge and expand at will. So, they did, and soon they grew bigger and bigger. Next, they forayed into the riskier, though more lucrative, investment banking business."

"These bastards kept encroaching on our business," Jones said.

"Sounds quite unbelievable, doesn't it?" said Brigitte. "The large commercial and regulated banks with their unlimited powers forced themselves into a market, turning it into a racket, in which they sold worthless mortgages in bundles with the blessing of the credit agencies they threatened. Then, they got themselves a tax break for their scam, and as a reward, were allowed to grow bigger—much, much bigger."

Parker Jones stood and walked to the liquor cabinet. "May I?" He asked.

"Of course, no need to ask," answered Brigitte.

Jones explained that these issues, while very concerning, would likely never result in a substantial correction in the market, but doubted a total crash would ensue.

Sam agreed. The MBS sold to trusting customers were rubbish. Sooner or later, the subprime borrowers would stop paying their mortgages, and investors would suffer. This, in itself, would not bring a collapse of the financial market.

Jones, who had walked over to the window, stared at the rain falling upon the glistening sidewalks. He sipped his whiskey quietly.

Unnerved by the long silence, Sam tried to explain his theory could be wrong.

"Why would our financial system have a meltdown? How is it even possible? This is America. We have the strongest economy in the world," Jones said.

"Greed and unlimited power," Brigitte offered. "You see, Mr. Jones, this is nothing but peddlers cheating each other of their unlimited wealth while screwing a few victims. The 80s and 90s saw the dismantling of most banking regulations. Fine, who cares? These regulations protected us from bank runs and crashes. But now, no longer did we have two systems of banking: regulated and unregulated, safe and risky. No longer did a safety net exist. And what came next, Mr. Jones, was pure craziness."

"What do you mean, pure craziness?" Jones asked.

Brigitte was staring at the proud hedge fund manager, who, apparently, had no clue what was to happen. "Upon release, a confined animal often behaves in the most exuberant of ways, and so did the large, once-regulated commercial banks. Their excesses came in the form of unbounded gluttony for more and more wealth." She said.

Jones turned to Sam inquisitively.

"Please forgive Brigitte," Sam said. "The banks possessed authority over politicians, as well as all areas of finance, including the Treasury and Federal Reserve. Their power had become unlimited. These banks had acquired the riches of the world. But now, with very little left to pillage, they decided to invent new schemes."

Jones stood and walked over to the liquor cabinet once more. Deep within himself, Jones knew the truth—the inexhaustible excess he had witnessed; the many fortunes made on absurd wagers he had refused to participate in until the partners forced him to. The bottle of whiskey trembled in his hand. His phone rang. It was Sameer. "The food." He turned to Sam. "Can you let my driver in?"

Brigitte walked over to the door and pushed the button to let him in. "Third floor. Number 306."

The three sat around the table. It was covered with Middle Eastern delicacies accompanied by the most delicious breads. A brand-new bottle of Johnnie Walker Blue Label stood ignored.

"My job as an analyst allows me to study a vast amount of data," Sam said. "The financials I reviewed over the last year have shocked me. For instance, Lehman Brothers has a leverage of 31 to 1. This means they owe $31 for every $1 they have in assets. $1 billion in assets and $31 billion in debt. $100 billion in assets and $3.1 trillion in debt."

"I can do the math," said Jones, irritated.

"Then you know what a massive amount of debt this is," Sam answered, raising his voice. "However, the real catastrophe is they're not the only ones; Washington Mutual, Fannie Mae, and Freddie Mac are others. The financial crisis I foresee will be major, Sir, and I mean major."

Parker Jones shuffled in his chair nervously.

"If some large institutions were to fail," Sam said, "a pronounced rise in unemployment and financial losses would follow. The magnitude of the crisis I foresee should not tip our entire financial system into oblivion, but the confluence of flaws in the system, like cancerous cells multiplying themselves into a deadly tumor, will trigger the upcoming crash."

"But we have insurance. AIG will cover these losses," Jones said.

"This is the unnerving and unfounded belief—AIG will rescue everyone."

Sam explained that AIG, the insurance giant, through its subsidiary AIG Financial Products in London, had extended its business to selling CDOs and CDSs, the riskiest of the derivatives market.

If the wave of foreclosures on unpaid mortgages grows to Sam's estimated forecast, the insurance giant will collapse.

"Ok, AIG collapses, and…?" Jones said, dejected. But he knew the answer. Lies and excess never bring success. Over the last few years, he had seen the folly the industry had embraced.

Neither Wescott nor Ms. Dumont had yet covered the derivatives market, the credit default swap or CDSs, and the Collateralized Debt Obligations, or CDOs, which had flooded the entire financial market—a market worth trillions, in which purchases were more like bets placed on such complex financial tools very few understood. Jones finally grasped the gravity of the situation. He reached for his glass. "How about the Feds? Could they do anything?" Asked Jones.

"The treasury is unwilling to see the extent of corruption and abuse currently committed, almost to the point of complicity. Bernanke believes the impact of the subprime market on the economy is contained and not an issue to be concerned with. The Federal Reserve is led by an egomaniac with unlimited power." Sam walked over to the board to find Greenspan's 2003 statement and read.

"Greenspan's grandiose delusion led him to believe that the '*derivative markets participants seem keenly aware of the counter-party credit risk associated with derivatives and take various measures to mitigate those risks.*' Pure foolishness," concluded Sam.

"Mr. Wescott, is there a way for us to mitigate our losses?"

"I believe we can, Sir. Your business has been safe and honest. It should take three to four days to identify and dispense of any and all risky interests we may currently have."

Parker Jones stood and walked over to the window. With his phone in hand, he dialed. "I want everyone in the office at 7 a.m. tomorrow," Sam and Brigitte heard him say.

When the call ended, Parker Jones said, "Mr. Wescott, thank you so much for bringing this to my attention." He picked his coat off the chair.

"Mr. Jones," Brigitte said, "there will be fortunes to be made from this upcoming crisis."

Parker Jones turned to her and offered a kind and handsome smile. "Miss Dumont, would you care to join your husband in leading our team?"

CHAPTER 18

THE AFTERMATH

...Hank (Paulson, Sec. of Treasury) ... was sitting in a chair. Ben Bernanke was sitting on a couch... Tim Geithner was on the line. It was an ambush. They told me that they wanted me to publicly announce that the FDIC would guarantee the liabilities of the banking system. They had even already prepared a script for me ...They wanted me to say that the FDIC was going to be guaranteeing everybody against everything in the $13 trillion banking system ... It was an overreach of the worst sort, and there was no doubt in my mind that Tim Geithner was the instigator.
— Sheila Bair, Chair of the FDIC, during the 2008 Crisis

We face a hostile ideology - global in scope, atheistic in character, ruthless in purpose, and insidious in method. Unhappily the danger it poses promises to be of indefinite duration.
— Dwight Eisenhower, 34th President, Farewell Speech,
January 17, 1961

WASHINGTON, D.C., 2011

Had there been uniformed soldiers marching toward our capital, their tentacles reaching out for our hidden treasures? Had there been a declaration of war, perhaps, or enemy soldiers at our doors? But no proclamation came forth, no formal war announced, no warning of an incoming pillage mentioned, and no bloodshed.

Their stark uniforms had been replaced by expensive suits, and malice had become their weapons. These evils spread like a discreet cancer; bit by bit, their diligent army propagated within our vital organs in subtle, well-intentioned moves. Soon, all areas of government had been infiltrated: The Treasury, the courts, the crooked politicians.

But a war had been declared—a well-planned and concerted war against our community, a war for the wealth of our nation.

The 2008 Financial Crisis was the sad outcome of our oligarchy's excesses: the result of a blind and immense greed for power and money. Kings, impervious to the reach of justice, they strolled about in their thousand-dollars suits, unaffected and undisturbed.

Our government, their minions—complicit in every way—ignored their crimes. They were, after all, too big to be sent away to pay for their sins. They were untouchables.

Our invisible enemies chuckled at the absurdity in which we conducted ourselves, a feeble and easily distracted enemy. So gullible.

Men are more inclined to suffer than to fight, to submit than to rise, and to shy away from the truth in fear.

So, the victors savored their spoils of war; our diminishing wealth sucked into a vacuum of insurmountable national debt. Today it amounts to $15 trillion but promises to grow. In the aftermath of the 2008 Crisis, these defiant and faceless royals rejoiced.

The financial crisis had been the most premeditated and despicable act committed by a tiny elite class against an entire society. It was the success of a century-old war for the wealth of our nation; a war no one dares mention; a war America lost long ago.

In his 1832 veto address, President Andrew Jackson wrote, *"It is to be regretted that the rich and powerful too often bend the acts of government to their selfish purposes."* He was correct.

A fortress had been constructed around these kings, princes, and dukes. Their army rejoiced at the challenge. At the U.S. Treasury, Hank Paulson ruled; his army of minions, weapons in hands, prepared for the battle. You see, Henry Paulson had been the CEO of Goldman Sachs. He was a good old boy who had been compensated a mere $37 million at Goldman Sachs in 2005 and around $16.4 million in 2006. His net worth was estimated to be over $700 million. Herbert Allison, who became the "TARP-Tsar," had been CEO of Fannie Mae and TIAA-CREF, and

President at Merryll Lynch. These men were the perfect insiders who would care little for the ne'er-do-wells in the lower stratus of society. These bankers were the puppet-masters, our government their puppets, the American people their resentful victims.

"The banks — hard to believe in a time when we're facing a banking crisis that many of the banks created — are still the most powerful lobby on Capitol Hill. And they frankly own the place," said Senator Dick Durbin of Illinois in 2009.

Secretary of State John Kerry, in his 2013 farewell speech to the Senate, said; *"The alliance of money and the interests that it represents, the access that it affords to those who have it at the expense of those who don't, the agenda that it changes or sets by virtue of its power is steadily silencing the voice of the vast majority of Americans..."*

Vice-President Al Gore declared, *"American democracy has been hacked. ... The United States Congress ... is now incapable of passing laws without permission from the corporate lobbies and other special interests that control their campaign finances."*

But unabashed by the crisis they had orchestrated, these bankers marched on; an obedient army seeking more treasures. The doors to the U.S. coffers were kicked in, our gold primed for the taking, while, as a result of the 2008 crisis, our poverty rate grew to 15.1%, and the banks' wealth increased. *"J.P. Morgan Chase grew 36% ... Wells Fargo more than doubled ...Bank of America grew by 32% ... compensation for the top twenty-five Wall Street firms in 2010 broke records at $135 billion,"* wrote Neil Barofsky, the Special Inspector General overseeing the Troubled Asset Relief Program, or SIGTARP.

America is run by a small group of powerful Kings hidden and protected by the men we elect to keep us safe. How can one truly believe there was justice when none of these criminals suffered the consequences of their misdeeds?

The aftermath of the 2008 crisis became a bloody mess in which fortunes were made by the criminals who committed the initial plunder. The villains continued their pillage.

Treasury Secretary Paulson initially requested a blank check for *"$700 billion* strictly for the purchase of mortgage-related assets, with no oversight supervisions, no reporting provisions..." Barofsky says in his book *Bailout*. Congress refused. So, Secretary Paulson negotiated some lame agreement that the dull Congress could agree on, but the Wall Street banks did not want.

Soon Paulson, the good little boy he was, changed TARP into a Capital Purchase Program or CPP. It was a free-cash infusion, and thanks to the American taxpayers, however broke they may have been, these banks received another $125 billion.

Their survival had fallen upon the ignorant populace. The commoners would pay the price for their kings' foolishness.

The Government Accountability Office published a study about the 2008 Financial Crisis. It estimated the real cost to the economy at more than $22 trillion.

The many crimes and fraud carried out by the large banks were soon recognized; "The SEC (Securities and Exchange Commission) accused Citigroup of making a $500 million bet against a bond it had created, marketed and sold" according to Barofsky. Bank of America was indicted for Racketeering in a Colorado Federal Court. JPMorgan Chase admitted to committing five felony counts over a period of six years. Wells Fargo would soon be fined $3 billion over a fake account scandal.

In the meantime, Americans who bounced a $28 check to feed their kids found themselves in prison.

"They (The American people) should be revolted by a financial system that rewards failure and protects those who drove it to the point of collapse and will undoubtedly do it again ..." wrote Neil Barofsky, Special Inspector General for TARP, the man assigned to protect the American people's money.

Is this, really, what America has become?

For now, it is.

Their soldiers kept on pushing, desiring even more of our treasures.

Soon came HAMP, the Home Affordable Modification Plan. Its goal was honorable—to help borrowers refinance their mortgage so they can afford to pay it. But once again, no one would stop the kings, not even the Special Inspector General for TARP, Neil Barofsky, who described the program as *"an unprecedented trillion-dollar playground for fraud and self-dealing."*

History proved him to be correct. Within years, J.P. Morgan Chase, Wells Fargo, Bank of America, and Citigroup had to defend themselves for defrauding borrowers trying to refinance through the HAMP program. They were found guilty and fined $25 billion. Bank of America was responsible for $11 Billion. These banks made billions through fraudulent behaviors, and the fines were minor penalties. None of their generals, lieutenants, or common soldiers went to jail. Why? Because *"At the highest levels, there is no separation between the people who run our biggest businesses and those in charge of our government,"* says John Perkins in his 2011 book, *Hoodwinked.*

Behind the veil of secrecy, these banks are the real kings. Their shareholders can afford to offer $135 billion in bonuses and still make immense profits.

Supreme Court Justice Felix Frankfurter (1939-1962) declared that *"The real rulers in Washington are invisible, and exercise power from behind the scenes."*

These rulers are, I believe, the men President Barack Obama spoke to when he said, *"My administration is the only thing between you and the pitchforks."*

Our government is ruled by an oligarchy comprised of many kings. It is disguised as a democracy but sadly, the Kings have won.

CHAPTER 19

MONARCHIES IN THE 21ST CENTURY

The modern banking system manufactures money out of nothing... Banking was conceived in inequity and born in sin. Bankers own the Earth. Take it away from them but leave them the power to create money, and with a flick of a pen, they will create enough money to buy it back again. Take this great power away from them and all great fortunes like mine will disappear, for then this would be a better and happier world to live in. But if you want to continue to be the slaves of bankers and pay the cost of your own slavery, then let bankers continue to create money and control credit.
— Sir Josiah Stamp, President of the Bank of England and the second richest man in Britain in the 1920s, speaking at the University of Texas

SARATOGA SPRINGS, NY. 2019

"To govern is not to rule," said Professor Lositano. "To govern is to manage the affairs of a community, a country, or a state. To rule is to exercise ultimate power and authority over a community, country, or state. In a democracy, there are no kings, no rulers, and there lies my question."

The Professor paused and looked around the classroom.

An hour earlier, Professor Lositano had entered the classroom. In his customary fashion, he was precisely three minutes late. It was a calculated move, for it enabled him to make a grand entrance. Arms spread wide, the palm of his hands facing skyward, he walked over to his desk and welcomed the class.

"Buongiorno. Come Va?" The Professor said in Italian.

Upon hearing his booming voice, everyone perked up a little.

"You are in the class called Monarchy and Government, E312 on the

315

Skidmore course catalog. If, by any chance, you are sitting in the wrong class, this is your opportunity to leave." Lositano paused while a tall student picked up his backpack and walked out of the auditorium.

The classroom seemed nearly empty, but to Lositano, the Italian-born sociology professor, it did not matter.

Short and stocky, Lositano let his long curly black hair fall onto his shoulders where it moved in an unruly dark mass. While the professor wore the most stylish Italian clothes, they strangely never seemed to fit him properly. Today, the brick-red pair of pants he wore were a little too long and certainly too tight at the waist. His striped, teal blue and bright green sweater was at least a size too large.

But Professor Lositano was an artist, a kind man with a warm heart and a sincere love for humanity. At times he wondered why these young students had selected his course. However, upon entering the classroom, he ignored these questions and stepped before his class just as an experienced performer would before his audience.

"Luckily, you will not be asked to study macroeconomics, nuclear fission, or electromagnetic signals. You will, however, be required to think and express yourself. Therefore, I strongly advise the double espresso from Peet's coffee shop on campus. Drink it straight up an hour before class, and as a result, our conversation will be more animated and consequently richer. For your effort, I will reward you with boundless gifts. Mainly, I will award you the good grades you all seek."

The diminutive Italian walked over to his desk, nonchalantly shuffled some papers, quickly gave up, and turned around.

"Introductions," he said, seeming to suddenly remember his class plan.

Lositano went on to speak about himself and shared his love for the city of his youth, Bergamo, forty kilometers north of Milan, in the Lombardi region. He described how beautiful the sunsets were over the Bergamo Alps. He lived in the fortified upper town on a tiny cobblestone street in a house whose yard, set away from the road, overlooked the valley. Whenever possible, the family ate on the patio, surrounded by the smell of herbs. Heaven," he concluded. "The food," he said but quickly stopped.

"You," he pointed forward. "A brief introduction."

Three rows back and in the center of the classroom sat Max Parsons who had enrolled in this class for the promise of easy credits. He had heard the professor was charming, fun, and never failed anyone. "He's like a renaissance artist," someone had told him. "The class is a lot of fun," another friend had commented. Max immediately registered for the class.

But Max Parsons, in his sophomore year at Skidmore College, only cared to be left alone. His goal was to do the minimum required to get the credit he needed while focusing on other matters, mainly the young and beautiful women who comprised more than 60% of the population on campus.

"Me?" Max inquired unconvincingly, pointing the finger at his own chest in disbelief. He waited but quickly realized no response would be forthcoming, and Professor Lositano, who had indeed singled him out now, seemed annoyed.

"My name is Max Parsons. I was born in Shanghai, where my parents worked as diplomats. I returned to sunny California at the tender age of four and spent the last 14 years living in Mendocino." Max continued for a bit. Soon, other students followed in what would prove to be a slow and agonizing process.

"A game," announced Professor Lositano once everyone had introduced themselves. "It's an easy one; word association. Ready, everyone?" He walked to the whiteboard.

"Mr. Max Parsons, would you be kind enough to help me?"

Max instantly wondered if he should just walk out of the classroom and go straight to the registrar's office to drop the class.

"Please stand to the left of the whiteboard. You will write each word our kind audience provides."

Max begrudgingly complied.

But Lositano was no fool, and to entice his young helper, he followed by asking a gorgeous young woman named Annabelle Winthrop to join him to the right of the whiteboard.

"Pardon me, but does anyone speak Italian in this class?"

A timid hand went up in the back row.

Max was shocked to see a stunningly beautiful brunette stand.

She and the professor started a conversation in Italian. Everyone looked at the gorgeous young woman who was now walking down a few steps to sit right up front. Her name was Christiana Tocci.

Max made a note of it.

Tall and thin, she wore colorful and fashionable clothes that were more appropriate on the pages of a Vogue magazine than on the Skidmore College campus.

"Please, Mr. Max, write the word 'King' on the top left of the board," Lositano said.

The young man moved closer to Annabelle, who smelled delightful, and wrote, King. He decided to stay by her side.

"I need everyone to offer words associated with 'Kings.' I know we are all unfamiliar with each other, but please, the only wrong answer is 'no answer.' Let's begin."

The students excitedly offered their word association. Max got into action, writing each word on the whiteboard:

"Rich, powerful, deceitful, above the law, dishonest, ruler, authoritarian, manipulator, liar, greedy, ruling authority, tyrant, superior, above all, lawless, monarch, magnate, majesty, overlord, sovereign, tycoon, imperator, dictator, baron, noble, count, governor, nobility, royalty, superior, eminence, lord, Sire, unpopular, secretive …"

"Bene. Bene, Excellente," the professor exclaimed.

Max was delighted. He now stood next to Annabelle Winthrop.

"Fantastic, here is a hypothetical situation," said Lositano. "You are the King of a distant land and believe in your absolute right to rule forever. Which of the words listed on the whiteboard are the most important to your continued success and longevity as King? Miss Annabella will read one word at a time and once it is agreed a necessary attribute by most of the class, she will write the word in the right column." Lositano said as he turned to the class and moved out of the way.

"Rich," said Ms. Winthrop in a clear and proud voice.

The class launched into a discussion.

The word "rich" was an obvious one and the class quickly agreed, but before selecting the word, the Professor asked the group, "Why do you believe wealth is of importance?"

The immediate response came thundering through the auditorium. "To buy things."

A few students burst into laughter. But once the commotion settled a bit, the questioning continued. Someone wondered out loud, "What kind of things should the king buy?"

The conversation quickly became moronic as two students went back and forth in a duel of words: Clothes! Jewelry! Paintings!

Max grew impatient and interrupted them. "I am sorry, but if the King hopes to survive for any length of time, he will require protection: Protection for the Kingdom and for its law-abiding citizens. Therefore, the King will have to create and financially support an army and a police force, the former to protect the Kingdom, the latter to enforce laws the Kingdom adheres to. These endeavors will be extremely costly. Therefore, some of his wealth will often be spent on these two important items." Max could feel Annabelle pat him on the arm.

"Cool," she was saying.

He couldn't believe it, and before turning to smile at her, he noticed Lositano wink at him as if to say, "You can thank me later, Mr. Max."

The professor walked to the center of the classroom. "Indeed, a poor king is not a king, my friends. Wealth is a prerequisite, and the richest king will often be the most powerful one. Now, before we proceed, does this wealth belong to the King or to the people of the Kingdom?" The class answered in unison: "It belongs to the King."

Lositano smiled. "Please, Ms. Winthrop, could you write, Personal Wealth."

The class agreed to combine the words rule, ruler, authoritarian, authority, above all, sovereign, dictator, and superior into the word "Ruler." The King's decisions are incontestable and are the laws of the land. The class agreed, and though kings have advisers, their decisions are usually the ones to be implemented.

Professor Lositano signaled Ms. Winthrop to enter the word "Rule."

She now stood close to Max, who, at six foot and one inch, with a muscular body, green eyes, and wavy blond hair falling past his wide shoulders, was a rare sample of her opposing sex. "Deceitful," she read in a distracted voice.

Max raised a hand and asked his teacher whether they should combine a few of the words: "Deceitful, above the law, dishonest, liar, and secretive."

"Though a king needs to implement certain laws to be forced on the people of his kingdom," Professor Lositano said. "We would all agree the King is above these laws. Studies of medieval times demonstrate kings cared little for the laws that they themselves enacted, and behaved in an unlawful manner, their reign forceful, violent, and often murderous. But this behavior changed over time, and kings became more discreet about their nefarious behavior. But there are so many examples where kings use 'Deception.' Let's look at a contemporary instance. The decision to invade Iraq was based on a document presented to the Congress. In 2016, the CIA revealed there was little to no justification to invade Iraq. However, that war cost the American taxpayers $800 billion, most going to private and powerful American companies, our new kings." Professor Lositano paused, checked the time on his Apple watch and continued.

"The King, in order to maintain his long-lasting reign, will need 'Personal wealth,' must 'rule' firmly and unquestioned, and will use 'deception' to hide his conduct. Through our word game, we have deduced these three traits or attributes would allow him to extend the length of his reign. Before we take a quick break, let's review the words remaining on our list. Ms. Tocci, any comments?"

Ms. Tocci stood and read the remaining words aloud: "Monarch, magnate, majesty, overlord, sovereign, tycoon, baron, noble, governor, nobility, royalty, superior," she paused. "Most of the words seem to imply a kind of status. They represent names for members of a noble class, a certain social class above or 'superior' to others."

The moment of silence that followed disturbed Ms. Tocci, who now doubted she had properly answered the question.

"This is what I think," she said, her voice trembling a bit.

Professor Lositano walked over to his desk and scanned the pink attendance sheet. His index finger pointing over the names, he scrolled down the page and stopped on a name, "Patrick Sutton" and looked up to see who the person was he had just called.

In the back row, a young man stood.

"Bene. Please, Sir, respond to Ms. Tocci's comments."

The young man combed his hand through his thick and curly red hair. "Well, I am not sure..." he said.

But the Professor interrupted him. "Mr. Pat, please come join us."

By the time the student landed before the short Italian Professor, he was blushing.

"Now, you can relax, Mr. Pat. I will ask Ms. Tocci to stand next to you and voice her opinion once more."

Christiana Tocci, the beautiful brunette whose uncertainty by this time had only grown, turned to Lositano, "Would you mind repeating the question?" She said in Italian.

"We are about to take a break, and you are doing extremely well. Let's review the answer you provided a moment ago, Ms. Tocci," he said, "to Mr. Pat, here."

She faced Mr. Sutton and offered a warm smile. Her rich hazelnut eyes twinkled a bit, and Pat Sutton relaxed. Ms. Tocci repeated her previous answer and the two agreed that kings relied on a fictitious class system to promote their superiority.

"The word 'monarch' comes from the Greek word monarkhēs," Professor Lositano said. "It has its roots in the words Monos, 'alone,' and arkhein, 'to rule.' We all know the monarchs, or kings of old ruled through fear and violence. Brute force was used to silence the voices of dissent. Any threat to a monarchy was met with death. Can you imagine living in the 10th century and openly criticizing the King?"

The class was amused, and a few grins appeared.

Annabelle turned to Max, a smile on her face.

"But as time passed, monarchs feared rebellion. By then, religion had grown more powerful, and men had become more educated. So, the kings allied themselves with the church and invoked a God-given right to rule. This divine right gave them absolute power, no longer subject to any earthly authority. Most common men will not go against the will of God," Lositano said. "The king, in order to survive, must establish and enforce an imaginary yet controlled Class System."

Annabelle and Max were asked to recap their discovery. The two looked at each other inquisitively, and Max invited her to proceed.

"A king, to survive, must possess four key attributes," she said. "He must have 'Personal Wealth,' needs to 'Rule' in order to impose his will on the population, will need to master the art of 'Deception' to protect his many transgressions, and finally, the King will create and maintain a 'Class System,' at the top of which he will remain, in perpetuity."

The Professor announced a fifteen-minute break, and the students quickly exited the classroom.

Annabelle and Max were the last to exit, smiling innocently at each other.

The Italian Professor walked to his office, where he set his Nespresso machine to make a Cappuccino.

A bit refreshed, the students returned to find Lositano at his desk, a large cup of coffee in hand.

"Let's continue," he said once everyone had settled. "By 1850, roughly 60 years after King Louis XVI of France was decapitated at the hands of revolutionary Frenchmen, most remaining monarchs had either abdicated or had been removed from power. Democracies sprouted around the world. New presidents governed for the betterment of the people who gave them the power to do so. Today, the world no longer has individuals with such enormous personal wealth. No longer do we have a society ruled by a tiny minority of individuals, where no one is above the law and under a system of three distinct classes." Lositano concluded. He took a sip and waited to see if the class responded.

The class was silent, intrigued, until Christiana Tocci stood and said,

"From the point of view of a foreigner witnessing the American experiment right before my very eyes, your statement is incorrect."

"How so?"

"Well, for one, we still have many people who are rich beyond belief."

Lositano walked to his desk and picked up a three-ring binder which he handed to Ms. Winthrop. "Miss Annabelle, could you read the first page, please."

Annabelle opened the binder.

"According to a 2017 Credit Suisse report, the globe's richest 1% owned half the world's wealth. The House of Saud, Saudi Arabia's ruling family, is said to be worth $1.4 trillion, and the Rothschild Family is believed to be worth between $350 Billion and $2 Trillion. Russia's President Putin alone is estimated to be worth over $200 Billion."

Kendra Wilson interrupted Annabelle. "I thought the guy from Amazon or Tesla were the richest men on earth?"

"At the highest level of wealth, men prefer to remain in the shadows. We all know about the 1%, but could anyone name who they are?" Asked Lositano.

The class looked at the professor. Each student waited for the next to answer. All remained silent.

"Could we agree that there exist a small group of individuals who possess one of the traits we had assigned our king: enormous personal wealth?" he paused for emphasis. "And could it be that these men are above the law?"

A rumble went through the class, as every student seemed to have an opinion.

Lositano continued. "A few years ago, I heard a very interesting interview on National Public Radio. It featured the sociologist Brooke Harrington who authored a book called *Capital Without Borders: Wealth Management and the One Percent.* The book documents her investigation of what the life of the über rich really looks like. To complete her work, she trained to be a wealth manager and embarked on a career working for the ultra-rich."

"Miss Annabelle, could you read the next section, please?"

Ms. Winthrop read.

"The lives of the richest people in the world are so different from those of the rest of us, it's almost literally unimaginable. National borders are nothing to them. They might as well not exist. The laws are nothing to them. They might as well not exist."

"In an interview with Chuck Collins for *The Nation* on June 21, 2017, Ms. Harrington stated the following:

"There's a certain group of well-to-do people who don't want to be subject to the laws that bind the rest of us. They don't want anarchy because that would be inconvenient. They still want roads and the rule of law. They want murderers to go to jail. They just don't want the laws to apply to them because it's a bummer."

"Sounds like our king. Mr. Max, could you read the next page, please?"

Max took the binder from Annabelle and read. "Excerpt from a book by Ferdinand Lundberg, *America's 60 Families,* page 225," Max began.

"...the course of justice under the antiquated American judicial system is what it has always been; the poor go to jail, the rich go free."

Lositano moved forward and closer to the class. "This statement was written in 1937. Who agrees it still applies today? Raise your hand if you do."

Every student raised their hands. Slowly, as the Professor looked around the room, each arm was lowered.

"Your point of view implies the laws, though pretending to be the same for all, appear to have a different outcome based on whether the accused is rich or poor? The rich go unpunished, while the poor remain in jail for long periods of time for trivial matters. And adding to this problem, the bail system allows the rich to pay, get out of jail, and hire the most

324

connected and expensive lawyer, while the poor, unable to cover their bail, find themselves in prison in a vicious circle in which poverty is their main crime," said Lositano.

The class remained quiet.

"Do you believe this line of thinking is common amongst your peers?" The class agreed.

Lositano walked back to his desk, turned to the class, and asked, "Can we all agree that in America, except for very few exceptions, there are two types of justice, one for the poor who often go to jail and one for the rich go who often go free?"

"Yes," answered Annabelle and Max in unison.

Ms. Tocci, amused to hear such a discussion in an American classroom, sat silent.

Beside her, Patrick Sutton was taking copious notes. *They seem quite illegible*, she thought.

On the wall behind the students, the clock read 11:30 a.m.

Another hour. Lositano thought, as he walked back to his chair and sat before the class. "Being above the law was part of Deception. But are there any other ways in which this small group may deceive us?"

"Well, there are many," said Patrick Sutton. "These Uber Rich own the corporate media which includes most television channels, they have turned the Stock Market into a casino and control most everything of importance; They finance lobbyists to enforce deregulation, and they own most of our politicians."

"While that is quite a statement, there is no deception if you know they are doing it."

"Well, I could not tell you who 'they,' the Über rich are," said Patrick Sutton. "And most often the media does not really cover their shenanigans. That's quite a deception, I would say."

"I agree, Mr. Sutton. Max, would you mind reading the page titled 'Lobbyist'?"

"Sure." Max flipped through the document and read. "In an episode of the CBS show *60 Minutes* on July 8, 2012, Lesley Stahl interviewed a lobbyist named Jack Abramoff about his work with Congress.

During the interview, Abramoff said the following:

'I would say, or my staff would say to him or her at some point, you know, when you're done working on the Hill, we'd very much like you to consider coming to work for us.' Now the moment I said that ... we owned them. And what does that mean? Every request from our office, every request of our clients, everything that we want, they're gonna do. And not only that, they're gonna think of things we can't think of to do.''

Talking about our politicians, in a 2018 speech at the University of Illinois, President Obama said the following.

"They promise to fight for the little guy even as they cater to the wealthiest and the most powerful. They promise to clean up corruption and then plunder away."

"Thank you, Mr. Max," said Lositano. "Could we all agree that when a certain class controls the media, hides behind lobbyists to enact the laws that they like, or defeat the ones they do not, that for all intents and purposes, Deception is a fact?"

The class agreed and Lositano moved on. "So, Wealth and deception, two of the four attributes we assigned our kings seem to apply to the Elite, this 1%, the Über rich."

Lositano walked back to his chair and sat before the class.

"At Gettysburg, Abraham Lincoln, probably the greatest American President, in honor of the people who had sacrificed their lives for democracy, stated the following: *'that government of the people, by the people, for the people, shall not perish from the earth.'* In 2014, Martin Gilens of Princeton and Benjamin I. Page of Northwestern University, two political scientists, wrote a research paper called 'Elites, Interest Groups, and Average Citizens.' Max, could you read the next page?"

The young man straightened and read.

"Gilens and Page's research paper asks the following question:

Who governs? Who really rules? To what extent is the broad body of U.S. citizens sovereign, semi- sovereign, or largely powerless?

"Here are parts of their findings:

'When the preferences of economic elites and the stands of organized interest groups are controlled for, the preferences of the average American appear to have only a minuscule, near-zero, statistically non-significant impact upon public policy...the preferences of economic elites (as measured by our proxy, the preferences of "affluent" citizens) have far more independent impact upon policy change than the preferences of average citizens do.'

'...What do our findings say about democracy in America? They certainly constitute troubling news for advocates of "populistic" democracy, who want governments to respond primarily or exclusively to the policy preferences of their citizens. In the United States, our findings indicate, the majority does not rule—at least not in the causal sense of actually determining policy outcomes.'

'...When a majority of citizens disagrees with economic elites or with organized interests, they generally lose. Moreover, because of the strong status quo bias built into the U.S. political system, even when fairly large majorities of Americans favor policy change, they generally do not get it...

'...Despite the seemingly strong empirical support in previous studies for theories of majoritarian democracy, our analyses suggest that majorities of the American public actually have little influence over the policies our government adopts.

'...But we believe that if policymaking is dominated by powerful business organizations and a small number of affluent Americans, then America's claims to being a democratic society are seriously threatened.'"

Max looked toward Lositano, who, with a nod of the head, thanked him.

"The subject of the study was to answer one question: Who rules? The study concluded the 'economic elite' seem to have a stronger voice than the one of the, I quote, *'average American'* or the *'majority,'* end of quote."

"Please, Ms. Annabella, could you read the following page?"

Max passed her the documents and stepped back.

"The following are excerpts from President Obama's speech at the University of Illinois at Urbana-Champaign on Friday, September 7, 2018:

'This Congress has championed the unwinding of campaign finance laws to give billionaires outsized influence over our politics; systemically attacked voting rights to make it harder for the young people, the minorities, and the poor to vote... It's a vision that says the few who can afford high-priced lobbyists and unlimited campaign contributions set the agenda, and over the past two years, this vision is now nearing its logical conclusion. So with Republicans in control of Congress and the White House, without any checks or balances whatsoever, they've provided another $1.5 trillion in tax cuts to people like me — who I promise don't need it — and don't even pretend to pay for them.

"In a healthy democracy, there's some checks and balances on this kind of behavior, this kind of inconsistency, but right now, there's nothing. Republicans who know better in Congress — and they're there, they're quoted saying, 'yeah, we know this is kind of crazy' — are still bending over backward to shield this behavior from scrutiny

or accountability or consequence, seem utterly unwilling to find the backbone to safeguard the institutions that make our democracy work.'"

Annabelle paused. The classroom had suddenly taken on a solemn mood.

"I repeat," said Lositano, *"the few who can afford high-priced lobbyists and unlimited campaign contributions set the agenda...'* I believe there is little doubt about who rules, and it is not the majority. To further support my point, I will ask Mr. Max to read the next quote."

The young man turned the page and read: "This is from 'America's 60 Families' written by Ferdinand Lundberg, in 1937 and 1938. Published by Vanguard Press. Page 3 of the book.

'The United States is owned and dominated today by a hierarchy of its sixty families...These Families are the living center of the modern industrial Oligarchy which dominates the United States, functioning discreetly under a de Jure democratic form of Government behind which a de facto government, absolutist and plutocratic in its lineaments, has gradually taken form since the Civil War. This de facto government is actually the government of the United States, informal, invisible, shadowy. It is the Government of money in a dollar democracy'."

"Ferdinand Lundberg described the ruling families as being an *'...informal, invisible, shadowy...'* government, a *'...modern industrial oligarchy...'*" Lositano paused. "But is America really an Oligarchy? Definition, anyone?"

A few hands went up, and the Professor pointed at a young man who stood immediately and proudly delivered his answer: "I believe an Oligarchy is when a small group of people has control of a country, organization, or institution."

"Well done," said Lositano. He turned toward the whiteboard and reviewed the list Max and Annabelle had created.

"Out of the four attributes which we found kings would need to survive, we could say three of these attributes apply to our current 'elite,' 1%, the Über Rich, our oligarchs. The people I would call our 'kings.' They have enormous personal wealth. They are masters of "Deception" and they "Rule." Let's look at the last attribute— the creation of a Class System."

Lositano pulled his chair from behind the desk and dragged it to the center of the class. He stopped a few feet away in front of the first row of students and turned to Annabelle and Max. "Please get yourself a chair and come join me."

The Professor waited until the students were settled beside him and pointing at a young lady, said, "Miss, could you please name the various social classes existing in America?"

"My name is Kendra Wilson. I would say there are three distinct social classes: The Rich, the Middle Class, and the Poor."

"Thank you, Ms. Wilson," Lositano said. "Now, no offense to you or anyone else because we have been conditioned to believe in this misleading assertion. The concept of three identifiable social classes is deceptive. It is designed to hide the real and much more nuanced truth. What is the amount of wealth required to be included in the 'rich class'? $1 Million, $10 million, or $100 million?" Professor Lositano asked.

The class remained silent. Most of the affluent families who sent their kids to Skidmore College had a net worth of at least a million dollars, many of them much more.

"Does a middle-class family earn $400,000.00 or $80,000.00 a year? It is quite a difference for most. The latter lives month-to-month, one catastrophe away from poverty."

The Professor walked to his desk, the remains of his Cappuccino by his Apple Watch. He ignored it. The subject of the conversation he was about to start was a difficult one—race and class.

"Let me ask if the class would agree with this statement: A middle-class African American family earning $150,000.00 a year, with both parents working and two young children, fit into the same class as an identical but white family, earning the same amount?"

Instantly, the tall Kendra Wilson stood. "No way."

The rest of the class remained quiet.

Ms. Wilson was the only African American student in the class.

The Professor walked to his chair and sat. "Miss Wilson, would you expand on your answer, please?"

"With all due respect to my fellow students, it is my belief segregation never completely disappeared. Racism is not only alive and well in America, it is actually growing. There is no need for me to elaborate. We are all cognizant of the repeated and unjust killing of young black men and the demeaning police stops in which minor infractions turn deadly. Whether we like it or not, racism is forever present in America. Only a racist man would scream 'you lie!' to a sitting president; the first African American President speaking during his joint address to Congress." She paused.

"My family is middle class, my parents tried to move to a white neighborhood but left it after a few years, unable to fit in, unable to make friends. We returned to a community where schools received lower funding, where the youth grew into the harsh reality of always being second-class citizens..." she was about to continue, but the Professor raised his hand to stop her.

"Thank you, Ms. Kendra. So, to the rest of the class, could you please answer my question: Would you agree a middle-class African American family earning $150,000.00 a year, with both parents working and two young children, fit into the same class as an identical but white family, earning the same?" Asked Lositano.

Annabelle asked the Professor if she could offer her point of view.

"Sure, Miss. Please."

She walked forward and close to where her fellow students were sitting. "I grew up in Brooklyn. My dearest friend was African American. As soon as the two of us found ourselves outside of New York City, I repeatedly witnessed instances when she was ignored and poorly treated. In most stores, it always seemed we were being watched. In restaurants, polite waiters or waitresses became impatient with her questions about the menu. I could never feel what she experienced being treated as such. So, it may be fair to say within each group exist another subgroup based on race. As you pointed out, Professor, to assign three social classes to such a various society is a perfect way to hide the enormous and unjust social differences. I believe the classes should begin with the 'ruling class,' or the ultra-rich, and go from there."

"Thank you, Miss."

"So it appears we live in a make-believe 'Class System' in which only three distinct groups exist. But once the question is asked to clearly define each class, we can quickly conclude this idea of three classes is bogus. Ladies and gentlemen, I am sorry, but our Democracy has been under attack for a while now. It did not start with the Russians and their interference in the 2016 elections, or the newly named 1%. It started hundreds of years ago, and sadly, we have been losing."

The class grew quieter, unsettled.

Miss Annabelle, would you mind?" He held his hand out for the document she held.

She passed it and he read. "This is a quote by John F. Hylan, Mayor of New York City' between 1918 and 1925:

'The real menace of our Republic is the invisible Government, which, like a giant octopus, sprawls its slimy legs over our cities, states and nation . . . The little coterie of powerful international bankers virtually run the United States government for their own selfish purposes.'"

"Is a New York City Mayor accusing "a coterie of powerful international bankers of ruling our country? Bankers?" said Losatino. "We know a lot about the history of the Medici, the famous Italian bankers which so many movies have been made about, but we know nothing about the Rothschilds, Morgans or the Rockefellers, Carnegies, Vanderbilts, DuPonts, and Astors, who all amassed enormous fortunes. Most of these people controlled banks and, I believe, used their power to rule from behind a veil of secrecy. But we have been warned.

President Jefferson said: 'I sincerely believe, with you, that banking *establishments are more dangerous than standing armies...'"*

Lositano continued and explained that, "Over the last hundred years, this *'... informal, invisible, shadowy'* power expanded its control to all sectors of our economy, finance, construction, utilities, etc. This 'shadow power' rules in secrecy. They install a puppet to govern, one behind whom they can hide, and who will carry the blame for whatever misery this elite group cares to afflict on the country—the 2008 Financial Crisis, the Crash of 1929, the Federal Reserve and so on."

The class was quiet, and the Italian Professor, for a moment, wondered what the students were thinking.

But, he continued, "The Economist, an international and highly respected organization, created a 'Democracy Index' which includes four categories: full democracies, flawed democracies, hybrid regimes, and authoritarian regimes. In 2017, the Economist downgraded the United States to a 'flawed democracy', based on the electoral process, civil liberties, the functioning of Government, political participation, and political culture."

"Sorry to interrupt Professor, but is America an Oligarchy?" asked Max.

"I believe there are two hundred years of history to prove it is so. In a 2015 interview, President Jimmy Carter said that our country is *'an oligarchy with unlimited political bribery.'* The records are there and easily found."

"So, you *do* believe America is an Oligarchy?" Asked Kendra Wilson, a tone of resentment in her voice.

"When a small group controls a country, it is called an Oligarchy. We concluded that kings would need four key attributes to survive and rule. They must have enormous personal wealth, be deceitful, rule and maintain a class system. Too often, we associate the richest men with people like Bezos, Musk, and Gates, but the richest prefer to live behind a veil of anonymity. So, we ignore the shareholders of our most powerful conglomerates or corporations, and we ignore the shareholders of the Federal Reserve Bank whose profit in 2016 was around $100 billion."

"That's an enormous profit. Isn't the Federal Reserve a governmental agency? How could they make such a profit?" Ms. Wilson asked.

"By creating money out of nothing, Miss."

"What?" Ms. Wilson said in disbelief.

"I know, Ms. Wilson. It's hard to believe. How many of you know the Federal Reserve is a private institution with little to no oversight?"

No one answered.

"During this class, we will discuss the Federal Reserve's right to issue money out of thin air and study its 100-year history." Lositano paused and looked at the clock. Twenty minutes left. "The subject of your assignment for next week is; Who owns America's $29 trillion sovereign debt?"

The class scribbled on their notebooks.

After a long summer recess, most of it spent in Bergamo, Lositano felt tired. "Any questions?"

Most of the students raised their hands.

"Let's proceed from left to right." The Professor said.

One by one, the students asked their questions. The Government was of particular interest.

Lositano repeated Lincoln's quote he had mentioned earlier; *"that government of the people, by the people, for the people, shall not perish from the earth,"* and wondered aloud, "Has that government perished?"

No response came forward, and the questions soon came to an end.

Beside Lositano, Annabelle and Max had remained quiet. The Professor turned to them.

"Is this all about money?" Annabelle asked in disbelief.

"John Adams stated the following, Miss: *'There are two ways to enslave a nation. One is by the sword. The other is by debt.'* Ezra Pound, the American poet, told us, *'Wars in old times were made to get slaves. The modern implement of imposing slavery is debt.'* Whoever owns America's debt owns America."

"So, what are we to do?" Said Max. "If we live in an oligarchy whose rulers have untold powers, wealth, and authority, it would seem an impossible task."

Lositano stood and walked to his desk. He rummaged through his leather bag and took out his iPad.

"Knowledge is power, is my first answer, Mr. Max, but then actions must follow, for complacency is the poison of the weak."

The Professor typed on his iPad, waited, and read,

> *"'While the Bill of Rights protects us from the tyranny of an oppressive government, many in the establishment would like the American people to submit to the tyranny of oligarchs, multinational corporations, Wall Street banks, and billionaires.'*

"This is from a speech by Bernie Sanders given in June of 2019. There are good and honest politicians, but change will be hard."

"Bernie Sanders is one senator amongst a hundred, and so many are crooked. It really feels like an insurmountable task," Max responded.

"From one are born the many. We must conclude our class. But I'll leave you all with this."

Professor Lositano woke his iPad. As he typed, he spoke slowly and shared what he was looking for. "This is from a service at the Marsh Chapel in Boston by the Reverend, Dr. Robert Allan Hill. It is called 'Hope is the Negation of Negation.' I would highly recommend reading the entire service online. Absolute genius. One second please."

Lositano, his index finger sliding down the page, scrolled through the service, found the part he was looking for, and read.

> *"'Hope, a sense that things are wrong and can be right-wised, is what gives us the angry courage, the courageous anger, to rise up, to resist out a tradition of principled resistance dating back to Amos of Tekoa, in the 8 century BCE, to struggle, to lose, to be defeated, and to get up again.'"*

Lositano calmly placed the iPad on his lap. "When men of the clergy speak such words, the seed of discontent is planted, and in time, when all hope has vanished, just as the French did in 1789, men will rise."

335

ACKNOWLEDGEMENTS

When the kindness of strangers leads one to achieve the unachievable, one must trust that the world is filled with marvelous people. *The Kings Have Won* may have remained but a dream without the steady guidance of a few incredible individuals. First and foremost, I must acknowledge author Ricky Wilks, whose infinite kindness and generosity inspired me to persist on this laborious and foolish task, author Mary Ford for her gentle and unending support, and finally, David Johnson's sharp wit and inspiring stories gave me the courage to complete this project.

Upon discovering the true facts behind such far-out events as the Burning of Washington, the Bank War, the founding of the Federal Reserve, or the 2008 Financial crisis, my initial response was usually one of disbelief and suspicion. But the truth is raw and wicked.

While most of the stories presented in *The Kings Have Won* were inspired by true historical events, it is nonetheless a work of fiction.

Finally, it is with a humble heart that I thank you, the reader for your inquisitive mind and our shared interest in American History. I hope you found these short stories informative and entertaining.
For more information, please visit www.adriengold.com to access our blog covering each chapter and detailing which part is fiction and which is true.

Thank you.

Adrien Gold

Made in the USA
Middletown, DE
09 April 2025

73996926R00195